MW01485247

Rudolph de Harak Graphic Designer

Rational Simplicity

With 534 illustrations

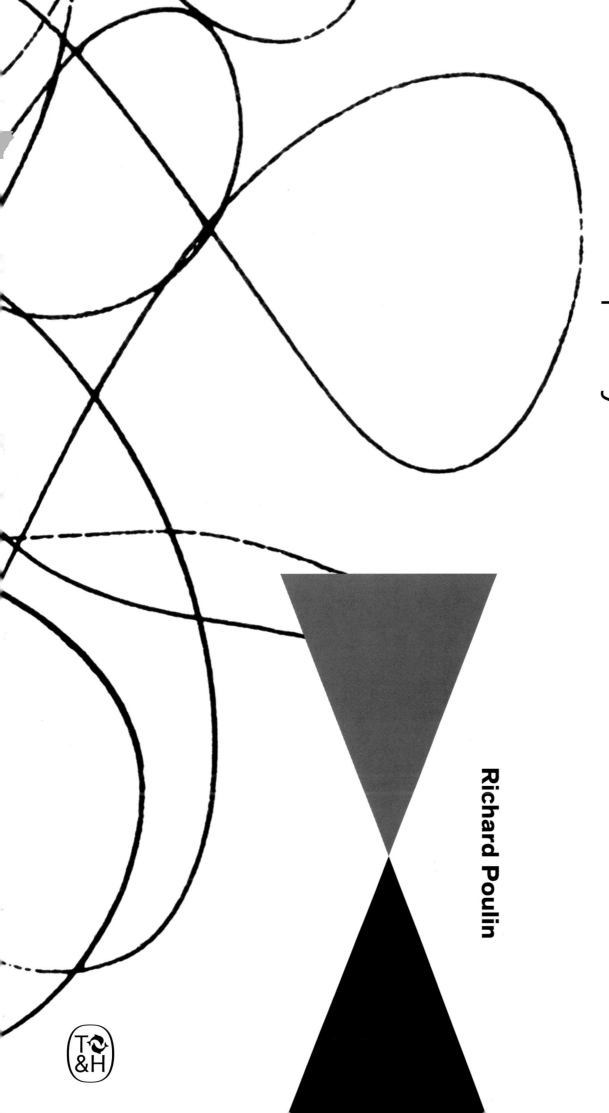

Rudolph de Harak Graphic Designer

Rational Simplicity

Richard Poulin

T&H

Cover, title page:
Magazine cover (detail),
Perspectives USA, no. 7,
Hamish Hamilton Ltd., 1954.

Endpapers:
Mimeographic study for
Print, vol. 11, no. 2, magazine
cover, February/March 1957.

First published in the United Kingdom in 2022
by Thames & Hudson Ltd, 181A High Holborn,
London WC1V 7QX

First published in the United States of America in 2022
by Thames & Hudson Inc., 500 Fifth Avenue, New York,
New York 10110

Rudolph de Harak Graphic Designer: Rational Simplicity
© 2022 Richard Poulin
Foreword © 2022 Thomas Geismar
Designed by Richard Poulin, Derek Koch, and Tyler Cheli

British Library Cataloguing-in-Publication Data
A catalogue record for this book is available from the
British Library

Library of Congress Control Number 2022931213

ISBN 978-0-500-02538-3

Printed in China by RR Donnelley

MIX
Paper from
responsible sources
FSC® C144853
FSC
www.fsc.org

Contents

Foreword

< De Harak with
Tom Geismar (*left*) during
construction of the
US Pavilion at Expo 70,
Osaka, Japan, 1970.

We are all, of course, reflections of, and creatures of, the times in which we grew up and came into maturity. In the mid-1950s, when I was a graduate student studying graphic design (at the time there was virtually no 'Graphic Design' taught in the United States at an undergraduate level), Rudy's small spot illustrations for *Esquire* magazine, his early record album covers and book covers were a definite influence. His work was consistently clear, bold, colorful, and meaningful in an abstract way.

In the late 1950s and early 1960s, through numerous publications, Ivan Chermayeff and I also became aware of the more fully developed Modernism movement in Europe. But while Ivan and I were intrigued by it, we took a typically American attitude towards it, and accepted it mostly as a style that we could use whenever appropriate. But Rudy fully adopted the philosophy behind the movement and accepted the idea that design could change the world. He believed the notion that good design meant 'cutting away all the unnecessary appendages, leaving only those elements that stated facts, thoughts, and ideas.' For example, he fully adopted the concept of using only one sans-serif typeface, always setting it flush left with tight margins.

But this whole-hearted adoption of a philosophy and methodology from overseas was typical behavior for Rudy because he approached all tasks that interested him with great intensity and enthusiasm. In 1968, we invited Rudy to join our team to design the building and exhibitions for the official United States Pavilion at the upcoming Expo 70 in Osaka, Japan. It was during those two years that I really got to know Rudy, as we shared a make-shift design office, and traveled together to Japan to oversee the installation of the project. It became clear that Rudy's enthusiasms went well beyond his absorption in European Modernist graphic design. He approached the design of the section on American Sports with great inventiveness and imagination, and he became enthusiastically involved in areas of sports where he had no prior interest. He was able to dig deep and develop unique ways to display artifacts and mementos that helped bring the exhibits alive.

This kind of deep, intense involvement would later be apparent in the highly imaginative 'digital clock' and entrance tunnel at 127 John Street and the roof-top airfield at 77 Water Street, both in Manhattan, and later by the design of his museum for the Cummins Engine Company, highlighted by his 'exploded' diesel engine suspended in the air.

Foreword

In many ways, Rudy was more like an architect than a graphic designer. His feeling for and understanding of materials, recognizing what they could do and how they could be joined, greatly absorbed his interest. He put together his own collection of mid-century, architect-designed chairs, and applied his fascination with materials and construction to other, more personal enthusiasms. When we were working on the design for Expo 70, Rudy would arrive at the office at 9:00 a.m., having actually arisen at 4:00 a.m., gone fishing for two hours, and then commuted to work. As he once said, 'I was a very, very dedicated fisherman.' Not surprisingly, he always fabricated his own fishing rods and lures.

For all that, Rudy never strayed too far from his graphic design roots. His design of all the information graphics, a key part of the then new Egyptian Wing of The Metropolitan Museum of Art, still stands today as an iconic example of using the classic elements of type, color, illustration, and diagrams to bring clarity and interest to an incredibly complex story. It is the information, not 'the style', that predominates. It could never have happened without Rudy's intense immersion in the subject and his unrelenting enthusiasm during more than a decade of work.

As Rudy later stated in an interview, 'I was always trying to do things that I didn't know. I was looking for answers to questions that I had never asked myself. I was looking always for a hidden order, or a hidden meaning.'

Tom Geismar
Founding Partner, Chermayeff Geismar & Haviv
August 2021

<Book cover (detail), *Technique of Executive Control,* by Erwin Haskell Schell, McGraw-Hill Paperbacks, *c.* 1960.

Introduction

'I don't believe in change for the sake of change. Change comes about through a natural process of development or because something needs improving. Modernism suggests a movement that is ahead of its time. If we do something that has been done before, we are not being creative, we are being redundant. Creativity, which is what Modernism is all about, is a constant searching process that promises a greater chance for failure than it does success.' [1]
        Rudolph de Harak, New York City, 1987

The year was 1977. I had just graduated from college and for the next few years was stuck in a series of dead-end, uninspiring design jobs. At this point at the start of my career, I was at a loss for what to do next. In a move that served as a life-changing lesson for me, I decided to identify the ten graphic designers in New York City that I most admired and send them letters in the hope that they might be open to an in-person interview. At the top of that list was Rudolph de Harak, and to my surprise he agreed to meet with me. Armed with a new portfolio that I had labored over for the past six months, I met with Rudy at his office. To my surprise, he offered me a position the next day and so began a working relationship with him that set me on a creative path that I am still traveling today.

        I was initially introduced to his work a few years earlier when I was in college. For four years, I worked five nights a week at Pratt Institute's art and architecture library. In retrospect, I always felt that, along with my first encounter with Rudy's work, my real education took place within those beautiful Tiffany-designed interiors, spending time in the stacks with a never-ending reserve of inspiring and memorable books and periodicals.

        Actually, four years before that, when I was a teenager growing up in New York City, I had unknowingly experienced Rudy's work at first-hand. I was visiting a friend who worked at 127 John Street when I first saw Rudy's monumental, three-story-high digital clock and the building's entrance — a galvanized, corrugated-steel tunnel, illuminated by multiple rings of blue argon-gas-filled tubes. I was still in high school at the time and had little, if any, knowledge or understanding of what architecture and graphic design were, but Rudy's redefined and reimagined urban landscape definitely left a lasting impression on my memory.

        I started working with Rudy as a staff designer in 1980. The design studio was organized in three teams, with everyone doing

everything from two-dimensional to three-dimensional work. If
you didn't understand something, or didn't possess a certain skill,
you were taught. It was a nurturing environment but, at times,
intimidating and overwhelming. Like any other creative force,
Rudy was intense and demanding. Not only of his staff, but more
importantly, of himself. If you were able to be responsive to him and
his needs, you could work effectively with him, and more importantly,
learn a great deal from him in a very meaningful way. I began to
understand that his intensity and demanding nature came from a true
and deep passion for design and for solving visual communication
problems. He took me under his wing and I was fortunate that he
gave me numerous challenges and opportunities that tested, as
well as broadened and enhanced, my conceptual understanding of
Modernist graphic design and of my own creativity.

For most of my tenure at the office, I literally worked six days
a week with Rudy. It was not a nine-to-five job — I mean, no design
job is — but I did everything. Within a short period of time, I became
an associate, and ultimately his partner, managing the creative,
administrative, and business development needs of the office during
his last years in New York City. It was a wonderful, intoxicating,
enlightening, and once-in-a-lifetime experience.

One of the main reasons for doing this book is that I always
felt Rudy was one of the unsung heroes of Mid-century Modernist
graphic design. He possessed a definitive and unique point of view,
which he stayed true to throughout his entire career, yet he and his
body of work have never been celebrated nor explored in depth. He is
an anomaly among his peers in the graphic design profession, yet no
one equals his diversity nor his accomplishments across the various
design disciplines.

In researching and writing this monograph on his life and work
for the past two years, I have come to learn that Rudy was a rare
individual — a thinker, a challenger, an advocate for new ideas, and an
inspiring colleague. He believed that all great ideas, and all significant
works of art and architecture, came from dreamers, visionaries, and
communicators. When he talked of this belief he always quoted the
great Modernist American architect Louis Sullivan: 'Nor am I of those
who despise dreamers. For the world would be at a level of zero
were it not for its dreamers — gone and of today. He who dreamed
of democracy, far back in a world of absolutism, was indeed heroic,
and we of today awaken to the wonder of his dreams. How deep this
dreamer saw into the heart of man. So would I nurse the dreamer of

dreams, for in him nature broods while the race slumbers. So would I teach the art of dreaming, as I would teach the science of thinking, as I would teach the value of action. He who knows naught of dreaming can, likewise, never attain the heights of power and possibility in persuading the mind to act. He who dreams not creates not. For vapor must arise in the air before the rain can fall.' [2]

Rudy's heroes were many, including Max Bill, Josef Müller-Brockmann, Armin Hofmann, Max Huber, El Lissitzky, László Moholy-Nagy, Alexander Rodchenko, Carlo Vivarelli, and Piet Zwart. These Modernists breathed new life into the world of graphic design, stripping away unnecessary ornament and excess and leaving only what was deemed essential. Their work was thoughtful and systematic, and the results were timeless. Four other significant figures were even more influential on Rudy's life and career — Saul Bass, Will Burtin, György Kepes, and Alvin Lustig. He was fortunate enough to have developed friendships with all of these men. First, in the late 1940s, while still living in Southern California, he became good friends with Bass and Lustig. A few years later, following his relocation to New York City, he finally had the opportunity to meet and become friends with his lifelong inspirations — Burtin and Kepes. 'In those days, and I believe it more so than today, we lived our design, slept little, and argued our philosophies with one another, late into the night,' he fondly recalled. [3]

Rudy was born in an era that was filled with global unrest and radical changes. At the time, a revolutionary experiment in new ways of thinking and living was underway, one that was to single-handedly alter the course of art and design in the modern world. It paved the way for a unified visual language that would eventually resonate throughout the world, dominating the remaining decades of the twentieth century. Modernism defined a new and fundamental approach to the design disciplines, including graphic design. Traditionalism, excess, and complexity were now looked down upon by many; this new way of thinking symbolized the beginning of greater individual freedom, epitomized by the pursuit of simplicity. It also reflected a new set of fundamental values and principles that started to emerge throughout society, so represented more than just a name of a style or a movement in design history — it is, and still remains, a philosophy, a state of mind, a way of living. This was the most valuable lesson that I ever learned from Rudolph de Harak.

In the latter years of his life, Rudy remained intensely interested and passionate about the visual world and his place

Introduction

> Book cover (detail), *Modern Physics for the Engineer,* edited by Louis N. Ridenour, McGraw-Hill Paperbacks, 1961.

within it. Always encountering new ideas to explore and new things to discover, his interest in life and his surroundings, large and small, kept him vibrant and energized until his last days.

I thought it would be fitting to end my introduction and begin this monograph with Rudy's own words in the hope that they will inspire the reader along their journey:

'The explosion of a de Kooning brush stroke, the dynamic peace in a Mies curtain wall, the wail of a baby, or the high-whine of a full-race Ferrari is communication. It's that dynamic symbology of Churchill's hand held aloft, with the fingers forming that famous "V" for victory, also, two hearts entwined, carved indelibly into the trunk of a tree, speaking out: "This is what I think … this is how I feel." Communication is commitment. Commitment is the essential element of communication. It is contact.' [4]

Rudolph de Harak, New York City, 1961

1. Rudolph de Harak, 'Some Thoughts on Modernism: Past, Present, and Future, Milton Glaser, Ivan Chermayeff, and Rudolph de Harak', in *Design Culture: An Anthology of Writing from the AIGA Journal of Graphic Design*, edited by Steven Heller and Marie Finamore, New York: Allworth Press, 2013, pp. 132–38.

2. Louis Sullivan, *Kindergarten Chats and Other Writings*, New York: George Wittenborn, Inc., 1965, p. 226.

3. Rudolph de Harak, 'Oral History Interview with Rudolph de Harak', interview by Susan Larsen on 27 April 2000 (transcript), in Ellsworth, Maine. Archives of American Art, Smithsonian Institution, Washington, DC.

4. Rudolph de Harak, 'In My Opinion', *Print*, vol. 15, no. 3, May/June 1961, p. 118.

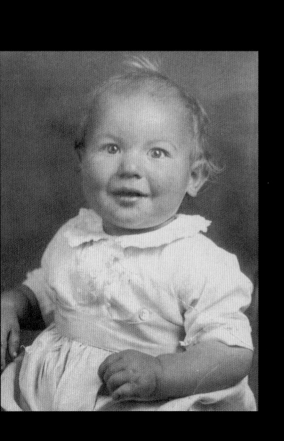

< Rudolph de Harak,
  Culver City, California,
  1924.

By the beginning of the 1930s, news of the Bauhaus and European Modernism had begun to spread across the United States to the west coast of California. Southern California, specifically the Los Angeles area, was fertile ground for this pioneering movement. And even more exciting was that this new 'language of vision' was being promoted throughout the country by European émigrés and former faculty members of the Bauhaus. Walter Gropius now taught architecture at Harvard University's Graduate School of Design in Cambridge, Massachusetts (1937–1952); Ludwig Mies van der Rohe became the head of architecture at the Armour Institute of Technology, later known as the Illinois Institute of Technology (ITT) in Chicago, Illinois (1938–1958); Josef and Anni Albers began teaching at Black Mountain College in North Carolina (1933–1949); and László Moholy-Nagy launched what was initially called the New Bauhaus in Chicago, Illinois (1937–1945).

Two other theorists and practitioners, Will Burtin and György Kepes, also carried with them the tenets of International Modernism when they emigrated to the United States in the late 1930s to build upon the legacy of the Bauhaus. Both men would have a significant influence on the course of visual communications and graphic design in the country over the following decades.

Burtin was a true visionary and pioneer of the Mid-century Modernist era, moving with ease from one discipline to another — architecture, exhibition design, information design, furniture design, and graphic design. His creative interests were boundless.

∨ Will Burtin, 1943.
US Army, Office of
Strategic Services.

György Kepes, c. 1940.

He was one of the first designers of the era to pursue a
seamless integration of graphic design and architecture and was to
become an inspiration for future generations of generalist designers
in the decades to come. As a young man, he decided not to finish
high school and instead accepted a four-year apprenticeship
in typography at the Handswerkskammer zu Köln in his native
Cologne. Following the completion of his graphic design studies,
he established his first design studio in 1927 and quickly became
one of Germany's leading creative minds. In 1938, he emigrated
to the United States following his refusal of numerous invitations
from the Nazi regime to become design director of its Ministry of
Propaganda. In a matter of months following his arrival in New York
City, Burtin received commissions from the Federal Works Agency,
an independent arm of the federal government which administered
public construction, building maintenance, and public works projects
from 1939 to 1949, and the pharmaceutical giant Upjohn. He was
also invited to join the faculty at Pratt Institute where he remained for
many years, becoming the chairperson of its Department of Visual
Communication in 1959. In 1943, he was drafted in the US Army and
worked at its Office of Strategic Services designing gunnery training
manuals for the US Army Air Forces, and then for the US Air Force.

In 1945, he simultaneously became the art director of *Fortune*
and *Scope* magazines, the latter a medical and pharmaceutical
magazine published by Upjohn. He held both positions until 1949
when he established his own design consultancy ultimately working
with clients such as Eastman Kodak, Herman Miller, IBM, Mead
Paper, the Smithsonian Institution, Union Carbide, and the United
States Information Agency (USIA). Throughout the 1950s and 1960s,
Burtin made major contributions to the discipline of information
design and data visualization, and to the understanding of complex
scientific information through his multidisciplinary work in editorial,
identity, poster, and exhibition design. As one of the founders of the
International Design Conference in Aspen, which served for more
than fifty years as a forum for the discussion and dissemination
of developments in the related fields of graphic design, industrial
design, and architecture, Burtin believed that 'man is the total sum of
his experience. His scale and focus must change continuously as he
studies, grows, and develops.' [1]

Kepes, one of the most influential and visionary minds of the
Mid-century Modernist era, was a painter, sculptor, photographer,
filmmaker, designer, writer, and educator. He initially studied painting
at Budapest's Royal Academy of Fine Arts, which in the early 1930s
was a hotbed of political and artistic unrest. After the completion of
his studies, he turned away from painting to filmmaking, which he
felt was a more effective and impactful visual medium for an artist
to express social and political beliefs. Following his move to Berlin,
he was invited to join the design studio of his fellow countryman,
László Moholy-Nagy, the Hungarian painter and photographer who
had taught at the Bauhaus. By 1936, due to the growing political
unrest in Germany, he immigrated to London, and then, a year later
to the United States. Moholy-Nagy had just become director of the
New Bauhaus in Chicago, which offered the first complete modern
design curriculum in the country. He invited Kepes to join him
there to start a light and color department, also the first of its kind
in the United States. During his tenure from 1937 to 1943, Kepes
expanded and refined his theories on the 'education of vision' and the

∨ Rudolph Valentino,
   c. 1925, gelatin silver print.
   Russell Ball, photographer.

influence of photography, cinema, and television on visual design and culture, which were detailed in his seminal reference book on visual communications and design education, *Language of Vision* (Chicago: Paul Theobald and Company, 1944). In 1943, he was invited to teach at Brooklyn College's Department of Design, headed by the Russian-born British architect and industrial designer Serge Chermayeff. His graphic design students included Saul Bass, who was later to introduce Kepes' avant-garde ideas to a broader audience through his iconic film posters and titles. Kepes was subsequently invited to establish a visual design program at the Massachusetts Institute of Technology (MIT) in Cambridge. In 1967, this program became the Center for Advanced Visual Studies, dedicated to developing new technologies and promoting creative collaborations between scientists, visual artists, and designers. He remained at MIT until his retirement in 1974.

Throughout his career and work, Kepes believed that 'visual communication is universal and international; it knows no limits of tongue, vocabulary, or grammar, and it can be perceived by the illiterate as well as by the literate.' [2]

In the years to come, Burtin and Kepes would develop new strains of Modernism that were to have a profound influence on Rudolph de Harak at the beginning of, and throughout, his fifty-year career. Their groundbreaking ideas set de Harak on a path that initially transformed the way in which he lived his life and how he thought about graphic design, and ultimately guided his understanding of his role and responsibility as a graphic designer and visual storyteller.

Beginnings in Southern California

Throughout the 1920s, industrial development in Southern California, and specifically in Los Angeles and its surrounding communities, was still in its infancy. The oil industry was just starting to expand in the region, as were manufacturing and aviation. However, the Hollywood film industry and silent film production which dominated the world throughout the early 1920s were already thriving. Within a ten-year period from 1920 to 1929, the population of Los Angeles and its surrounding communities more than doubled from approximately 500,000 to over 1.2 million residents, in large part due to the expanding film industry. In the following decade, Southern California also attracted a great many artists and intellectuals who had fled Europe. The film industry provided employment for many of these individuals, but it also attracted people from all walks of life to Los Angeles, attracted to the optimism, prosperity, and vitality it offered. The region rapidly became a mecca for artists and designers searching for a community of like-minded individuals.

In 1924, the de Harak family lived at 4160 Irving Place, a small, one-story Spanish-style Art Deco bungalow located on a tree-lined street in Culver City in western Los Angeles. It was located a few blocks from the main entrance to the Metro-Goldwyn-Mayer (MGM) studios on Washington Boulevard. One of the main reasons why Alice and Francis de Harak chose this location to raise their young family was that they loved anything and everything about the movies, especially MGM. They had both worked as extras in several of the studio's films, and ultimately named their youngest son after

the silent-film star Rudolph Valentino, who was extremely popular throughout the 1910s and 1920s.

Rudolph Falla de Harak, their sixth and youngest child, was born on 10 April 1924. At the time of his birth, his siblings included four sisters, Leonie (age 12), Holly (age 11), Dolly (age 7), and Daisy (age 2), and his brother Earl (age 4). His older sister Mildred, born in 1918, died eleven months after her birth, and his younger brother Marshall, born in 1927, died that same year, also at eleven months of age.

Alice Elizabeth Falla, de Harak's mother, was of British descent, and was born on 24 July 1883 in Lewisham, England, a southern suburb of London. In 1911, she emigrated from Vancouver, British Columbia to the United States with her new husband, Francis, whom she married that same year. Francis de Harak was of Czechoslovakian descent, and was born on 3 May 1884 in Moravia, then part of Austria-Hungary, and now in the Czech Republic. He was an aspiring chef when he arrived with his new bride in the United States. At the time, he thought that being Czechoslovakian would be a disadvantage to any potential job opportunities in the States, so he decided to add the 'de' to his last name. From that moment on, he stated that he was of French descent.

Alongside a variety of other jobs, Francis worked as a title writer for MGM and other film studios located in the Los Angeles area. One visual oddity of silent films was that they frequently used onscreen title cards, also known as intertitles, which consisted of frames of text, either hand-drawn or printed, inserted intermittently between sequences of film footage for a variety of purposes — to narrate story points, to present key dialogue, and sometimes even to comment on the action for the movie-going audience. In an interview decades later, de Harak fondly recalled that his mother, Alice, had told him that Francis had beautiful script handwriting, and that the studios came to him time and time again to handwrite title cards. It seems that this was the only creative connection that de Harak would ever have with his father. His parents divorced in the early 1930s and he never saw his father again. In April 1973, Francis de Harak died at the age of eighty-eight in Long Beach, California.

Screenland's Culver City

Founded by Harry Culver in 1917, Culver City was one of the first epicenters of the motion-picture industry, primarily as the home of the vast Metro-Goldwyn-Mayer studios. Throughout the silent era, the city was well known as 'The Heart of Screenland'. Little did movie-goers know that their favorite 'Hollywood' movies were actually being produced several miles away in Culver City. The first building on the lot that was to become the MGM studio complex was a huge edifice with classical colonnades fronting Washington Boulevard. During the Prohibition era, it was joined by speakeasies and nightclubs scattered up and down the Boulevard. In 1924, Goldwyn Pictures merged with Metro Pictures and Louis B. Mayer Pictures, forming Metro-Goldwyn-Mayer Studios, better known as MGM. Eventually sprawling over more than 180 acres, MGM Studios was a city within a city. Its vast campus included multiple soundstages, false streets, an artificial lake, police and fire departments, telegraph and post offices, a water tower and

well, a laboratory, and backlot amenities such as electrical, paint, and locksmith shops, as well as wardrobe, make-up, property, lighting, art, and camera departments. Over the years, MGM would produce countless classic films on its Culver City lots, including *The Wizard of Oz* (1939), *Singin' in the Rain* (1952), and *Ben-Hur* (1959).

In addition to his part-time work for various film studios, and prior to de Harak's birth, Francis primarily worked as the head chef at Pickfair Estate, home of Mary Pickford and Douglas Fairbanks, known as Hollywood's first 'it-couple'. In subsequent years, he continued to work as a pastry chef at exclusive restaurants, country clubs, and hotels located up and down the California coast, including the Arlington Hotel in Santa Barbara, the Palace Hotel in San Francisco, and the Los Angeles Country Club, as well as the San Marcos Hotel in Chandler, Arizona; and the Paso del Norte in El Paso, Texas.

After Alice and Francis divorced in the early 1930s, Alice was left to single-handedly support her entire family by taking in laundry and assisting friends and families in their Culver City neighborhood with various domestic chores. She was, and remained until her death in October 1947, the emotional and financial anchor of the de Harak family. Show business and entertainment were also in Alice's blood. She was somewhat of the proverbial 'stage mother', and while living in Culver City supplemented her family's income by giving dance and music lessons. When her daughters, Holly and Dolly, were teenagers, respectively thirteen and sixteen years old, she had them pose as adults and perform professionally under her maiden name, first as the Falla Twins, then as the Falla Sisters. They performed modern interpretive dance in the style of American dancer Isadora Duncan, and became well known throughout the United States, as well as in Europe and South America. In the 1930s, the Falla Sisters performed in numerous stage productions and were featured in several movies and Broadway musicals, including *Thumbs Up!*, a musical and comedy revue which ran for 156 performances at the St James Theatre in New York City in 1935. During World War II, Holly and Dolly de Harak's dancing careers as the Falla Sisters ended, and they ultimately retired from show business, married, and raised their respective families.

Eastbound to Chicago

At the beginning of 1934, at the height of the Great Depression, Alice decided to move east to Chicago with Leonie, Holly, Dolly, Daisy, Earl, and de Harak, thinking that there would be more performing and theatrical opportunities for her daughters, as the Chicago World's Fair had opened the previous year under the title *A Century of Progress International Exposition.* During the Prohibition era,

∨ De Harak with his sister
Daisy, Chicago, Illinois,
1934.

Chicago established itself as one of the major metropolitan centers in the United States, and was notorious for its crime, gangsters, and speakeasies. Faced with high unemployment and food lines, many turned to crime as a way to deal with their poverty. The Chicago World's Fair, a showcase of science and industry held to celebrate the city's centennial, was located on the banks of Lake Michigan and attracted over 39 million visitors in its first year. Attendees experienced the latest in rail travel, automobiles, 'Moderne' architecture (a more streamlined take on Art Deco), and entertainment, including performances by burlesque star Sally Rand and singing trio the Gumm Sisters — the youngest of them was Judy Garland. The fair was also a venue for firsts: the first Major League All-Star Baseball Game was held at Comiskey Park (home of the Chicago White Sox); the first streamlined locomotive trains for the Union Pacific Railroad were exhibited, as well as the Denver Zephyr for the Chicago, Burlington and Quincy Railroad; and Cream of Wheat breakfast porridge, Juicy Fruit chewing gum, and Pabst Blue Ribbon beer were all introduced.

Unfortunately, the Chicago World's Fair did not provide Alice and her daughters with the performing and theatrical opportunities that they had hoped for. The de Haraks stayed in the Windy City only until the summer of that year. From Chicago, they packed themselves and all of their belongings into their new Graham-Paige sedan and drove east to New York City, finally settling in Astoria, Queens.

Growing Up in Astoria, Queens

By the end of the summer, de Harak, now ten years old, and the de Harak family were settled in Astoria, a middle-class and commercial neighborhood in the New York City borough of northwestern Queens. Originally called Hallett's Cove, the area was renamed for John Jacob Astor, the first American multimillionaire, with the hope that he would invest in the new neighborhood. His investment never materialized, but the name stayed nonetheless. In the 1930s and 1940s, it was predominantly working class, with a diverse local population of English, Greek, Irish, Italian, Jewish, and Scottish families. Bernard Nolan, a boyhood friend of de Harak's, recalled their early teen years growing up in Queens: 'Astoria was a blue-collar community with a wide mix of ethnic groups, almost exclusively white ... Religious differences rather than ethnic ones seemed to drive family parental biases when I lived there, yet the children of my generation mixed well both in school and socially.' [3]

In a 2000 interview, de Harak reluctantly described his family life and early childhood growing up in Astoria 'as a disaster'. [4] He further explained, 'We really had very little family life ... I never had a sense of a very close family or of a lot of laughter ... There was never a book in the house, except for the Bible and *Science and Health with Key to the Scriptures*.' [5] The latter was Mary Baker Eddy's treatise on the Christian Science faith, published in 1875. De Harak also remembered a typical evening with his mother, sisters, and brother: 'There was very little money in those days for just about anything, and there wasn't all of the technological amenities that we have now ... But I do recall the one thing that we would do is, after dinner, we would all sit around the radio and we would listen to the various radio family shows, such as: *Jack Armstrong*, *The*

∨ The Metropolitan
  Apartments, Astoria,
  Queens, New York,
  c. 1930.

  Alice de Harak, Astoria,
  Queens, New York, 1937.

All-American Boy, *The Shadow*, *Little Orphan Annie*, and *Black and Blue*.'[6]

De Harak and Nolan attended P.S. 141, a public junior high school in Astoria. Throughout the Depression-era years, public schools in New York City always kept their doors open at night so that they would be a communal haven for young people in the neighborhood. Emphasis during these gatherings was mostly on sports with the school's gymnasium in constant use. Nolan fondly recalled: 'In my early teens I would retreat from my house of misery to the sanctuary of my friends' homes where food, warmth, and the stability that goes with an intact family was always abundant. My best friend in those tender years was Rudolph ('Rudy') de Harak … Mrs. de Harak always treated me like one of her own.

Rudy and I shared common interests in music, sports, and going to dances.'[7]

The de Haraks lived in the Metropolitan Apartments, or 'the Mets' as they were known at the time. This was a large apartment complex built by the Metropolitan Life Insurance Company as an experiment in affordable, low-rent public housing, and was designed by American architect Andrew J. Thomas, described as 'the undisputed master strategist of courtyard apartment house design in the 1920s'[8] by the American architect and author Robert A.M. Stern. The complex occupied two blocks between Ditmars Boulevard, 33rd Street, 21st Avenue, and 35th Street, and consisted of twelve five-story U-shaped buildings arranged around the perimeter of a central open green space — they are still standing today.

In his pre-teen years, de Harak admitted to not being at all interested in fine art or the graphic arts other than comic strips. 'I did like to draw. I remember lying on the floor and copying *Dick Tracy* and being very, very enamored with some of the newspaper cartoonists: Milton Caniff, who did *Terry and the Pirates* … and Alex Raymond, who was really a marvelous draftsman. And he did the strip for the Hearst papers called *Flash Gordon*, and also *Jungle Jim*. Interestingly enough, he also did a strip called *Secret Agent X-9*, which was written on a daily basis by novelist and mystery writer Dashiell Hammett. I was very interested in those things, and was always taken with the cartoon strip, *Krazy Kat*.'[9]

George Herriman, the first African-American cartoonist of note, introduced his most famous character, Krazy Kat, in 1910, and a daily

strip followed in 1913. By the 1920s, *Krazy Kat* was popular with intellectuals, artists, and critics, receiving praise for its Modernist experiments with new forms of visuals and language, as well as its poetic, dialect-heavy dialogue, its fantastic, shifting backgrounds, and its bold, experimental page layouts. In 1924, cultural critic Gilbert Seldes' article 'The Krazy Kat Who Walks by Himself' gave serious attention — perhaps for the first time — to what many considered a 'low art', proposing that Herriman's strip was 'the most amusing and fantastic and satisfactory work of art produced in America'. [10] Notable fans included Charles Chaplin, Walt Disney, Umberto Eco, W.C. Fields, Ernest Hemingway, James Joyce, Jack Kerouac, Willem de Kooning, Gertrude Stein, and a young and impressionable de Harak. Herriman was also a primary influence on cartoonists such as Robert Crumb, Will Eisner, Jules Feiffer, Charles M. Schulz, Art Spiegelman, Chris Ware, and Bill Watterson.

It was these early interests in comic-strip serials that began de Harak's introduction to the world of fine art and Modernism in the 1930s. He continued with his drawing, especially in junior high school. The results seemed to impress his art teacher at P.S. 141, who suggested that he apply to New York City's School of Industrial Art.

School of Industrial Art

In November 1936, four New York City art teachers came together to establish the School of Industrial Art, located in a dilapidated warehouse building at 257 West 40th Street between Ninth and Tenth Avenues in Manhattan. It had first been envisioned as a continuation school — one that students who had already left school attended for half days so that they could continue their education, taking vocational classes relevant to their current or future jobs. However, when it opened, the School of Industrial Art had transformed into one of the first vocational high schools with an emphasis on commercial art in New York City. It had an initial enrollment of 129 full-time students, all of them male, and a staff of eight teachers.

Due to limited resources, skilled artists were recruited to serve as teachers. While they were licensed in art, they taught everything including mathematics and science. Six months after its opening, fifty-nine full-time female students joined the student body. By the end of 1939, the faculty grew from eight to twenty-nine, and enrollment reached over five hundred full-time students. An advisory

< *Krazy Kat* comic strip by George Herriman, c. 1930.

∨ De Harak outside the Metropolitan Apartments, Astoria, Queens, New York, 1937.

J.I. Biegeleisen. *Silk Screen Stenciling as a Fine Art*, New York: McGraw-Hill Book Company, Inc., 1938. Title-page designed by Rockwell Kent.

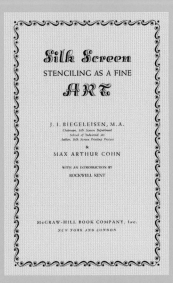

commission composed of art-industry leaders was formed to assist in the development of curricula and the placement of graduates into the real world. As the School of Industrial Art continued to grow, an elementary school building located on East 51st Street was added to the campus and used as an annex for several years. Since both of these buildings had originally been built in the 1860s, many facilities considered essential to a modern high school were in a state of disrepair. Following an extensive review of alternative locations, and a certain amount of local-government opposition, the school identified a new home — a former annex building to Benjamin Franklin High School, located on East 79th Street on the Upper East Side of Manhattan. In September 1960, the School changed its name to the High School of Art and Design and relocated to 1075 Second Avenue, where it remains today. In the years following de Harak's graduation in 1940, many of the School's alumni became notable for their creative work in the fields of art and design, including graphic designer, art director, and photographer Henry Wolf (1943); singer and artist Tony Bennett (1945); fashion designer Calvin Klein (1960); Pulitzer Prize-winning author and cartoonist Art Spiegelman (1965); actor, playwright, and activist Harvey Fierstein (1969); fashion photographer Steven Meisel (1971); artist and photographer Lorna Simpson (1978); and fashion designer Marc Jacobs (1981). Many members of the School's faculty also became well known for their creative work, including cartoonist Alvin Hollingsworth and artist Tom Wesselmann.

One of de Harak's most influential teachers at the School of Industrial Art was Jacob Israel Biegeleisen, a Polish-American screen printer, educator, and author of several books on the screen-printing process. Biegeleisen taught classes in screen printing at several New York City high schools, including the School of Industrial Art, where he supervised its screen department and served as the Chairman of its Art Department for over twenty-five years. Biegeleisen was a well-known, knowledgeable, and highly skilled practitioner of the screen-printing process, both in the classroom and the workplace. Writing in 1963, he stated: 'My knowledge of the subject is … not limited to reading about it in books or consulting with others. My own personal experience as a daily practitioner in the field goes back more than twenty-five years and extends to the present day. During my long internship, I have had occasion to work in every department of the screen shop: as a printer, paint mixer, layout and lettering artist, stencil man, manager, estimator, and consultant.' [11]

While at the School of Industrial Art, de Harak studied everything from lettering and mechanical drafting, to drawing and silk screening. While he was never the type of student who applied himself with great diligence, he did learn visual and technical skills that would serve him well later in life. He admitted that he didn't attend many of his classes in high school because, in his words, he was 'always trying to hustle some way to make a buck'. [12] He later described his last two years at Industrial Art as 'a very, very difficult time … I was forced into a work ethic … When I got back from school, which was at 4:00 p.m. in the afternoon, I didn't go home. I went directly to the local drugstore, where I worked from 4:00 p.m. in the afternoon until 10:00 p.m. at night. I worked very hard for a year-and-a-half, and my pay was $5.00 a week. And, of that, I turned $4.00 of it over to my mother. So, that went on, actually, until I graduated, which was in 1940.' [13]

∨ De Harak and Bernard
Nolan (*left*), location
unknown, 1941.

De Harak in Compiègne,
France, 1945.

De Harak was also good friends with Anthony Benedetto, later to be known as legendary vocalist Tony Bennett. The two had met in 1938, when Bennett's family moved into the Metropolitan Apartments. Both boys attended P.S. 141 and shared a love of music, art, and drawing. Following Bennett's failure to be accepted into the prestigious High School of Performing Arts in Manhattan, de Harak suggested he apply to the School of Industrial Art instead. While Bennett initially regretted attending Industrial Art and not being able to go to Performing Arts, years later he came to a different realization: 'All I did was learn technique; how to make stained-glass windows, how to do silk screen, how to do lithographs, sculpture, painting, photography. It was a wonderful experience.' [14] In his 1998 autobiography *The Good Life*, Bennett described de Harak as one of the few people in his life at the time who continuously encouraged him in his love of art and music: 'He became a dear friend of my family's, and even came to think of my mom as his 'other mother'. We hung out together because of our mutual love of jazz and drawing. In fact, Rudy took up the saxophone as a kid. I remember it well because in the summertime, when everybody had their windows wide open, the whole building could hear Rudy blowing away, learning his scales. Eventually, he became quite a proficient sax player.' [15]

De Harak's old schoolmate, Bernard Nolan, later recalled his friend's efforts to kickstart his career: 'Rudy was blessed with intuitive talents leaning mostly to the graphic arts and music. He graduated from the School of Industrial Art in New York City at the age of sixteen where his talents could be nurtured by practical training. I can still visualize Rudy and his large portfolio containing samples of his work, hoofing around Manhattan trying to break into the world of graphic arts. He even had a sample comic strip in that portfolio, one of those 'superhero' applications called 'The Polkadot'. Fittingly, Rudy's hero wore a polka dot mask as he flitted about vanquishing evil. Sadly at the time, Rudy could not penetrate the world of graphic arts.' [16]

When de Harak graduated from the School of industrial Art in 1940, the country was still in the throes of the Great Depression, with unemployment at a record high. However, he was luckier than most of his classmates, since his first job was loosely related to commercial art. Within a month following graduation, both de Harak and Nolan found jobs at Heading, Incorporated, a Long Island City textile-printing plant that produced fabrics and textiles for draperies and upholstery. They worked in the plant's printing shop, which made silk screens and zinc plates, etching the plate's fabric patterns or painting them directly onto the silk screens. After working at Heading for more than two years, de Harak was drafted into the 78th Infantry Division of the US Army in 1943. At the age of eighteen, he would be away from his family for the first time, looking reluctantly towards his future and the unknown.

U.S. Army 78th Infantry and World War II

In September 1939, Nazi Germany invaded Poland and World War II began. Two years later, on 8 December 1941, the United States entered the war, following the bombing of the American fleet at Pearl Harbor by the Japanese the previous day. The 78th Infantry Division

> *Jazz*, pencil drawing by
> de Harak, c. 1940.

was ordered into military action in the Spring of 1943, having completed basic training, advanced training, and maneuvers at Camp Butner, North Carolina. The division embarked from New York City, sailing to the United Kingdom in October 1944, and crossing the English Channel to France in late November 1944. After landing in France, it moved to Belgium, and then on to Germany to prepare for combat. De Harak later described his combat experience: 'I went in as a replacement. I was a rifleman in a line company, the 4th Infantry Division, and somehow managed to squeak through all of Normandy, the liberation of Paris, the run through Brittany into Belgium, the Siegfried Line, and then into the Hürtgen Forest, and the Battle of the Bulge. I think, if my memory serves me right, in twenty-one days in the Hürtgen Forest, we lost 10,000 men. It was a pretty brutal experience.' [17] In an interview, fifty years later, he would only use three words to describe this time in his life: fear, loneliness, and hopelessness.

The Battle of the Bulge was described by British Prime Minister Winston Churchill as 'undoubtedly the greatest American battle of the war' [18] and was the Nazi regime's last major offensive against the Western front. Its failure paved the way to victory for the Allied forces. De Harak was in the thick of the fighting for months. He was injured on 11 February 1945 following a fierce firefight, taken off the line to a field hospital, reclassified into non-combatant service, and was finally stationed for nine to ten months in Compiègne, a small town located approximately forty miles north-east of Paris. To maintain his sanity while convalescing, he turned to drawing as a means of escape, making his first attempts at visual storytelling. After almost four years of military service, de Harak was discharged and shipped back to the States, arriving in New York City on New Year's Day, 1946. He was twenty-one years of age.

Return to Southern California

After spending a few weeks in New York City to reconnect with friends, de Harak decided to return to California and reunite with his family who had moved back to the Los Angeles area while he was overseas. With no specific training or career prospects, he took a manual-labor job in a concrete-block factory, as well as delivering commercial cans of milk to local restaurants at night. After six months of what he called 'hard labor', [19] and uncertain about his future prospects, he decided that he had enough and quit his job.

> *Köln Alone...*,
> colored pencil drawing
> by de Harak, 1945.

He was determined to find a job in which he could thrive, so he went to a local employment agency. Fortunately, he met an inquisitive counselor who took an interest in him. De Harak recollected that she simply asked him what he wanted to do and what interests he had. He jokingly responded, 'I want a job where I don't have to lift anything heavier than a pencil.' [20] He also told her that he liked to draw and paint. Soon after, she found him a position as a mechanical art apprentice at a small art studio and production house, California Advertising Art Service, that serviced the needs of local advertising agencies in Los Angeles.

Initially, he was hired to produce mechanical art, a task for which he had no skills or training. To further complicate this situation, no one at the studio knew anything about these skills either, so he took it upon himself to learn: 'I just figured if the printer or the engraver, as the case may be, had to work with this kind of material, they must have it all over the place, and they must know exactly what they wanted. So, at night, I would go to the printer's or to the engraver's, or both, and they were always eager to help, because it was in their interest, from a business point of view, but also in their interest from a craft point of view, that they would get something that they could work with, with the least amount of trouble. So, I really learned from the printers and the engravers, what was the best way to produce a mechanical.' [21] At that time, de Harak's new job was referred to by many in the profession as a 'layout artist'. The design historian Philip Meggs describes the role of a layout artist as 'a pair of hands doing what he was told. He had value as an artist with drawing ability and a sense of placement, but no one would consider asking him to solve a problem, or even ask him to think about the problem.' [22] Following the end of World War II, the graphic design profession grew by leaps and bounds in the United States. While to a certain degree, this could be attributed to the development of new technologies in typesetting, printing, and paper manufacturing, this transformation was given additional momentum by America's embrace of European Modernism, and related avant-garde art movements such as De Stijl, Purism, Surrealism, Dadaism, Cubism, and Futurism.

This was also a period full of opportunity and growth for de Harak, with the roles of graphic design and of the graphic designer starting to be defined in new and meaningful ways. While he had little if any knowledge of these developments at the time, his responsibilities and skills as a layout artist were quickly evolving, encompassing those that we associate with the profession of graphic design today. After five or six months at California Advertising Art Service, de Harak proudly recalled: 'I got very good at it, and in a very short period of time. Interestingly enough, I ended up running that office … The boss was rarely there, he was always out playing golf, and so it worked out that I was really doing all of this stuff, and I also was going to see clients, and deliver work to them, and so on. A lot of responsibility. I was twenty-two years old at the time.' [23] As his confidence grew, de Harak began to hone his craft as a mechanical and layout artist. Soon after, he was promoted to studio manager. One of his early independent assignments, an illustration and advertisement for a local business — the Los Angeles Coat & Suit Manufacturing Association — was entered into an annual design competition by his supervisor and won a merit award from the Art Directors Club of Los Angeles. De Harak was astonished, unable to believe that he could receive recognition and acclaim for his work. In many ways, this was the start of his new career in graphic design.

Around this same time, de Harak had another defining moment in his young career. He reconnected with a former high school classmate, Hal Tritel, who was now a graphic designer and happened to be working in the same office building in downtown Los Angeles. Tritel had been valedictorian of de Harak's graduating class at the School of Industrial Art in 1940, and de Harak later credited Tritel with introducing him to the world of Modernist graphic design. Following his service in the armed forces during World War II, Tritel arrived in Los Angeles in 1945 and soon began his career as a graphic designer. As a freelancer graphic designer on the fringes of the film industry, he worked for Seven Arts Productions and Hill-Hecht-Lancaster Productions (most notably, on the poster for the 1955 Academy Award-winning film, *Marty*).

De Harak fondly remembered that 'Hal was a whiz … he was very, very smart, very bright. He was an intellectual, and a very talented chap. And he took me under his wing and started to introduce me to museums, and recommended books for me to read.' [24] To de Harak, his entire world and outlook now seemed brighter and ripe with opportunities. It was during this time that Tritel invited him to attend lectures at the Art Center School in Los Angeles given by two renowned Mid-century Modernist European émigrés, Will Burtin and György Kepes. Founded as a private college in 1930, the Art Center School (renamed Art Center College of Design in 1965) offered students classes in advertising, publishing, industrial design, painting and drawing, and photography. It was one of the first art institutions in the country to have a faculty solely made up of working professionals from those fields. Following the end of World War II, enrollment skyrocketed due to an influx of veterans who wanted to pursue the opportunities for higher education and vocational training provided by the G.I. Bill, which offered financial and social benefits to service personnel. This growth led to a move to larger facilities; the start of a full, year-round schedule of class offerings; and a year later to becoming an accredited four-year art and design educational institution.

De Harak later recalled that these two lectures at the Art Center School in particular had made a profound and lasting impact on his life: 'The first was a lecture by Will Burtin, 'Integration: The New Discipline in Design'. Burtin not only spoke about design and communications, but he presented an exhibition of his work, which moved the viewer through a series of experiences which were described as the four principal realities of visual communication: the reality of man, as measure and measurer; the reality of light, color, texture; the reality of space, motion, time; and the reality of science.

He was the first person I had heard use the term 'visual communications'…A month or so later, I also had the opportunity of hearing György Kepes. At the time I didn't fully understand everything he had to say; yet I knew that his words were very important to me, and I recall my excitement, as I was able to draw parallels between what he was saying about the plastic arts and what Will Burtin had said concerning the realities of visual communications.' [25] Both lectures were pivotal for de Harak and set him on a life and career path that he would never veer far from. Years later, he admitted to a friend that 'he was blown away' [26] by Burtin's words. These experiences marked the beginning of de Harak's realization that it was possible for him to communicate visual information that could transcend common graphic conventions and become art. He also quickly came to the conclusion that he could have a viable vocation in graphic design while simultaneously experiencing deep personal fulfillment. He quit his job as a mechanical and layout artist and committed himself completely and wholeheartedly to his new profession in graphic design.

In 1948, de Harak and Tritel opened their own design studio. Assembling Tritel's previous work, as well as some hypothetical work that the pair quickly put together, a portfolio was compiled and they started to make the rounds. In less than a year, de Harak started to do freelance work for Monogram Art Studios, a New York City-based design firm. Monogram was starting to work for Columbia Records on redesigning a portion of the CBS Columbia Records library. De Harak's design solutions were somewhat naïve, and were derivative of contemporaries he admired such as Saul Bass, Paul Rand, and Alvin Lustig. However, this early work provided him with an opportunity to evaluate his approach to graphic design and visual storytelling. Whatever de Harak's design solutions lacked from a conceptual perspective at this point was made up for in the breadth of his experimentations in shape, form, color, scale, image, composition, and typography. De Harak described these challenging times fondly: 'We would go out and see people, and try to get freelance work. And we worked out of a basement that was really kind of marvelous…And there was a group of us that worked together, and it was a pretty exciting time, trying to learn new things…I rarely went to bed. I would just go to sleep, exhausted, because I would spend all of my time reading, trying to do some writing. I bought a camera, taking photographs, experimenting with emulsions, and going to museums, and painting.' [27]

Kindred Spirits and Like-Minded Modernists

As the graphic design community started to flourish in Southern California, there was an obvious and vital need for many designers to connect and come together to discuss their work and, most importantly, feel that they were part of a larger sympathetic group. Following the Kepes lecture, de Harak was fortunate to meet a few kindred spirits and like-minded Modernists including Saul Bass, Louis Danziger, John Follis, and Alvin Lustig. Soon after, they established the Los Angeles Society for Contemporary Designers. While the organization was short-lived, it was one of the first occasions when a group of multidisciplinary designers, representing graphic, product, industrial, and exhibition design, came together

∨ De Harak with Saul Bass
(*right*) at an Alliance
Graphique Internationale
(AGI) conference in
Solvang, California, USA,
1985.

to share their ideas and collective work with the public at large. De Harak later explained that the reason for forming the society was purely a matter of survival: 'We were a young, very enthusiastic group trying to function in a desert, which is what Los Angeles was at the time.' [28]

Throughout his celebrated forty-year career, Saul Bass received global recognition for his work in graphic, film, industrial, and exhibition design, and was best known for his animated film title sequences, film posters, and corporate identities. In 1996, de Harak wrote a remembrance of his lifelong friend for the Los Angeles chapter of the American Institute of Graphic Arts (AIGA): 'I first met Saul in 1947. Two years later, I made the decision to leave Los Angeles and move to New York. Knowing that Saul was from New York, had studied and began his career there, I called him and asked if he would meet with me and perhaps give me his opinion on the advisability of such a move. We did meet, and I shall always remember his concern, sensitivity to my situation and the many pertinent questions he asked. Saul was both very generous with his time and helpful ... I think Saul was unaware of it, but his attitudes, values, broad information and curiosities made a great and long lasting impression upon me. The way in which he looked at and thought about things was indeed unique and was certainly the root of his specialness as a communicator.' [29]

Louis (Lou) Danziger is perhaps best known for introducing the visual principles of European Constructivism to Mid-century Modern advertising and graphic design in America. Danziger fondly remembered the founding members of the Los Angeles Society for Contemporary Designers as a group of 'crusaders who were deeply committed to doing and furthering Modernist design which we felt important to contributing to a better society ... We wanted to gain recognition for our work and encourage modern design appreciation throughout the Los Angeles' business community.' [30]

California-native John Follis was a multidisciplinary designer, author, and educator with a surprising range of work and interests, including graphic, exhibition, editorial, and furniture design. He is considered by many to be one of the founding fathers of environmental graphic design — his book *Architectural Signing and Graphics* (New York: Watson-Guptill Publications, 1979) was the first comprehensive 'how to' reference book on this emerging design discipline, and featured de Harak's work as one of its twenty-five case studies.

A self-taught designer, writer, and educator, Alvin Lustig was one of the first American designers to approach his craft and profession in a non-specialized manner. He believed that all design was a matter of form and content, and that the role of the designer was that of synthesizer, not of style maker. During his brief career, Lustig's diverse work ranged from books and book jackets to furniture and interior design. In an introduction to a lecture on the work of Lustig, de Harak shared his insights with audience members: 'Alvin had a strong influence on my work, as he also had on the design community at large. In those days all of us younger designers and, I'm convinced, the older ones, too, watched in anticipation for Lustig's next design solution. Of the many designers in the United States and Europe whose work I admired, Alvin Lustig's visual poetry and graphic design magic perhaps touched me the deepest. Alvin Lustig really believed that good design could change the world.' [31]

By this point, the profession and practice of graphic design across the country were being led by a group of European émigrés, who were inspiring young American graphic designers such as Bass, Danziger, Follis, Lustig, and de Harak to make their own individual marks on the profession and the world. In 1950, de Harak decided to move back to New York City in search of better and more challenging opportunities. Upon his arrival, he quickly embraced the influences and tenets of the newly emerging 'International Typographic Style'.

1. Will Burtin, 'Integration: The New Discipline in Design', *Graphis,* vol. 5, no. 27, January/February 1949, p. 230.
2. György Kepes, *Language of Vision*, Chicago: Paul Theobald and Company, 1944, p. 13.
3. Bernard Thomas Nolan, *Isaiah's Eagles Rising: A Generation of Airmen*, Bloomington: Xlibris Corporation, 2002, p. 37.
4. Rudolph de Harak, 'Oral History Interview with Rudolph de Harak', interview by Susan Larsen on 27 April 2000 (transcript), in Ellsworth, Maine. Archives of American Art, Smithsonian Institution, Washington, DC.
5. Ibid.
6. Ibid.
7. Bernard Thomas Nolan, *Isaiah's Eagles Rising: A Generation of Airmen,* Bloomington: Xlibris Corporation, 2002, pp. 39–40.
8. Robert A. M. Stern, Gregory Gilmartin, and Thomas Mellins, *New York 1930: Architecture and Urbanism Between the Two World Wars*, New York: Rizzoli International Publications, Inc., 1987, p. 419.
9. Rudolph de Harak, 'Oral History Interview with Rudolph de Harak', interview by Susan Larsen on 27 April 2000 (transcript), in Ellsworth, Maine. Archives of American Art, Smithsonian Institution, Washington, DC.
10. Bas Schuddeboom, 'Milton Caniff,' Lambiek Comiclopedia, 30 December 2020, https://www.lambiek.net/artists/c/caniff.htm.
11. Jacob Israel Biegeleisen, *The Complete Book of Silk Screen Printing Production*, Mineola: Dover Publications, 1963, p. viii.
12. Rudolph de Harak, 'Oral History Interview with Rudolph de Harak', interview by Susan Larsen on 27 April 2000 (transcript), in Ellsworth, Maine. Archives of American Art, Smithsonian Institution, Washington, DC.
13. Ibid.
14. David Evanier, *All The Things You Are: The Life of Tony Bennett*, Hoboken: John Wiley & Sons, Inc., 2011, p. 36.
15. Tony Bennett, *The Good Life: The Autobiography of Tony Bennett*, New York: Atria Books, 1998, p. 37.
16. Bernard Thomas Nolan, *Isaiah's Eagles Rising: A Generation of Airmen*, Bloomington: Xlibris Corporation, 2002, pp. 40–41.
17. Rudolph de Harak, 'Oral History Interview with Rudolph de Harak', interview by Susan Larsen on 27 April 2000 (transcript), in Ellsworth, Maine. Archives of American Art, Smithsonian Institution, Washington, DC.
18. Robert Rhodes James, ed., *Winston S. Churchill: His Complete Speeches, 1897–1963, Vol. VII, 1943–1949*, New York: Chelsea House Publishers, 1974, p. 7095.
19. Rudolph de Harak, 'Oral History Interview with Rudolph de Harak', interview by Susan Larsen on 27 April 2000 (transcript), in Ellsworth, Maine. Archives of American Art, Smithsonian Institution, Washington, DC.
20. Ibid.
21. Ibid.
22. Philip B. Meggs, '50 Years of Graphic Design: The Shape of the Decades. The 1940s: Rise of the Modernists', *Print*, vol. 43, no. 6, November/December 1989, p. 68.
23. Rudolph de Harak, 'Oral History Interview with Rudolph de Harak', interview by Susan Larsen on 27 April 2000 (transcript), in Ellsworth, Maine. Archives of American Art, Smithsonian Institution, Washington, DC.
24. Ibid.
25. Ibid.
26. Ibid.
27. Ibid.
28. Steven Heller, 'Rudolph de Harak: A Playful Modernist', *Baseline*, no. 45, 2004, p. 28.
29. Rudolph de Harak, 'Remembering Saul Bass.' n. l., 1996.
30. Louis Danziger, Interview by Richard Poulin, 19 March 2021.
31. Rudolph de Harak. 'Introduction to Alvin Lustig.' n. l., n. d.

∨ Album cover, *Eddy Duchin Reminisces, Eddy Duchin with Rhythm Accompaniment,* CBS Columbia Records, 1948.

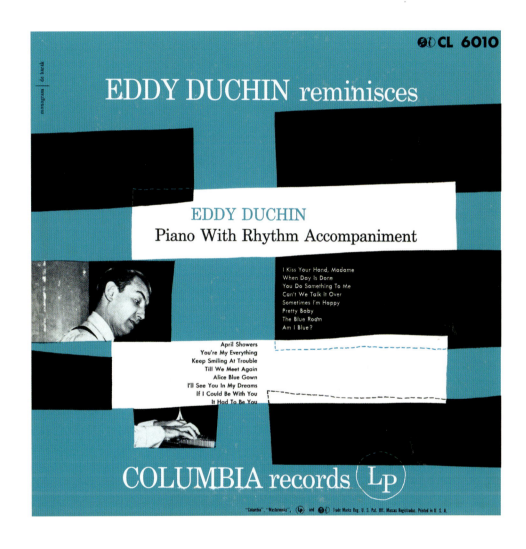

⌄ Album cover, *Xavier
Cugat and His Orchestra*,
Rhumba with Cugat,
CBS Columbia Records,
1948.

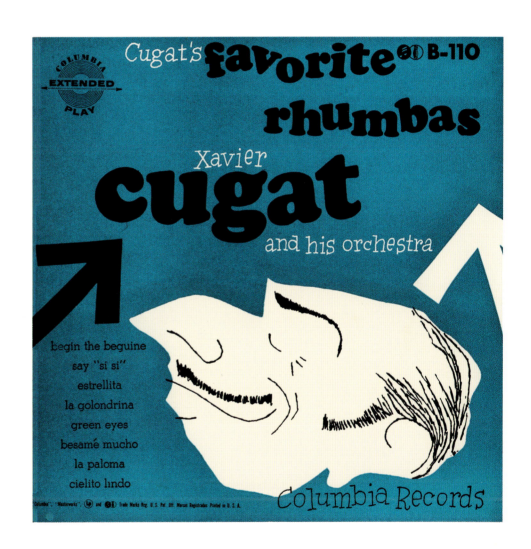

∨ Album cover, *Xavier Cugat and His Orchestra, Cugat's Favorite Rhumbas*, CBS Columbia Records, 1948.

∨ Album cover, *Les Brown
and His Orchestra:
Sentimental Journey,*
CBS Columbia Records,
c. 1949.

> Album cover, *Les Brown
and His Orchestra:
Dance Parade,*
CBS Columbia Records,
1949.

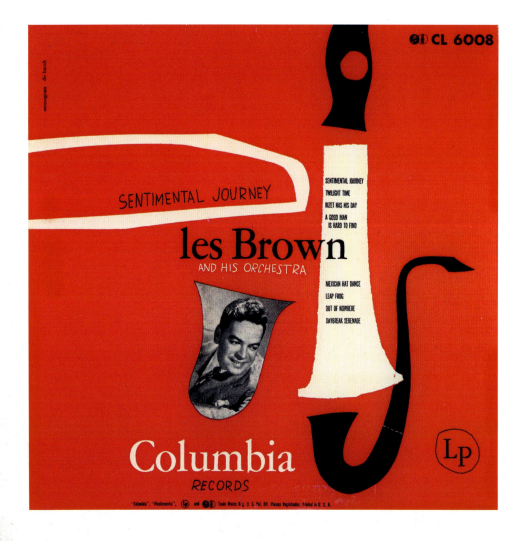

CL 6060

DANCE PARADE

SOPHISTICATED SWING
A FINE ROMANCE
'TAIN'T ME
SENTIMENTAL RHAPSODY
LOVER'S LEAP

les Brown
AND HIS ORCHESTRA

I'VE GOT MY LOVE
TO KEEP ME WARM

JUST ONE OF
THOSE THINGS

DARDANELLA

Columbia
RECORDS

LP

< Magazine cover (detail),
Graphis, vol. 13, no. 70,
Graphis, Inc., 1957.

Immediately following the end of World War II, New York City became one of the leading economic and cultural centers of the world. It was here that European Modernism first found its home in America and would prove to be a powerful and pervasive force throughout the country for decades to come. Newly constructed glass and steel office towers rose throughout Manhattan, representing the triumph of corporate America, but also that of the International Style. The latter was a major architectural movement that emerged in Western Europe during the 1920s and 1930s. Its moniker was originally coined by American architectural historian Henry-Russell Hitchcock and American architect Philip Johnson for their 1932 groundbreaking exhibition at the Museum of Modern Art (MoMA) in New York City on what was considered at the time as avant-garde architecture. It was rooted in the earlier developments of Modernist design principles, primarily from the Bauhaus, and was characterized by the simplification of form; a rejection of ornament; the honest and obvious expression of a building's structure; and the use of functional, utilitarian materials such as concrete, steel, and glass.

Just as Modernism swept across American architecture in the post-war period, a new objective rationalism was taking hold of American graphic design during this same time period. This 'International Typographic Style', also known as 'Swiss Style', had first emerged during the 1920s and 1930s in Russia, the Netherlands, and Germany. Its philosophy and tenets evolved directly from the

Weimar Bauhaus, the De Stijl movement, and Jan Tschichold's highly influential manifesto, *Die neue Typographie* (Berlin: Verlag des Bildungsverbandes der Deutschen Buchdrucker, 1928), in which the philosophy and practice of Modernist graphic design were first expressed.

Further refined in Switzerland during the 1950s, the International Typographic Style was based on the visual principles of order, function, and clarity, and rapidly established itself as one of the most influential design movements of the twentieth century. Its reliance upon pure geometry, asymmetrical compositions, sans-serif typefaces such as Akzidenz-Grotesk (H. Berthold AG, 1896), mathematically-constructed page grids, and related proportional systems transformed graphic design. Early examples often featured typography as a primary design element, and not just as text; later work reflected a preference for photography over illustration or drawing. Its tenets shared many characteristics with those of the International Style in architecture — both aspired to transcend style, national identity, and an individual's point of view — and both were enthusiastically embraced worldwide. The International Typographic Style became part of mainstream consciousness, providing graphic designers with a unified visual language that has prevailed for the last ninety years, and remains a major force that resonates with many contemporary design disciplines.

Rebirth in New York City

De Harak remained in Southern California for four years, but at the end of 1949 he realized that there was nothing left for him personally or professionally on the West Coast. He desperately wanted to succeed in his new profession and decided that he would be in a better position to do so if he was in New York City. In February 1950, he travelled by train cross-country back to the East Coast to look for work. He had a very limited portfolio and hardly any work experience but was fearlessly determined to find a job that would be right for him. Initially, he met with little success. He later described this frustrating experience, reminiscing that he had received 'a number of offers that didn't seem quite right, and twenty times that number of turn-downs; I saw a lot of people. Actually, I practically lived in Grand Central Station. I was staying with a friend all the way out in Corona in Flushing, Queens... It was about a forty-five-minute or an hour ride into Manhattan. And, in those days, you could take showers in Grand Central Station, and use their lockers. And I would keep all of my stuff there, and I would arrive early in the morning, and stay all day, trying to find work, and then go home in the evening. It was a long haul.' [1]

New York City transformed at a rapid pace in the 1950s, and fortunately de Harak was now at the center of these changes. He had returned to a city that was on the verge of a new age and a new understanding of creative freedom, and one with a new set of Modernist values, ideas, and trends that were the counterpoint to long-held mainstream beliefs in social, cultural, and religious values. Among these developments were many that would have a major impact on the course of Mid-century Modernism, as well as on de Harak's burgeoning career as a graphic designer. In 1950, the Museum of Modern Art (MoMA) launched an influential series of

⌄ *Seventeen* magazine
cover, February, 1950.

'Good Design' exhibitions. A year later, the first major installation of Abstract Expressionist work, the *9th Street Art Exhibition*, featured work by such artists as Willem de Kooning, Jackson Pollock, and Mark Rothko, among others. The same year, author J.D. Salinger introduced the world to Holden Caulfield in his provocative coming-of-age novel *The Catcher in the Rye*. In 1954, Seymour Chwast, Milton Glaser, Reynold Ruffins, and Edward Sorel started Push Pin Studios. Jerome Robbins' *West Side Story* opened on Broadway in 1956 and became a turning point in American musical theatre. In 1957, the travelling exhibition *Swiss Graphic Designers* — featuring work by Karl Gerstner, Armin Hofmann, Richard Paul Lohse, Josef Müller-Brockmann, Siegfried Odermatt, Emil Ruder, Carlo Vivarelli, and others — introduced the International Typographic Style to the United States. The Seagram Building, designed by Mies van der Rohe, was completed in 1958 and immediately became a Modernist icon. The following year, the Guggenheim Museum, designed by American architect Frank Lloyd Wright, opened on Fifth Avenue.

In those first few months following his return to New York City, de Harak became obsessed with learning, experimenting, and experiencing as much as he could while simultaneously looking for a job. 'I hardly slept,' he remembered. 'I read books, did drawings, took pictures, melted negatives in boiling water, all sorts of marvelous things.' [2] He also started to paint. Modern art, and specifically Abstract Expressionism, became a major influence — he particularly admired the work of Franz Kline, Willem de Kooning, and Robert Motherwell. Painting became a means of self-expression, and also a major visual element in his graphic design work. In the spring of 1950, at the age of twenty-six, de Harak finally landed his first professional job, as promotion art director at *Seventeen* magazine, then located at 11 West 42nd Street in Midtown Manhattan.

Seventeen Magazine

Seventeen magazine began as a monthly publication geared towards inspiring teenage girls to become model workers and citizens. Soon after its debut, the magazine took a more fashion- and romance-oriented approach, while also promoting self-confidence and independence. It was first published in September 1944 by American businessman Walter Annenberg's Triangle Publications.

As its visionary founder and its first editor-in-chief from 1944 to 1953, Helen Valentine enhanced the role of teenage girls as consumers of popular culture by presenting them with role models that included working women, and also with information about their personal and professional development. During the early 1950s, *Seventeen* magazine was also fertile ground for a select group of young and talented artists, illustrators, and graphic designers. Led by the legendary magazine art director Cipe Pineles, its design staff and regular contributors included Leonard Baskin, Seymour Chwast, Eva Hesse, Sol LeWitt, Richard Lindner, Ad Reinhardt, Ben Shahn, Jerome Snyder, Saul Steinberg, and now de Harak.

Will Burtin, who had been such an influence on de Harak's passion for graphic design, also had his design offices at 11 West 42nd Street. De Harak later recalled, 'I didn't get to meet him at that time until thirteen years later when we became good friends...but just to know that he was in the building was just so thrilling to me.' [3]

> De Harak's first spot
illustration for *Esquire*
magazine, May 1953.

∨ 488 Madison Avenue,
New York City, 1951.
Wurts Bros., photographer.

After a few months working at the magazine, de Harak's outlook on his emerging career suddenly took an even more positive turn when *Seventeen* relocated to 488 Madison Avenue.

488 Madison Avenue

Completed in 1950, 488 Madison Avenue — known as the Look Building, after the influential magazine — was one of the first commercial office buildings in New York City to reflect the influence of the International Style. At the time, Mies van der Rohe's dictum of 'less is more' was just starting to impose itself on the American urban landscape. The Look Building was also known as one of the city's most influential hubs of creative activity. De Harak once described working there as 'just marvelously crazy...I mean, talk about these wonderful coincidences...in our building were *Look*, *Fleur*, *Esquire*, *Coronet*, *Apparel Arts*, and the William H. Weintraub Agency...It was a beehive of design.' [4] Everyone who was anyone in publishing and advertising in New York City during the 1950s worked at 488 Madison Avenue: Allen Hurlburt was art director at *Look*; Paul Rand was art director at the Weintraub Agency; Art Kane was an art director at *Seventeen*; and Henry Wolf was art director at *Esquire*. Fortunately for de Harak, all four of these men would soon become his friends and creative colleagues.

After only eighteen months at *Seventeen* magazine, de Harak became frustrated with the commercial culture at the magazine and quit his job. Subsequently, he went to work for an advertising agency but soon realized that taking the position was also a mistake and resigned. This was the last full-time job he would ever have. He reflected on his mind-set at the time: 'I think it was too hard for me to work for somebody. It's not that I didn't want to, but I was very strong in my convictions and the way I wanted to work is antithetical to the way most advertising agencies think. Actually, I didn't take direction too well. Therefore, going out on my own was a choice of necessity, not so much something I wanted to do.' [5] While two of his earliest jobs were in promotion and advertising, de Harak was never interested nor intimately involved in the world of advertising. He was always proud to say that he intentionally steered clear of the 'hard sell'. Whether he planned it or not, he found, throughout his career, that he was always on the periphery of the mainstream graphic design profession. He also realized, upon leaving *Seventeen*, that he still had a great deal to learn about his craft and profession. Even so, he was still inspired and passionate about numerous aspects of the visual world and the creative process, from photography and fine art to literature and music. And he was also beginning to understand what he needed to connect with in order to define his own point of view — his own voice.

Interests and Opportunities

When he left *Seventeen*, de Harak was living in a small apartment on West 58th Street in Midtown Manhattan, which also doubled as his studio. The kitchen was his darkroom but could only be used at night since he did not have the means or the money to black it out when needed. Photographic prints were processed in his kitchen and

DE HARAK

washed in his bathtub. While he realized very quickly that being a purist was unlikely to be marketable in the commercial world, he stood by his intuitive convictions and started to pursue freelance work. One of his first major commissions came from his friend and colleague, Henry Wolf. De Harak became good friends with Wolf while they were working at 488 Madison Avenue. Along with Art Kane, they shared a mutual passion for design, fine art, jazz music, and photography — the three of them took weekend outings together to explore New York City and its surroundings with their cameras. Since his arrival in New York City, de Harak had become extremely interested in avant-garde photography and film, especially the work of Man Ray, Luis Buñuel, Salvador Dalí, and Hans Richter. He also became an avid experimenter, at first with his newly purchased Rolex camera which he quickly realized was ineffective as a visual tool. He soon traded it in for a new Leica III camera, and started buying and testing different films, experimenting with different emulsions, and teaching himself about various film-processing techniques. It was through these friendships and initial experiences that he learned to control his camera, and also discovered that content could follow concept.

Henry Wolf was one of the leading graphic designers, photographers, and art directors of the twentieth century. During the 1950s and 1960s, while serving as art director at *Esquire*, *Harper's Bazaar*, and *Show* magazines, he influenced American editorial and magazine design with his unorthodox layouts, experimental typography, and inventive photography. While working at the monthly American men's magazine *Esquire*, he commissioned illustrative and photographic work from de Harak, as well as graphic designers Jerome Kuhl and Roy Kuhlman, photographers Bob Cato and Jay Maisel, and artist Andy Warhol.

Esquire had initially flourished during the Depression era under the leadership of editor and co-founder Arnold Gingrich. In the 1940s, the magazine was transformed into a more refined publication, with an emphasis on men's fashion and literary contributions by high-profile authors, including André Gide, Ernest Hemingway, F. Scott Fitzgerald, and Alberto Moravia. In subsequent years, the introduction of Alberto Vargas's illustrated pin-up girls and New Journalism authors such as Joan Didion, Norman Mailer,

∨ De Harak in his New York City studio, 1955. Jerome Kuhl, photographer.

Gay Talese, and Tom Wolfe boosted the popularity of the magazine and its circulation.

From 1953 to 1958, Wolf commissioned de Harak's most visible work to date — a series of monthly spot illustrations for the magazine. These unusual editorial collages, forty-one in all produced over a period of five years, were referred to by de Harak as 'jazz-like improvisations and a kind of 1950s Dada'. [6] Composed from found print ephemera, his own photographs, and drawings that he had either collected or produced over the past few years, these impromptu conceptual compositions reflected his ever-growing interests in abstract expressionism, photographic experimentation, and visual communications.

Among his early work, de Harak took tremendous care over, and had particular pride in, those pieces that he actually prepared for reproduction himself. For example, his *Esquire* collages were always submitted to Wolf as individual composite photographic prints — even if the collage included a variety of visual elements, such as typography, multiple images, or line art, de Harak would always prepare each final composition as a single piece of registered film. He admitted years later in an interview that his earlier technical training allowed him to take great joy in doing things with a high degree of skill and precision. De Harak's self-discipline was boundless. If he ever needed anything, he found a way to make it happen, and he always looked to do it better time after time.

In the spring of 1952, after living and working in his combined apartment and studio for almost a year, de Harak moved to an actual working design studio on West 55th Street, which he shared with graphic designer Jerome Kuhl, whom he had first met while working at 488 Madison Avenue. Kuhl would become a good friend and the subject of many of de Harak's photographic experiments in the next few years.

A New Way of Thinking

In the early 1950s, Midtown Manhattan was the epicenter of the American music industry and home to the headquarters of three major recording labels — Columbia, Decca, and RCA Victor — as well as numerous music publishers and recording studios. At the beginning of the decade, the music industry started to re-evaluate how its products were being packaged and merchandised to the American consumer. New ways of thinking were emerging that would ultimately change the manner in which music recordings were marketed to the listening public. It would also produce a multitude of freelance opportunities for a considerable number of young graphic designers, including de Harak.

Founded in 1887, Columbia Records was one of the first major record labels to take a new and innovative approach to album packaging and cover art as markets, technologies, and graphic design evolved in the 1930s and 1940s. This wave of change initially started in 1939 with the hiring of Alex Steinweiss, a twenty-three-year-old graphic designer, as its first art director. That same year, Steinweiss created the first illustrated album cover for a 78 rpm vinyl record. Previously, albums consisted of three to four records packaged in sleeves, packaged in a cardboard jacket held together with a leatherette binding, stamped with the artist's name and the record's title. Steinweiss referred to this unappealing and unimaginative solution, which was displayed in the same manner as a book on the retailer's shelves, as a 'tombstone'.

Steinweiss believed that an album cover should communicate an immediate first impression, and function as a visual accompaniment to the recorded music. He was the first art director who thought that the cover art needed to reflect the style of the recording and its artist, while also grabbing the consumer's attention, just as a film or theater poster would. In 1948, he introduced new packaging for the launch of the 'LP', Columbia's cutting-edge long-playing 33⅓ rpm microgroove vinyl record. His innovative design solution consisted of a thin cardboard jacket sleeve covered with printed paper that simultaneously protected the vinyl record and promoted the new recording and its artist. The sleeve was made from a large cardstock sheet with printed art, and had a square paper sheet printed with liner notes glued on its back. While this new approach was initially rejected by Columbia executives as too costly, once they saw that the sales of albums with Steinweiss-designed covers jumped considerably, they acquiesced. With additional advances in full-color, offset-printing technologies, including the introduction of larger presses with faster results, illustrated and photographic-based album covers soon became the norm, and were quickly adopted by the other major American record labels.

During the 1940s and 1950s, Columbia was fertile ground for a number of influential art directors and graphic designers, who initially worked for Steinweiss. Jim Flora was recruited by Steinweiss in 1942. De Harak was a freelance art director in the early 1950s and hired S. (Sadamitsu) Neil Fujita to work full-time at the label. De Harak and Fujita shared a preference for featuring photography and bold typography rather than illustration, which added a new and distinct identity to Columbia's releases. Fujita was made art director in the mid-1950s, and was followed over the next two decades by John Berg, Bob Cato, and Mati Klarwein who all added their own personal vision to an already eclectic and visually diverse history to the design of album covers.

Monogram Art Studios worked extensively with Columbia Records during the early 1950s on redesigning a large portion of its Columbia Masterworks library, with de Harak designing his first album cover for the label in 1951. This led him to similar work for Circle Records, Oxford Recording Company, Plymouth Records, Pontiac Records, and Remington Records. De Harak's extensive work for Monogram and Columbia Masterworks during the 1950s, which amounted to seventeen album covers completed over a period of seven years, also functioned as a series of personal lab experiments in which he explored the use of black-and-white photography; photographic processes and techniques; abstract and geometric forms; printed ephemera; various typographic styles; and hand-drawn organic and ethereal shapes and forms. All were linked conceptually and visually to the musical content of each album. This important work foreshadowed his work for Westminster Records in the 1960s, where he was able to use his new-found voice in a meaningful, unique, and groundbreaking way.

Circle Records, a jazz record label founded in 1946 by music aficionados Rudi Blesh and Harriet Janis, commissioned de Harak to design the cover for jazz pianist Ralph Sutton's album *Ralph Sutton at the Piano*, released in 1952. The following year, this cover was recognized by the Art Directors Club and the American Institute of Graphic Arts (AIGA); selected for the Museum of Modern Art's (MoMA) *Recent Acquisitions, 1946–1953: Department of Architecture and Design* exhibition, which ran from December 1953 to February 1954; and selected for the typography and advertising section of a major exhibition drawing on MoMA's collections, *American Art of the Twentieth Century*, held at the Musée d'Art Moderne de la Ville de Paris from March to May 1955.

Talking about this time in his career, de Harak recalled: 'I was particularly influenced by Alvin Lustig and Saul Bass, who were poles apart. Bass, who was a very content-conscious designer, would get a strong idea and put together a beautiful design based on that idea. Lustig, on the other hand, was a strong formalist, much less concerned with content, but deeply interested in developing forms and relating type to them. I too went off in that direction and [became] dedicated to the concept of form. I was always looking for the hidden order, trying to somehow either develop new forms or manipulate existing form. Therefore, I think my work was more obscure, and certainly very abstract. Sometimes it was hard for me to understand why my solutions fell short. But one thing I did was happen to sharpen my design sensibilities to the point that my work generally fell into a purist category.' [7]

Even when new client commissions and freelance opportunities began to come his way in the early 1950s — including book jackets for Rinehart & Co. and New Directions Publishing Corporation — de Harak was still having a hard time financially. He later described his dire living situation at the time: 'I was doing almost regularly, every month, these little kind of Dada illustrations for *Esquire* magazine. And I would get $75.00 each for them. And, if I was lucky, I would maybe do two or three of them in a month, ... and maybe doing a book jacket, I would squeeze by with the rent, and get to go to a movie or something.' [8]

Teacher, Mentor, and Advisor

To make ends meet, de Harak began teaching what was called at that time an 'advertising design' class at Cooper Union in 1952. Located in the East Village, Cooper Union was founded in 1859 by Peter Cooper, and was one of the first institutions in the United States to offer free education to working-class children and women. Inspired by the École Polytechnique in Paris, it granted each student a full-tuition scholarship. This prestigious opportunity terrified de Harak, but also challenged him in ways he was yet to understand. He recalled, 'I hadn't been a designer long, but what I lacked in experience I made up for in my commitment and my enthusiasm, so much so that Cooper Union asked me to come back the next year.' [9] The request surprised him at the time, but his commitment and enthusiasm proved to be a catalyst for him developing into one of the most influential teachers at Cooper Union for more than thirty years. In 1979, he was appointed the first Frank Stanton Professor of Graphic Design, the first permanently endowed chair in graphic design in the United States. De Harak retired from Cooper Union in 1986.

Later in his career, de Harak described his love of teaching: 'I very much enjoyed teaching the sophomore year at Cooper Union.

They had had a year of foundation, and had made a decision to study graphic design. And so I really took them deep into graphic design. And, of course, it was a vicarious experience for me, because I had no schooling. And here I was, at a really top university, and it was like I was going to school.' [10] To de Harak's credit, most of his former students concurred that he always brought an intelligence and passion to his classes that were unparalleled in their learning experiences. As an educator, his standards were extremely high and never wavered. He lived by a set of ideas and values that were both practical and pragmatic, and which he integrated into every aspect of his personal, academic, and professional life. Describing his teaching philosophy and his goals with his students, de Harak stated that he always wanted to: 'enrich and broaden their aesthetic senses, to give them a much better understanding of typography, which is the root of graphic design. If you think about it ... about 99.9 per cent of everything you see is typography, and the rest is illustration, photography, and symbols. So, one has to — if you're going to be a graphic designer, you have to either love, or learn to love, typography. If you don't, you should do something else.' [11]

Graphic designer and curator Ellen Lupton, a former student of de Harak's and a staff intern at his office in the early 1980s, recalled that 'Cooper Union was a maelstrom of competing design ideologies in the 1970s and 1980s. The school is the alma mater of Milton Glaser, Seymour Chwast, Herb Lubalin, and Lou Dorfsman, giants of the design world ... Another powerful force was Rudolph de Harak, a teacher and designer whose rational, systems-based design methodology contrasted with the eclectic populism practiced by Glaser and others.' [12]

In the years that followed, de Harak was also a visiting professor and lecturer at the School of Visual Arts (1962–1964), Parsons School of Design (1973–1978), and Pratt Institute (1973–1978), all in New York City; as well as Kent State University (1976) in Kent, Ohio; Yale University (1979–1980) in New Haven, Connecticut; and Alfred University (1987) in Alfred, New York. Over the course of his extensive teaching career, de Harak influenced generations of young graphic designers that continued to develop new ideas and approaches to their work and careers based upon the rational tenets of Modernism. Former student and fellow Art Directors Club Hall of Famer Roy Grace, who graduated from Cooper Union in 1962, reminisced about de Harak and his advertising design class: 'Rudy brought a sense of value, elegance, and eloquence into his classes none of us had ever seen before. He taught us how important priorities, goals, and vision were and to fight for what you thought was right. He also said, "If you're in this business for the money, get out! If you love what you're doing, the money will come."' [13]

Don Crews, who graduated in 1959, fondly remembered that 'Cooper Union was a fantastic place to be in the 1950s. It was full of like-minded students and instructors who appreciated willing learners.' [14] He also recalled that de Harak's art-based theories and

∨ De Harak conducting a class critique at Cooper Union, New York City, c. 1958.

> *Santa Claus, c.* 1955.
Rudolph de Harak,
photographer.

Andy Warhol, 1955.
Rudolph de Harak,
photographer. De Harak
photographed Warhol
at his own West 58th
Street studio in New York
City using a Rolleiflex
camera with a 3.5
Schneider Xenar lens.

∨ *Brass bed,* 1955.
Rudolph de Harak,
photographer.

classroom environment were 'always instructive with useful critiques. He taught the importance of ideas and how to think and how that thinking leads you to find innovative directions.' [15] Crews met his future wife, Ann Jonas, in de Harak's second-year graphic design class. Following their graduation from Cooper Union, Jonas went to work at de Harak's new office and Crews would be hired by de Harak later that year as an assistant art director at *Dance Magazine*, where he was consulting art director. They would work with de Harak on and off for the next ten years, culminating with their overseeing of a small design team that produced the exhibition and interpretive graphics for the Canadian Pavilion's 'Man, His Planet, and Space' exhibition at Expo 67 in Montreal.

Jean Marcellino, who graduated from Cooper Union in 1958, also remembered de Harak's class with pleasure: 'It was really an introduction to the principles of graphic design. Like so many others, I was greatly influenced by him. In some ways, he set me off on my entire career. When speaking of him to others, I always say "Rudy de Harak introduced me to the concept of a concept."' [16] Robin Plaskoff Horton, who was on his design staff in the early 1980s, remembered, 'Rudy taught me to be a design thinker. He was my lifelong role model, having instilled in me that good design begins with solid strategic thinking and analysis. Later, as an art director at Burson-Marsteller, I mentored my designers to approach design in the same manner.' [17]

In a 1977 *Graphis* profile, Nicholas Chaparos, Director, School of Design, University of Cincinnati, from 1981 to 1986 wrote about de Harak's teaching: 'His students appreciate his enthusiasm and respect for each individual's sense of integrity, and many recall the times spent with him with deep feeling and emotion. He's difficult, but it's precisely that giving of himself, demanding of others, and sharing of professional experience that have made him a catalyst for so many careers…he is at once gentle yet an emphatic disciplinarian, always the teacher.' [18]

Survival Tactics

After teaching at Cooper Union for almost three years and being paid $4.00 to $5.00 an hour per class, while also attempting to find new clients at the same time, de Harak accepted the harsh reality that his freelance graphic design practice was going nowhere and that he had to quickly re-evaluate his income sources if he was to survive in New York City. One possible solution was to expand his teaching opportunities, so he turned to friend and colleague Alvin Lustig for advice, who provided de Harak with several letters of reference so that he could apply for full-time teaching positions at other colleges and universities. In the summer of 1952, de Harak applied to Tyler School of Art in Philadelphia, Pennsylvania; Bennington College in Bennington, Vermont; and Sarah Lawrence College in Bronxville, New York. None of these opportunities came to fruition.

As a fallback position, de Harak quickly assembled a portfolio of his photographic work, which earned him assignments for *Esquire* and *Apparel Arts* magazines, as well as with several advertising agencies. De Harak spent approximately two years as a studio photographer while simultaneously continuing with his freelance graphic design practice. When looking back at this time in his life, he was always grateful that photography had been such an integral part

of his early training and interests. He always felt it made him a better graphic designer and visual storyteller. One of his most successful freelance photographic commissions came from Italian architect Romaldo 'Aldo' Giurgola, *Interiors* magazine's art director from 1952 to 1957. De Harak recalled reviewing his photographic portfolio with Giurgola at their initial meeting. It included a black-and-white photograph of a game of bocce, which he had taken on the Lower Eastside on Second Avenue. Giurgola was very excited about this image and asked if he would consider making it into a cover for the magazine. De Harak complied but decided to turn it ninety degrees on end so that the shadows read more prominently and dramatically. It proved to be one of the most successful magazine covers that he created during the 1950s.

Professional Pursuits

In the spring of 1953, de Harak's work was included in the Sixth Annual Exhibition of the Book Jacket Designers Guild, hosted by the American Institute of Graphic Arts (AIGA). This was a much-needed boost to his self-confidence and determination, as it was the first time that his work had been recognized by his peers since his relocation to New York City from Los Angeles. The exhibition included book jackets designed by a range of luminaries, including Alvin Eisenman, Milton Glaser, Janet Halverson, Alvin Lustig, Reynold Ruffins, and Saul Steinberg, placing de Harak alongside an established and renowned group of now peers and colleagues.

As he became more involved with the practice of his profession, he also became more involved with the graphic design community. In 1954, he became a member of AIGA, and he would continue to be involved with and support it the remainder of his career. Founded in 1914, the American Institute of Graphic Arts (AIGA) remains the oldest and largest professional membership organization for design and is now known simply as 'AIGA, the professional association for design'. Its members practice all forms of visual communications, including graphic design, typography, interaction design, user experience, exhibition design, environmental graphics, branding, and identity. The organization's aim is to be the standard bearer for professional ethics and practices for the design professions.

In the summer of 1954, de Harak traveled to Europe — the first visit since his military service — to absorb different cultures and meet designers that he admired, and these trips became an annual occurrence: 'It was really a marvelous adventure since I was never making any money, but on practically nothing I would get these charter flights. And every summer, I would take a full month off, and I would fly to Europe. I would decide to do, let's say, Sweden and Denmark, and look up all of the designers. Actually, it was interesting, because at this time I was getting a reputation ... European designers were terribly interested in what the Americans were doing. I came to know every important designer in Europe. And I remember just sitting for hours, listening.' [19]

One of the first designers that he contacted, and ultimately met, was the Swiss Modernist Max Bill, who had been one of his earliest influences. Bill is widely recognized as the single most decisive influence on Swiss graphic design, and on the International Typographic Style, through both his theoretical writings and his rational Modernist work. He believed that the perfect combination

< In 1954, de Harak and American photographer Jay Maisel photographed Geoffrey Holder and his dance company rehearsing Trinidadian dances for the New York Summer Dance Festival. From 'On and Offstage: Pictorial Highlights of the First Annual New York Summer Dance Festival,' *Dance Magazine,* vol. 28, no. 9, September 1954, pp. 32, 34–37.

∨ Kunstgewerbemuseum Zürich exhibition poster, Max Bill, 1931.

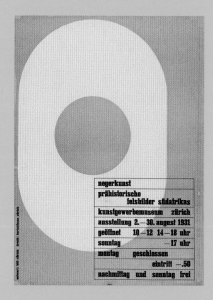

*Make-ready (i. e. making the press ready to print) is defined as the extra amount of paper needed to further guarantee that an offset printing project is running correctly on a printing press. At this time, defects such as imperfections in paper stock, improper distribution of ink and printing pressure, and poor registration can be detected and corrected prior to continuing with the main printing run.

of form, function, and beauty would result in the magical quality known as *gestalt*. Born in Winterthur, Switzerland, Bill studied at the Bauhaus, and counted Josef Albers, Wassily Kandinsky, Paul Klee, László Moholy-Nagy, and Oskar Schlemmer among his teachers. In 1950, he joined with typographer and graphic designer Otl Aicher and the writer and activist Inge Scholl to establish the Ulm School of Design (Hochschule für Gestaltung-HfG Ulm), a design school initially created in the tradition of the Bauhaus, but which later developed its own approach to design education integrating art and science. The school was notable for its progressive four-year curriculum, which included graphic design, architecture, industrial design, film, and also semiotics — the general philosophical theory of signs and symbols. The majority of Bill's work was solely based on cohesive visual principles of organization and was comprised of purist forms — modular grids, sans-serif typography, asymmetric compositions, linear spatial divisions, and mathematical progressions.

This was also the period in which de Harak started to design several magazine covers that gained considerable attention, not only from his peers and colleagues, but from the wider reading public. The art and culture magazine *Perspectives USA* was published in multiple languages from 1952 to 1956 in an effort to promote American values in Europe as part of a 'cultural cold war' with the Soviet Union. The magazine was edited by James Laughlin, the founder and publisher of New Directions Publishing, and published in America by the nonprofit organization Intercultural Publications, with funds from the Ford Foundation. While de Harak was the only graphic designer besides Lustig to design more than one cover for *Perspectives*, an impressive list of Mid-century Modernist talent produced covers during the magazine's four years of publication, including Herbert Bayer, Leo Lionni, and Paul Rand.

In 1955, the Museum of Modern Art (MoMA) organized the first and largest American modern art exhibition ever to be sent abroad, with over 500 works from the museum's collection. This groundbreaking exhibition, *American Art of the Twentieth Century,* was on view at the Musée d'Art Moderne, Paris from March through May 1955. Alongside paintings, sculpture, prints, photography, and industrial design were examples of posters, book jackets, album covers, newspaper and magazine advertisements, street signs and lettering, brochures, packaging, and more. Herbert Bayer, Leo Lionni, Alvin Lustig, Noel Martin, Paul Rand, and de Harak were among the graphic designers whose work was selected. Specifically, three of de Harak's album covers — *Budapest String Quartet: Quartet in F Major Ravel, Quartet in G Minor, Opus 10 Debussy; International Song Festival*; and *Ralph Sutton at the Piano* — were included in the exhibition, as well as his stationery program for his newly established office.

As with his earlier spot illustrations for *Esquire*, de Harak always had an intuitive connection to found materials and how he could coax spirited visual stories from them. His first cover for *Print* magazine was a case in point. When asked specifically about this approach, he stated: 'These mimeograph impressions were done as a result of a discarded piece of paper I found in the wastebasket of a public stenographer's office. It was a make-ready* sheet of sorts and was covered with blobs of ink that formed the intriguing pattern found in the first illustration. This aroused my curiosity and encouraged me to make the following experiments reproduced here.

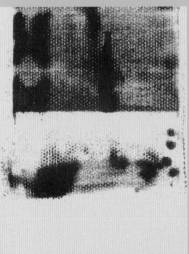

∨ Mimeographic studies
for *Print*, vol. 11, no. 2,
magazine cover,
February/March 1957.

Naturally the limitations of the mimeograph and its inflexibilities were dictating factors to the final result; however a certain amount of control was possible…and it was delightful to see the genesis of an idea expand by means of repeated attempts on the same theme.' [20] The *Print* editors enjoyed his efforts for their cover, praising its 'original and striking results'. [21]

De Harak was always intrigued with the manipulation of found materials into abstract forms and compositions and continued this conceptual exploration with his magazine cover for *Graphis*. He once described this solution for this particular project as 'a sense of abstraction that was born out of a system. At the time, I was very excited about this cover because I was exploring systems. I was attempting to make this connection — flatness to flatness, shape to shape, and a divergence of color.' [22]

Independence and Growth

In the summer of 1954, de Harak married Berenice Mignon Lipson, a concert pianist, in New York City. Three years later, he and Berenice had their first child, a son Dimitri Alexander, born on 27 July 1957. They lived in an apartment on East 40th Street until late 1961, when they divorced. Berenice (de Harak) Gruzen died in 1998 at the age of seventy-three after a successful career.

Since his alternative career as a successful studio photographer turned out to be less fulfilling emotionally, creatively, or financially than he had hoped, in 1958 de Harak threw caution to the wind, opening a small office at 795 Lexington Avenue, hiring a few of his students from Cooper Union, and promoting his design consultant services under the name Rudolph de Harak Incorporated. Years later, he reflected on this milestone: 'I came to the realization that I really wanted to work for myself, and had to work for myself, I just, somehow I didn't have the temperament to have a boss standing over me. I mean, you always end up having bosses, but it was… important just to be on my own.' [23] With patience and perseverance, a few commissions started to come his way, the most important from the Kurt Versen Lighting Company, founded in 1920 by Kurt Versen, a Swedish lighting designer, with an archetypal Modernist ambition of combining art and science. This would be the beginning of a twenty-year-long business relationship, with de Harak designing everything from its symbol, logotype, stationery, and business forms to its identity standards, packaging, and product sales catalogs.

During the 1950s, de Harak became increasingly adept at engaging with the formal principles of the International Typographic Style while simultaneously pushing the limits of his own graphic design concepts. He continued to consider the potential of abstraction, geometry, and color, as well as various photographic techniques. This is evident in the work he did as *Dance Magazine*'s consulting art director from 1954 to 1964. In many ways, the 1950s was a time of exploration and experimentation for de Harak — not only was he trying to find a place for himself within his profession and his practice, but he was also employing a wide range of visual languages to help further define his own voice. Among the most successful of these experiments were his abstract images, created through simplification and distillation, and solely dependent upon their intrinsic form rather than on narrative content or pictorial

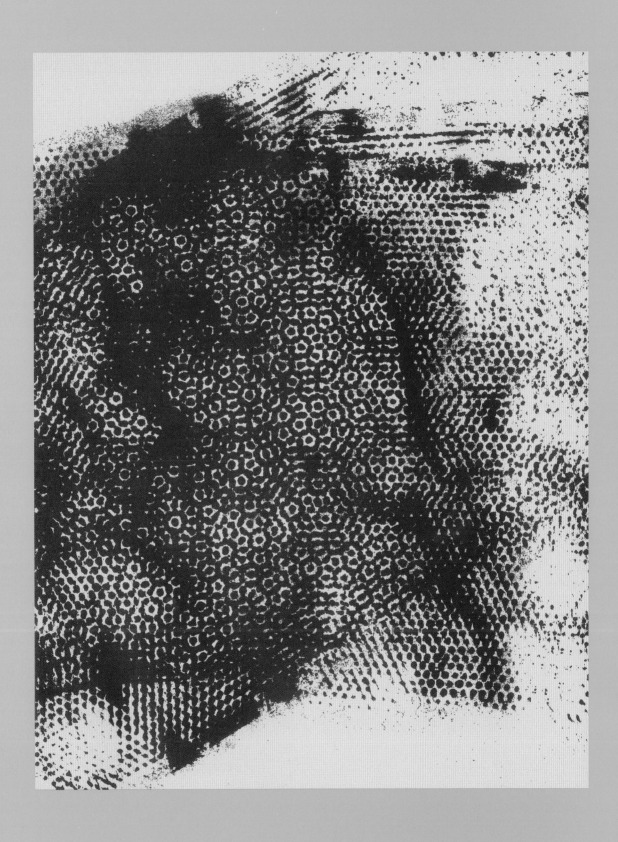

⌄ Mimeographic study
for *Print,* vol. 11, no. 2,
magazine cover,
February/March 1957.

∨ BLM Berthold-Layout-
Musterblätter Akzidenz-
Grotesk-Serie
(H. Berthold AG Akzidenz-
Grotesk) portfolio with
specimen sheets, c. 1957.

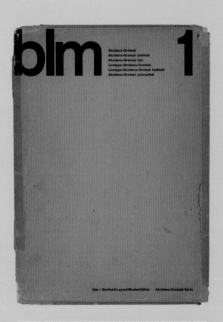

representation. De Harak would frequently rely upon abstraction
in his early work as a means to communicate visual messages
which the viewer could connect with immediately, intuitively, and
most importantly, emotionally. He created abstract images that
were always sensory experiences that reshaped the familiar into
the expressive. They were reductive and free of objective content,
context, and meaning. His abstract images were consistently
interpretive, imaginative, impressionistic, non-representational,
and purely of his own making.

Berthold's Akzidenz-Grotesk

In addition to exploring the potential uses of abstraction and
simplified visual form, de Harak was also refining his approach and
usage to typographic form. Up to this point, he had intentionally
limited himself to using only a few typefaces in his work, including
the sans-serifs Franklin Gothic and News Gothic, both designed
by Morris Fuller Benton in 1902 and 1908, respectively. Then in
the late 1950s, he discovered a sans-serif typeface that reflected
all the aspects of the rational simplicity he sought, and would be
a primary visual element in his work for decades to come. 'There
was something about the purity of its letter form that dealt with
straight-ahead information, without embellishment. I felt the same
way about the typewriter...that old Remington typewriter face, was
a beautiful, straight, concise, systematized thing that really worked,' [24]
he recalled. When describing its impact and influence on American
graphic designers during the 1950s, design historian and author
Philip Meggs described de Harak's ongoing quest for visual clarity,
rational order, and simplicity, and also noted that 'Rudy was one of
the first graphic designers to obtain specimen sheets from European
foundries of Akzidenz-Grotesk since it was still not available in the
United States.' [25]

De Harak further explained that 'this was a very exciting
and crucial point in my life.' [26] Months earlier, he had written to the
Berthold Foundry in Berlin requesting type specimen sheets of
Akzidenz-Grotesk. The foundry's response was generous, sending
him approximately one hundred large specimen sheets, with
letterforms measuring up to ninety-six points. This was a turning
point for his understanding of, as well as his approach to, the use
and context of typographic form. Once he had these specimen
sheets in hand, he would cut letters apart and reassemble them as
main headlines for his work. This hands-on process provided him
with the high degree of perfection that he was always striving for in
all of his work.

Akzidenz-Grotesk was originally released by the Berlin-based
foundry H. Berthold AG in 1898. 'Akzidenz' was intended to convey
its use as a typeface for commercial print runs, such as business
cards, invoices, forms, and letterheads, while 'Grotesk' was a
standard name for sans-serif typefaces during this period. This was
the first time a unified and systematized type family had been made
available in extensive weight and style variations within one original
font. Its simple, neutral appearance is void of the adornments and
flourishes that were so prevalent in the decorative sans-serifs of the
late nineteenth century. Its monoline structure, with all letterform
strokes sharing a similar width, conveys formal perfection, along with

superior clarity and functionality. Relatively unknown for a half-century after its introduction, it achieved iconic status in the post-war period as the preferred typeface of many Modernist typographers and graphic designers, swiftly becoming the hallmark of Swiss graphic design, and the International Typographic Style.

The year 1959 turned out to be a watershed year for de Harak and his newly established design consultancy. Multiple commissions started to come his way. While he had no way of knowing it at the time, the unorthodox, Modernist approaches that he had developed and refined during the last ten years would further define his work in the future. His continuing reliance on the bold Modernism of Akzidenz-Grotesk would effectively anchor his design thinking, as well as providing him with a neutral, rational, and simple design element to marry with the growing palette of memorable images that he was now creating. Additionally, his extensive explorations and experiments with color, form, optical illusion, and photography would strengthen his ability to confront the design challenges that he would encounter over the next decade.

1. Rudolph de Harak, 'Oral History Interview with Rudolph de Harak', interview by Susan Larsen on 27 April 2000 (transcript), in Ellsworth, Maine. Archives of American Art, Smithsonian Institution, Washington, DC.
2. Rudolph de Harak, interview by Steven Heller, February 1987 (transcript), in New York City. Steven Heller Collection, School of Visual Arts Archives, New York.
3. Ibid.
4. Ibid.
5. Ibid.
6. Steven Heller, 'Rudolph de Harak: A Playful Modernist,' Baseline, no. 45, 2004, p. 28.
7. Ibid.
8. Rudolph de Harak, 'Oral History Interview with Rudolph de Harak', interview by Susan Larsen on 27 April 2000 (transcript), in Ellsworth, Maine. Archives of American Art, Smithsonian Institution, Washington, DC.
9. Ibid.
10. Ibid.
11. Ibid.
12. Ellen Lupton, Mixing Messages: Graphic Design in Contemporary Culture, New York: Princeton Architectural Press, 1996, p. 44.
13. Roy Grace, 'Rudolph de Harak Inducted into Art Directors Club Hall of Fame.' The One Club for Creativity, 1989. https://www.oneclub.org/adc-hall-of-fame/-bio/rudolph-de-harak
14. Don Crews, Wilder Award Acceptance Speech, 28 June 2015, American Library Association Annual Conference.
15. Ibid.
16. Jean Marcellino, Interview by Richard Poulin, 19 April 2021.
17. Robin Plaskoff Horton, Interview by Richard Poulin, 19 April 2021.
18. Nicholas J. Chaparos, 'Rudolph de Harak', Graphis, vol. 33, no. 193, 1977, pp. 444–45.
19. Rudolph de Harak, 'Oral History Interview with Rudolph de Harak', interview by Susan Larsen on 27 April 2000 (transcript), in Ellsworth, Maine. Archives of American Art, Smithsonian Institution, Washington, DC.
20. Rudolph de Harak, 'Mimeo-Imagery,' Print, vol. 11, no. 2, 1957, p. 68.
21. Ibid.
22. Rudolph de Harak, interview by Steven Heller, February 1987 (transcript), in New York City. Steven Heller Collection, School of Visual Arts Archives, New York.
23. Rudolph de Harak, 'Oral History Interview with Rudolph de Harak', interview by Susan Larsen on 27 April 2000 (transcript), in Ellsworth, Maine. Archives of American Art, Smithsonian Institution, Washington, DC.
24. Rudolph de Harak, interview by Steven Heller, February 1987 (transcript), in New York City. Steven Heller Collection, School of Visual Arts Archives, New York.
25. Philip B. Meggs and Alston W. Purvis, Meggs' History of Graphic Design, 4th ed., Hoboken: John Wiley & Sons, Inc., 2006, p. 370.
26. Rudolph de Harak, interview by Steven Heller, February 1987 (transcript), in New York City. Steven Heller Collection, School of Visual Arts Archives, New York.

ML 4132

Grieg

The
Philadelphia Orchestra
Eugene Ormandy
conductor

Peer Gynt Suite

No. 1, Opus 46

Liszt
Hungarian Rhapsody No. 1
Hungarian Rhapsody No. 2

Originator of the Modern Long Playing Record

Columbia Lp   Masterworks

< Album cover, *Grieg, Peer Gynt Suite No. 1, Opus 46, Liszt, Hungarian Rhapsody No. 1, Hungarian Rhapsody No. 2, The Philadelphia Orchestra*, Columbia Masterworks, 1952.

∨ Album cover, *Strauss Waltzes, Brahms Eight Hungarian Dances, Pittsburgh Symphony Orchestra*, Columbia Masterworks, *c.* 1950.

Album cover, *Debussy, Two Nocturnes, Respighi, The Pines of Rome, The Philadelphia Orchestra*, Columbia Masterworks, *c.* 1950.

Album cover, *Liszt, Sonata in B Minor, György Sandor, Piano*, Columbia Masterworks, *c.* 1950.

Album cover, *Liszt, Concerto No. 2 in A Major, Weber, Concertstück in F Minor, Opus 79, Robert Casadesus, Piano, The Cleveland Orchestra*, Columbia Masterworks, 1952.

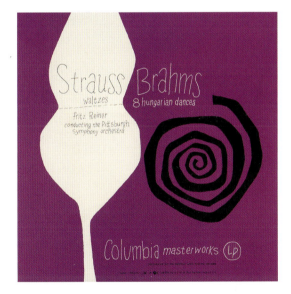

the golden era seri

presents

benny
goodr
comb

after you've g
gilly
stardust
breakfast fe
benny's bu
as long as i
on the alam
liza
shivers
ac-dc curre
slipped dis
a smo-o-o-th

columbia

LP
LONG PLAYING · MICROGROOVE
NONBREAKABLE

< Album cover (detail),
Benny Goodman Combos,
Columbia Masterworks,
1951.

∨ Album cover, *Erroll Garner,
Solo Flight,* Columbia
Masterworks, 1952.

Album cover, *Rachmaninoff,
Cesare Siepi, The Little
Orchestra Society, Anton
Stepanovich Arensky, The
Miserly Knight, Variations on
a Theme by Tchaikovsky for
String Orchestra, Opus 35,*
Columbia Masterworks, 1952.

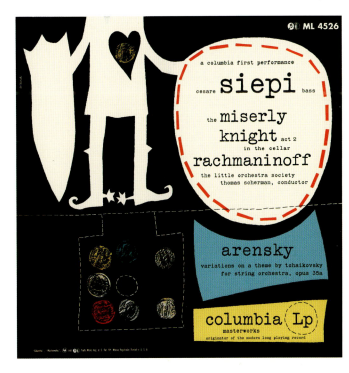

⌄ Album cover, *Benny
Goodman and his
Orchestra,* Columbia
Masterworks, 1951.

Album cover, *Benny
Goodman Combos,*
Columbia Masterworks,
1951.

> Album cover (detail),
Erroll Garner, Solo Flight,
Columbia Masterworks,
1952.

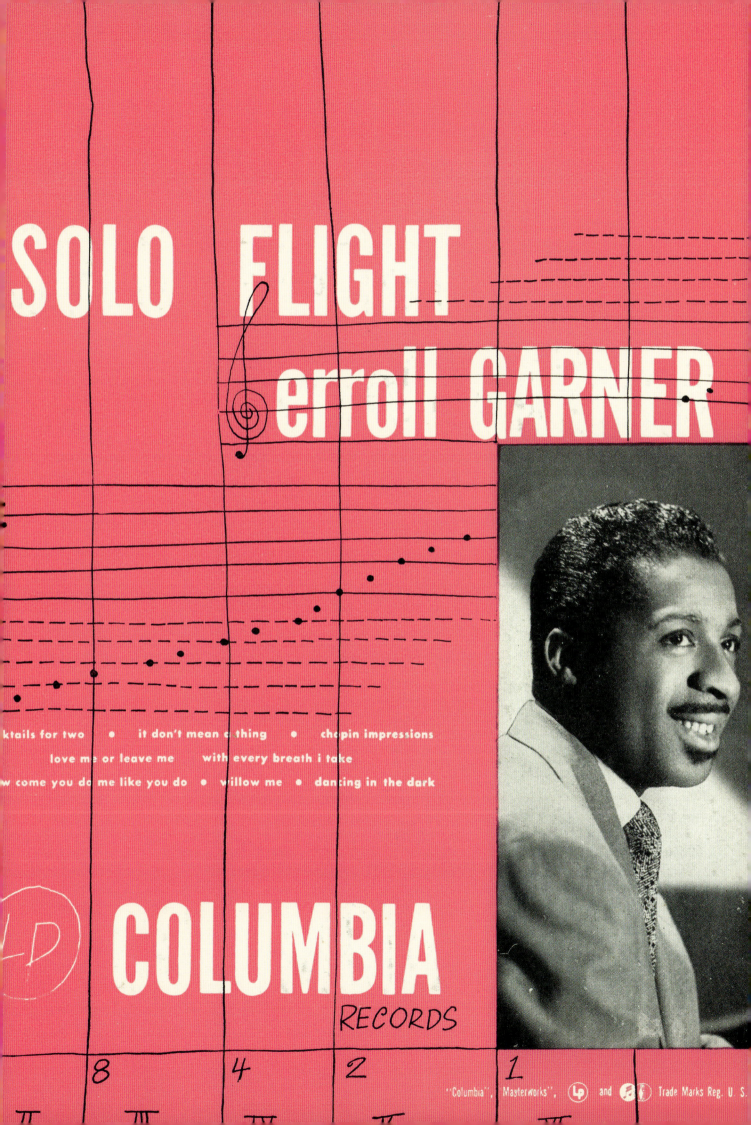

∨ Album cover, *Ravel,
Quartet in F Major,
Debussy, Quartet in G
Minor, Opus 10, Budapest
String Quartet*, Columbia
Masterworks, 1953.

∨ Album cover, *Sibelius, Symphony No. 5 in E Flat Major, Opus 82, The Cleveland Orchestra,* Columbia Masterworks, 1955.

> Album cover, *Beecham Berlioz Overtures,* Columbia Masterworks, 1955.

Album cover, *Harry James and his Orchestra, All Time Favorites,* Columbia Masterworks, 1955.

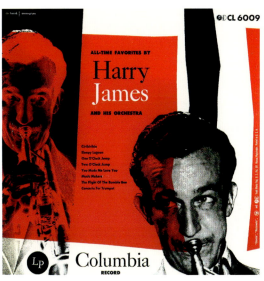

∨ Album cover, *Beethoven,
Sonata 23 in F Minor,
Opus 57, Appassionata,
Mozart, Fantasy for Piano,
Sonata No. 15 in C Major,
Alfred Kitchin, Piano,*
Plymouth Records,
c. 1952.

> Album cover (detail),
*Ravel, Quartet in F Major,
Debussy, Quartet in G
Minor, Opus 10, Budapest
String Quartet,* Columbia
Masterworks, 1953.

quartet in f major **rave**

quartet in g minor, op. 10 **debu**

budapest string quartet

(J. Roisman and A. Schneider, *violins*; B. Kroyt, *viola*; M. Schne

monogram

 *columbia* ma

THOVEN

no. 23 in F minor, op. 57 "APPASSIONATA"

ZART

for Piano, k. 475   Sonata no. 15 in C major, k 545

HIN, *pianist*

L-413

Ralph **at the piano**

Sutton

CIRCLE RECORDS Long Playing Microgroove 33⅓ RPM

∨ Album cover, *Beethoven,
Symphony No. 7 in A
Major, Opus 92, Vienna
Symphonic Society
Orchestra, Kurt Wöss,
Conductor,* Remington
Records, 1951.

∨ Album cover, *Anton
Bruckner, Symphony
No. 3 in D Minor, The
Salzburg Mozarteum
Orchestra,* Remington
Records, 1953.

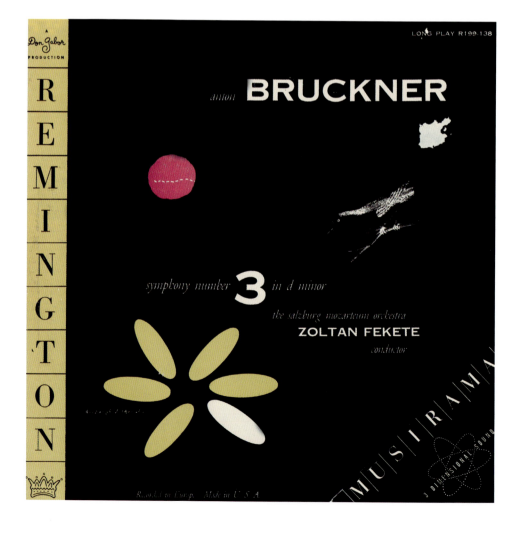

> Album cover, *Hindemith, Sonata for Bassoon and Piano, Sonata for Two Flutes, Sonata for Flute and Piano,* Oxford Recording Company, *c.* 1959.

Album cover, *Fania Chapiro, A Piano Recital,* Oxford Recording Company, *c.* 1959.

Album cover, *Mozart Trio in E Flat Major for Piano, Clarinet, and Viola, Haydn, Sonata in G Major for Flute and Piano,* Oxford Recording Company, *c.* 1959.

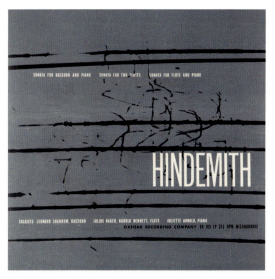

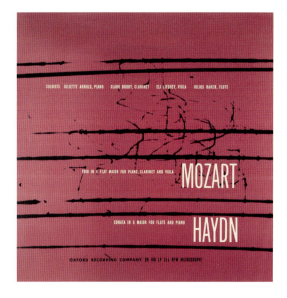

Spot illustrations, *Esquire*,
1953–1958.

When all is said and done, what does a killer really want?

DE HARAK

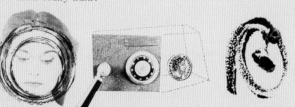

THE LAST DEFENSE by JAMES J. SIMONDS

WHAT surprised him most was that he felt no fear. He stood there and thought of what he was going to say. The words flowed in his mind and, unspoken, they seemed convincing. He waited patiently, his head bowed and his eyes partly closed. Thinking.

"You may begin now, John."

John Reynolds began to clear his throat, then realized it wasn't necessary. The pause gave a nice effect to his first words.

"I was eighteen before I got into any trouble."

"Just a moment. Is that as far back as you want to go?"

"Yes."

"All right, John, go ahead."

"When I was eighteen, I got good-looking. Before that I'd been skinny and I had pimples. But then my face cleared up and I filled out, to around a hundred and eighty. Am I going into too much detail?"

"Whatever you think will matter."

"All right. It seemed to me that from then on I had nothing but trouble, in one form or another. There were girls then, always pestering around, teasing me." There hadn't been really, aside from that one. But even now John's mind raced as he thought of her, her slender waist and her flaring hips. "There was one girl in particular. Estelle Rook. She was a . . ." He stopped. "What am I going to say? You took a look at her, you knew what she was. She had brown hair and blue eyes, or grey, or green maybe. What does it matter? When I saw her she was always wearing jodhpurs, light tan, very tight. I believe she was twenty-two."

The weariness he'd often felt came back as he thought of her. He said, "I was working in a stable off Central Park. I took care of the horses, her horse and five others. She never looked at me. I saw her picture in the paper one Sunday, part of a bunch of pictures taken at a horse show, and that's how I found out she was married. She never wore her rings when she rode. But by then it didn't make any difference—about her being married, I mean. I couldn't think of anything but her. She was a light shining in the dark of my mind. I couldn't sleep. I hated her husband because he was old and had money, but mostly because he had her."

"Harold was only thirty."

"I know. But I was nineteen. And one day she smiled at me! I looked behind me to see if anyone else was there and it made her laugh."

He closed his eyes and instantly he saw her again as she was that day, her hips insolent in the tight jodhpurs, the silent clamor of the contoured V of flesh exposed at the open throat of her blouse.

"After that she always spoke to me. Just 'Good morning' at first, but it got to be more and more until one day she asked me to have breakfast with her. We went to a little place off the park. There were booths by the windows and the sun came in and sparkled on the dishes. It was wonderful to be there with her. Then every morning after her ride we went back there and I sat across the table from her and . . . hungered. One day I told her I loved her."

"Did you?"

"No," he said, after a moment. "I wanted her, but I didn't love her. I told her I did, though. I told myself that, too, if it helps any."

He went on. "Right then and there things began to pick up speed. She told me about her husband, how he drank, how he abused her. I asked her to go out with me that night and she said, 'Yes.' At ten o'clock she picked me up in her car and we drove into the park. She let me hold her in my arms, for a moment, then she pushed me away and we talked. But this talk was leading somewhere. There was direction to it. I didn't too

much want to go, but then she let me kiss her. She said she loved me."

"Do you think she did?"

"Oh, God, no. She didn't even want me. But what does a kid of nineteen know? I believed what she told me and she did say she'd go away with me. It seemed like she mentioned the money as an afterthought. Twenty-five thousand dollars' worth is a lot of afterthought, but she made it sound like that. All that money was in the wall safe in her apartment, going to waste when it could take us wherever in the world we wanted to go. I thought of lying in the sand with her on a Mediterranean beach and that thought hypnotized me. She told me the combination to the safe; I memorized it. She gave me a gun; I put it in my pocket. She told me her husband would be drunk; I believed her.

"I waited outside the apartment building for twenty minutes, then I walked up the stairs to the fifth floor. That gave me plenty of time to realize what I was doing and, if I wanted, to change my mind. I opened the door to 5-D and as I did I took the gun out of my pocket. I don't know why. Only that I had seen people do it in the movies and it seemed natural.

"The living room was dark except for a crack of light under the bedroom door. I felt along the wall and found the safe. I was wondering how I would read the numbers in the dark—I didn't even have a pack of matches with me—when I reached up and turned the knob. I felt a connection break and a heavy electric bell began to ring. The bedroom door opened and a man came through it. He turned the lights on and I swung around and faced him. He was a tall man, heavy, big in the shoulders, but even then he didn't look mean or surly as Estelle said he always was. There was no doubt about one thing, he was cold sober. We stood and looked at each other as that bell kept ringing and ringing. When I tried to move, my legs felt like they were asleep. I backed away from the man, an inch at a time, it seemed like. Through the bedroom door I could see Estelle picking up the telephone. She was in her slip and it surprised me that she didn't look as I had imagined she would. I had been so used to seeing her in jodhpurs that she looked unreal in her slip. But then everything else seemed unreal and out of focus too.

"I was still backing toward the door when Estelle's husband took a step forward. I tried to run backwards and I started to slip on the polished floor. Somehow I fell sideways against the television set and my elbow hit the screen. The tube exploded and it was a moment before I realized the gun had gone off in my hand. I remember thinking that now there was no reason for that bell to keep ringing and it annoyed me that it did. What I thought, though, and what I felt really didn't matter. It may now. What did matter was that I shot Harold Rook through the heart.

"It seemed only a moment before I heard the sirens. Estelle had been calling the police. While she was talking to them, they heard the shot. My prints were on the safe and when they came in I was standing there with the gun in my hand. It was about over then."

"You didn't tell your authorities of Estelle's part in this?"

"No. It would have been useless, I didn't even try. She had what she wanted then—her husband's money. Who would have believed me?"

"And so you were convicted and executed?"

"Yes."

"And now you want justice."

"No." For the first time John Reynolds raised his head and opened his eyes wide. "No. I've had justice. Now I want mercy. Even down there they wanted me to have that. At least they kept saying so up to the end. It was the last thing I heard—'May God have mercy on your soul.'" ⧛

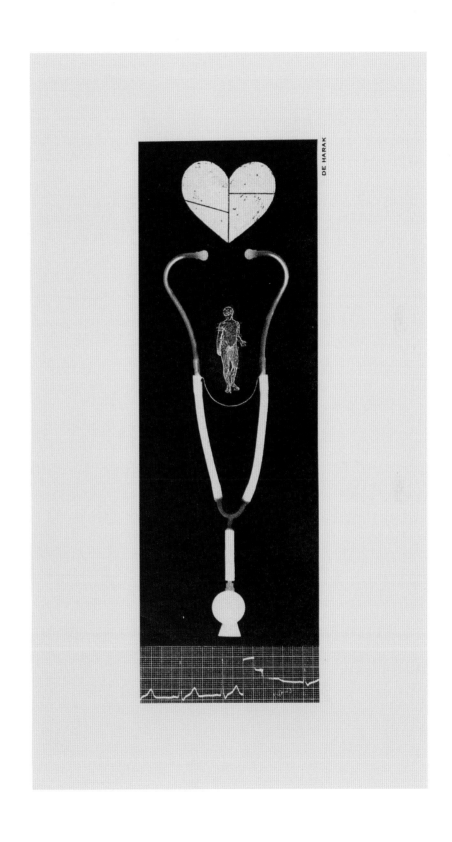

DE HARAK

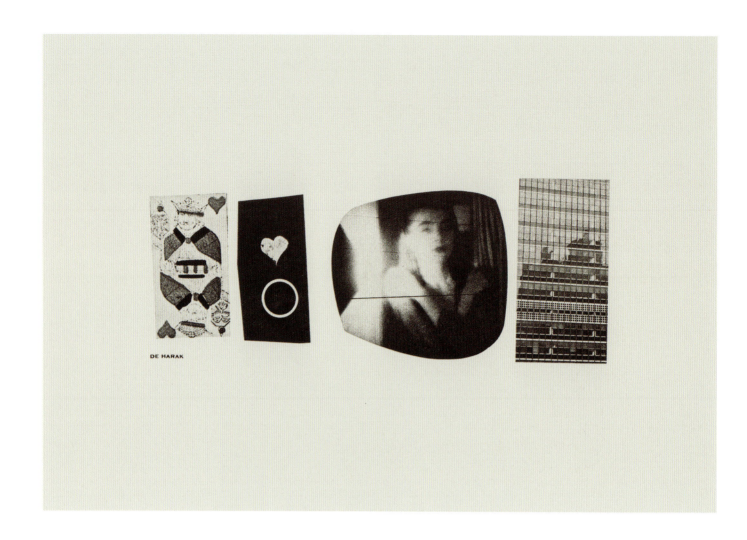

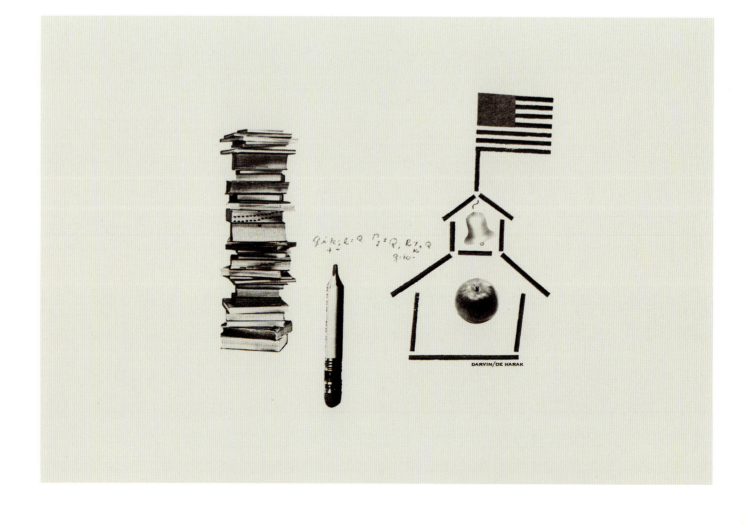

The irritable life and early death of Comrade V-8   **by ALBERT PARRY**

KREMLIN CAR LOT

IF you are a big shot in Russia you don't have to own and maintain a car. The government does it for you. The Kremlin gives you an automobile, and quite an expensive one at that.

It isn't a gift, to be sure. The car is yours to *use* only, and if you fall from Malenkov's grace you lose the use of the car among other good things of life (and perhaps life itself). But while you are in good Soviet standing, you have not only the car, but free maintenance, gas, oil, repairs and garage, and a chauffeur, all paid for by the government. If you are a high official, you may get two cars, or even more.

The largest and best Soviet car is the seven-passenger ZIS-110, manufactured at the Plant in Honor of Stalin (*Zavod Imeni Stalina*, or ZIS; 110 apparently stands for the number of experiments which finally produced this model). American experts recently visiting in Moscow recognized it as a rather inferior copy of our 1940 seven-passenger Packard. This ZIS-110 is a long, sleek, black-and-chrome job, often with white-wall tires, streamlined and fast moving, with many comforts, including automatically operated windows. Its price, according to a story in the Moscow *Ogonyek* (Little Light) of March, 1952, is in the neighborhood of 150,000 rubles, or, at the official Soviet rate of exchange, $37,500.

A six-passenger ZIS and a somewhat similar ZIM (built in a plant named for Molotov) are only a little less costly. They are newer models, and get more mileage per gallon of gasoline. For wider distribution there is the five-passenger Pobeda (meaning Victory), which, according to *Ogonyek*, costs a mere 16,000 rubles, or $4000. Least expensive (though no price is given) is the low-powered Moskvich (meaning the Muscovite), produced with a station-wagon body as well as a regular car body.

These vehicles are definitely for sale to the public; in fact, the government which makes them is pushing them with every trick known to Soviet salesmanship. A Moscow car-selling agency is merely an imitation of an average American automobile showroom, but to a Russian there is nothing average about it: it is the acme of awesome luxury. The writer of the *Ogonyek* story, warming to his work, shows how a Moscow automobile showroom looks through the eyes of a car buyer from the provinces:

"The store was large and seemed half empty. Only farther away, against its back walls, stood small counters. Little round tables, sofas, palm trees in green barrels gave the appearance of a reception room in some State ministry or other. Out of habit, the eyes of Semion Polikarpovich groped for the little window of an information bureau. But his glance was stopped by a light-grey Pobeda which stood behind a slightly sagging thick rope of crimson velvet."

The joys of buying, owning and driving a Pobeda car are described in the *Ogonyek* story with high-pitched exultation. Semion Polikarpovich, the buyer from the Ukraine, is represented as a medium-rank village official, fairly prosperous but not too rich. And he buys that Pobeda for himself, out of his own savings, not for the good of all the local comrades. The whole tone of the story, done on instructions from the Soviet propaganda office, is: "You, too, can save sixteen thousand rubles to buy a car like that!"

Soviet propagandists are presently trying to show that many, very many Soviet citizens are now proud owners of cars. But their slip shows whenever they forget themselves and give exact figures. Thus the Moscow *Izvestia* of November 14, 1951, boastfully announced that in Magnitogorsk a total of 387 engineers, technicians and workers had bought cars of their own (61 Pobedas and 326 Moskviches). But Magnitogorsk, "the Pittsburgh of the Urals," is a steel-making center of 220,000 inhabitants—so the ratio is one privately owned car for every 569 people.

Despite the government's efforts its vehicular merchandise sells slowly, partly because the prices are high, and partly because the poor private owner has to take care of his car almost entirely on his own. "We have a steadily increasing number of car owners," brags an editorial writer in the Moscow *Literaturnaya Gazeta* (Literary Gazette) of May 27, 1952. "But why so little attention to their needs?"

The bill of particulars that follows is pretty depressing. "Suppose you drive into a strange town and decide to stay overnight. Where would you put your car for the night? It is not such a simple matter. As for having your car washed and filled with gas and oil, or having minor repairs made, why, in many places of our country it is entirely unthinkable."

Do you want a spot to rest your own weary Soviet bones? You might as well stretch out on the back seat of your Pobeda or Moskvich. "There is hardly any construction of summer hotels in our country," *Literaturnaya Gazeta* continues. "Even at our liveliest, most frequented points we see scarcely any places where a traveler could find shelter and rest before setting out on the next leg of his tour. Is it so very difficult to provide such resting places? We don't think so. We are not asking for anything special, but merely for light summer-type structures or just plain tent combinations."

But suppose you don't even dream of travel— you just want to stay in your Soviet town and use your car for local transportation. Woe is to you, comrade, just the same.

In Kharkov, a Ukrainian city of 833,000, suburbanites who own cars can hope to have little garages of their own, but nothing else. Here is, for example, a suburb for workers and engineers of the famous Kharkov Tractor Plant. Some of them own cars, and do have garages, but according to the April 8, 1952, issue of the Moscow *Trud* (Labor), the main daily of the Soviet trade-unions, "there isn't a single auto-repair shop" in the entire suburb. A similar and more detailed complaint, this one from a group of Soviet car owners in the rich industrial Donets Basin, was published in *Literaturnaya Gazeta* on October 23, 1951.

"No one bothers to service privately owned cars here," the owners wrote, somewhat bitterly. "Our troubles start, and our cars become a veritable burden, should any one of us want to have his car checked, or to replace a part (even the simplest), or to paint over a scratch, recharge the batteries, or vulcanize the tires. There isn't a single shop at Stalino, Makeevka, Gorlovka, Zhdanov or any other city of this region that would do any work for privately owned cars. There isn't even a shop that would undertake to give a car a wash."

(These cities, by the way, are no country crossings. Stalino—formerly Yuzovka or Hughesovka, founded in 1870, by a Mr. Hughes, an enterprising Welshman—has 500,000 inhabitants; Makeevka, 300,000; Gorlovka, 150,000; and Zhdanov—formerly Mariupol—150,000.)

"We are also upset," the complaint wails on, "by the fact that this absence of checking and repairing facilities for our cars leads to accidents on the Donets Basin roads. Cars are worn out before their time."

The bureaucratic apparatus of the Soviets is set in motion from time to time to correct this melancholy situation, but nothing ever happens —perhaps because there are plenty of government service stations to take care of the bosses' cars. A recent *Trud* had an interesting story about an attempt to set up garages for privately owned cars.

On December 2, 1950, the Moscow office in charge of USSR's automobile and tractor sales ordered its Stalino sub-office to establish "an automobile prophylactorium" in the region. A deadline was set: January 1, 1951. The deadline came and went, and nothing was done.

In February, 1951, the regional authorities ordered their local sub- (Continued on page 151)

DE HARAK

THE MARKSMAN

He hunted to kill, but killing was only one of his pleasures

by ROBERT SWITZER

THE black bear came down to the stream, walking the way bears always walk, all hunched over like a monkey hugging a football, her head low and reasonably alert but not alert enough because 200 yards away Henderson lay on the rocky shelf and used the 30-30 on her perfectly. She went down as though she had been lassoed around a front paw, the leg sliding inward across her chest, the leg sliding inward across her chest, the leg sliding inward across her chest and slightly on one side, with no fuss at all, disappointingly, gracefully even, just going forward and down as if unhurt, as if only lazy from the sun.

Henderson turned his head and said, "Dangerous beasts, aren't they?"

"Not very," Jerry said with a fine admiring grin. "Not a bit when you shoot like that."

Henderson grunted or snorted or did something which said distinctly, Nothing to it, and Jerry thought, *Sometimes I think I'm not particularly fond of you, sir.*

Jerry stood up but Henderson merely sat up, lit a cigarette, and blew smoke into the clear morning air.

He can't even be bothered going over to look at it!

"Skin it," Henderson said.

Yes, sir. I'd never have thought of it myself.

Carrying his rifle, Jerry half climbed, half jumped down from the shelf and went over to the bear, carefully, watching for life. There was none and he laid aside his rifle and drew his skinning knife.

There is killing for food, which is one thing, and there is killing for sport, which is another thing, and then there is killing for the sake of killing, which is indecent, but this man is killing just to show how easy it is, and that is even more indecent.

The afternoon before, a hound had come racing around a corner of the hunting lodge, tail flailing vertically, horizontally and in erratic circles, as if a tail traveling on only one plane would be an understatement. Eileen stood in the doorway and watched the mountain-scarred station wagon stop and two men get out. One was young, under thirty, hatless, face very tanned and hair sun-bleached and he was Jerry; the other was older, but still young, forty-five perhaps, and this second man was exceedingly handsome. If you saw a photograph of him (and you sometimes did because at the age of nineteen he had discovered a revolutionary way of beating eggs and had led a rather wealthy life ever since) you would say unfairly that he not

only had a first-rate photographer but one who also knew all there was to know about retouching. He was big, no taller than the younger man, but heavier, and his hair was black and thick with grey glinting at the temples. His mustache was expertly groomed and there were specks of grey in it, too. *By George,* she thought, *he's just as beautiful as his pictures.* She walked down to the car and Jerry introduced them. "Mr. Henderson, this is my wife, Eileen." She put out her hand and Henderson took it and they smiled at each other, and Jerry, also smiling, watched them, thinking: *I'd hate to be a judge at this beauty contest—it would be an awful decision to have to make.* While Jerry unloaded the station wagon, she learned that Henderson was glad it was late in the season and he was their only guest; he had come hoping for just that. He was surprised that they lived here the year round; the Rockies had always impressed him as a fine place to visit, but he didn't know that he'd like to be surrounded by them all the time.

In the evening they sat before the fireplace and Jerry went through the ritual of telling humorous hunting stories which Henderson only half listened to and wished he could hear less of because he was realizing more and more that Eileen was really quite attractive and in a decent environment could be much more so. He finally excused himself—he wasn't sure whether it was in the middle of one of the young man's stories or not—and went to his room.

"It seems to me," Jerry said, "I intercepted some thoughtful glances thrown your way by our new friend. Did you notice anything like that?"

"Certainly," she said. "How bushed do you think I am?"

He grinned and said, "Good. He looks like a mink-coat and Mexico-winter man to me."

While in his room Henderson was thinking: *I hate waste and I don't like her being wasted on that young lout. The thing is, she probably hasn't had a chance to know any better. I think maybe we'd better shove that lout of hers around a bit and sort of help her to separate the men from the boys. Yes, I think that's the thing to do.*

So the next morning they had gone out and Henderson had butchered the bear and they came back to the lodge and Jerry gave Eileen the news.

"One shot!" she said. "Where did you learn to shoot like that?"

"There was nothing sensational about it,"

Henderson said. "After all, sporting rifles are made by superb craftsmen. They're built to shoot straight. If you line the sight up with the target and don't yank on the trigger, there's no reason why you should miss."

"As easy as that?" she said. "I never found it as easy as that."

"Well," he said, "you have to hold the gun steady, of course, and allow something for distance and movement, but there is nothing difficult about it—nothing nearly so difficult as all these hunters would have you believe."

Which, even for Henderson who was not subtle, was a rather obvious back-of-the-hand to Jerry whose occupation was primarily that of a hunter, if such a childishly easy pastime could be called an occupation.

"Nothing personal there, naturally," Henderson said, smiling, his eyes crinkling up, real friendly-like.

I am a businessman, Jerry thought, *and the customer is always right.* "Of course not," he said pleasantly, and to get away from this, he said, "I'm going to take old Pete and go north this afternoon. See what I can line up for tomorrow."

"Make it good," Henderson said. "Something a little more violent than that black bear would be all right. How about a grizzly?"

"I'll do my best," Jerry said. "Grizzlies are getting mighty scarce around here, though."

"Yes?" Henderson said, and it was there in his voice, the implication that a man who knew what he was doing could find a big thing like a grizzly bear.

They lunched and Jerry left immediately for the north, a 30-30 under his arm, with Pete dashing on ahead and around about in the unbelievable ecstasy of a hound going hunting. It was a lovely afternoon, very warm for this late in the year. At Henderson's suggestion, Eileen accompanied him down to the stream where they sat on rocks close to the clear, icy water.

"You know," Henderson said, "I find this rather hard to believe—that your husband would leave you alone here with a strange man."

"Why?"

"Well, you people don't know me. I might be some sort of fiend."

"Are you?" she asked smiling.

"Unfortunately," he said, smiling back and looking very handsome, "no."

"Then why would Jerry worry?" she said, chuckling to herself as she remembered his parting words to her: "You *(Continued on page 142)*

DE HARAK

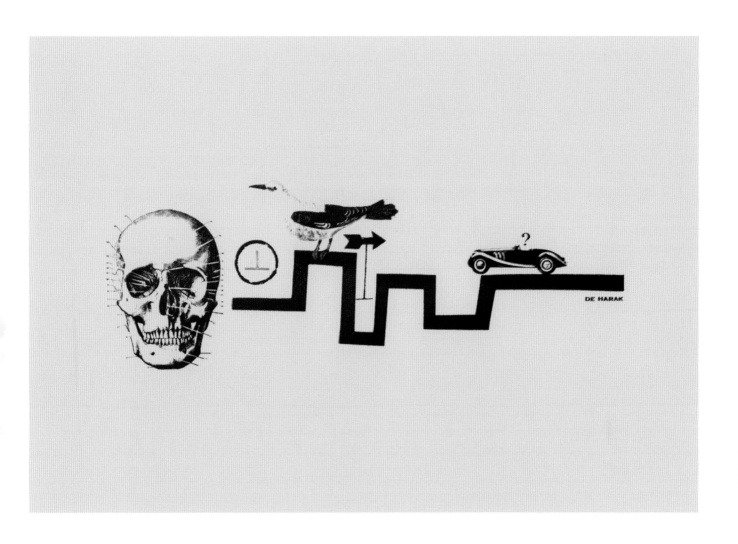

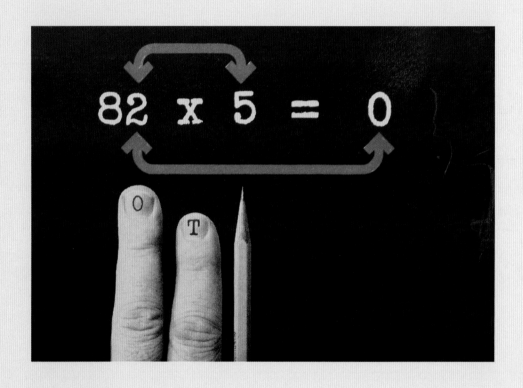

DE HARAK

> Magazine cover (detail),
Perspectives USA, no. 7,
Hamish Hamilton Ltd.,
1954.

BEAUTY AND THE BUST

Build 'em, buy 'em, or ignore 'em?—the deficient damsel's dilemma   by **VICTOR WARREN QUAYLE**

S OCIAL HISTORIANS of the future may, or may not, refer to the middle twentieth century as the Uplift Age, but be that as it may, Hollywood, TV and the fashion designers have exalted the female bosom in a manner unprecedented in modern times. Probably not since the reign of England's lusty Charles the Second has an adult world been so preoccupied with the highly functional outcroppings of flesh and glands and muscle that adorn a normal woman's chest.

Millions of women have been made breast conscious by this emphasis upon what are known, physiologically speaking, as the mammary glands. The increasingly frank revelation of the bust, and the general acceptance of the subject as a topic of more-or-less-polite conversation, has been a phenomenon of comparatively recent years (at least in America), and has had a terrific impact upon the western world's social and economic life.

The manufacture of that artful device coyly known as the "falsie" has zoomed into a multimillion-dollar industry. Countless thousands of flat-breasted women, overwhelmed by the requirements of an age that has produced a Mae West, a Dagmar, a Marie Wilson and a Jane Russell in one generation, have gone scurrying in search of aid less artificial than the falsie; they have poured fortunes into the exchequers of beauty experts and physical culturists in an effort to remedy the deficiency by special diets and exercises, which have produced some remarkable results.

Few persons, presumably, are qualified to state what effect mammary exposure has had upon the moral fiber of the nation, but the trend has a sharp significance to students of modern behavior, many of whom believe that it represents a healthy revulsion to the dour school of opinion that mistook discomfort for morality, and a final revolt against the last vestiges of prurient prudery in America.

Not all sociologists share this liberal viewpoint. The question of whether to bare the bosom or not to bare it has become a bone of controversy gnawed alike by those who see no evil in the current glorification of the female façade and those convinced that the trend is but one more neurotic symptom of the general moral breakdown of our times, linked, by a pattern of association, to sexual promiscuity, corruption and crime. While the controversy simmers, realistic women have had to accept the iron dictates of a fashion that demands they put up the best front possible —speaking literally as well as figuratively.

It may be a sad commentary upon our civilization, and upon the efficacy of higher education, but in certain employment circles a well-filled sweater is as great an asset as a Phi Beta Kappa key. All of us live in a world in which we had little part in the making, but today's woman, however she may dislike the thought, must face the fact that in this modern world the glamour jobs—and the glamour men—most frequently go to the girls who have what it takes to keep a strapless evening dress in a vertical position. The reaction of the intelligent woman has been a reflex conditioned by necessity. Those who have 'em display 'em to advantage; the have-nots resort to the development salon or the falsie counter and view the latter measure as a pardonable deception, although there is a case on record of a husband who sued for divorce when he found that his wife's sizable "development" was due to the garment industry, instead of nature.

Fashions in clothing—as well as fashions in morals—are said to run in cycles, which may comfort those inclined to be distressed by the present tendency of the feminine neckline to descend. The Victorian age, which eventually imposed its harsh concepts of morality upon the speech and manners and costumes of most of the civilized world, experienced, at its beginning, a violent repugnance to the excesses of the Regency period.

Belles of that remarkably free-and-easy age had somewhat revolutionary ideas of what was *de rigueur* in feminine apparel. They lifted their breasts with tight bands of cloth that puffed them out like inflated balloons, wore almost no underclothing, and actually doused their transparent dresses with water, so that the material would cling to their bodies.

Preachers of the fire-and-brimstone school fulminated against the curvaceous hussies who embellished early-nineteenth-century London society, but it is a matter of record that pneumonia slew more of them than did ecclesiastical wrath. And just as Victorian living was, in a sense, a last gasp of Cromwellian Puritanism, so did the antics of the gay Regency belles represent a nostalgic regard for the piping days of naughty Charles the Second and an atavistic resentment of the dour Oliver Cromwell whom Charles succeeded.

Someone has said that if there had been no such thing as immorality before Oliver Cromwell, the old Puritan would have given it a reason for existence. The leader of the revolution that overthrew and beheaded Charles the First, Cromwell was a zealot who walked fully after the Lord who, to him, was a vengeful and tribal deity rather than a benevolent and forgiving Creator. In Cromwell's reasoning, bodies were vile things, so women swathed their provocative flesh in many layers of clothing.

Bosoms were regarded as standard parts of female equipment, necessary in providing sustenance for the infants who were, theoretically, the future guardians of Puritan prejudice and power. When not busy hunting down Royalists or engaged in the massacre of Irish peasants, Cromwell and his son forced upon England a code of morals as savagely repressive as any the world had ever known. Without making apologies for the libertinism of Charles the Second, it may be said the Restoration was like a breath of spring and a flame of light, after the cold darkness of intolerable winter.

The Merry Monarch, Charles, loosened the moral stays of all Europe. A devil-may-care adventurer of frankly lecherous tendencies, Charles scattered the abodes of his mistresses like way stations across London and adjacent areas, and for the first time since antiquity the female bosom burst forth in all its pristine splendor. Along with other women of the period, Nell Gwyn, the street-gamin orange vendor who became his favorite, bared her plump white shoulders and breasts in gowns slashed almost to the navel. As a matter of fact, modern couturiers are at a loss to understand just what kept the bosoms within the bodice, so abandoned was the décolletage. Many of the more daring demoiselles painted their nipples instead of their fingernails, received gentlemen callers in their baths, and regarded adultery as a commonplace. It was a profligate age, a period of unbridled license, and it doomed itself with its own excesses. Yet the blithe, lascivious spirit of Charles wrestled for centuries with the grim shadow of Oliver Cromwell, and was never decisively beaten until Victoria and her stern German consort, Albert, brought nineteenth-century England to their own strict way of life.

America seems to have happily escaped the full fury of both Cromwellian prudery and Restoration debauchery. True, our Pilgrim forefathers were steeped in the acid of gloomy Puritan belief, and some of their Blue Laws still survive, but even the elders of the Plymouth Colony knew a sense of freedom that had been stultified in England.

The men who pushed back the colonial frontiers were aware of the pleasures of the flesh, but not preoccupied with them. During the late colonial years and the beginnings of the young republic, the bust was admired but not overemphasized, and women seldom allowed the dictates of fashion to ride roughshod over their sense of *(Continued on page 109)*

∨ Magazine cover,
Perspectives USA, no. 7,
Hamish Hamilton Ltd.,
1954.

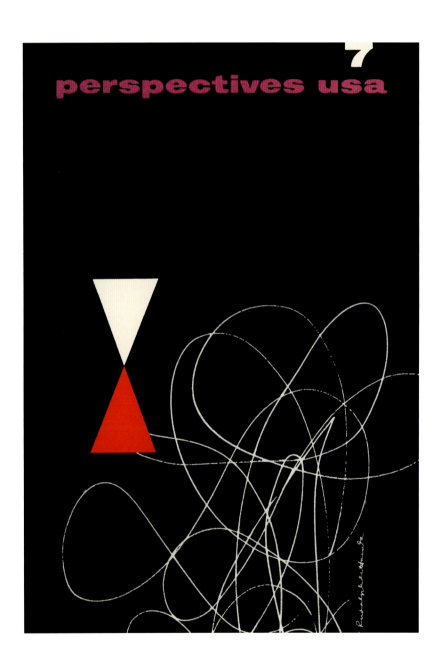

"The
Man
with
the
Golden
Arm"

a play by Jack Kirkland; based on the novel by Nelson Algren; directed by Louis MacMillan; sets and lighting by Paul Morrison
Tuesday through Friday, 8:40 p.m.; Saturday 6:40 and 9:40 p.m.; Sunday, 2:40 and 8:40 p.m.

∨ Magazine cover, *Dance Magazine,* 'Special Holiday Issue,' vol. 33, no. 1, Dance Magazine, Inc., January 1959.

Magazine cover, *Perspectives USA,* no. 12, Hamish Hamilton Ltd., 1955. This magazine cover for *Prospetti,* the Italian edition of *Perspectives,* drew inspiration from Italian Renaissance tiles. The magazine's interior was designed by Alvin Lustig.

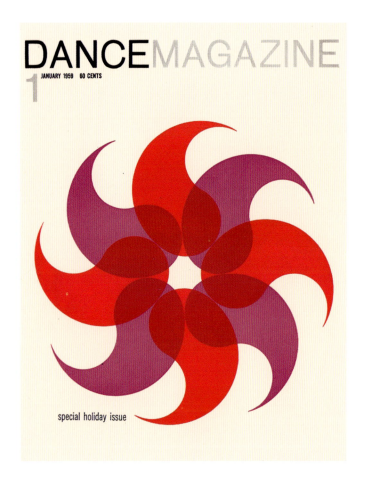

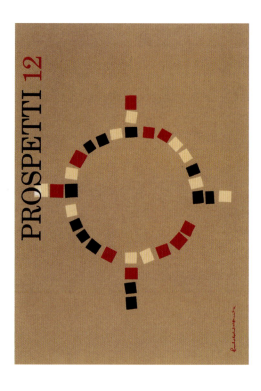

⌄ Magazine cover, *Interiors*,
Whitney Publications,
April 1953. Rudolph
de Harak, photographer.

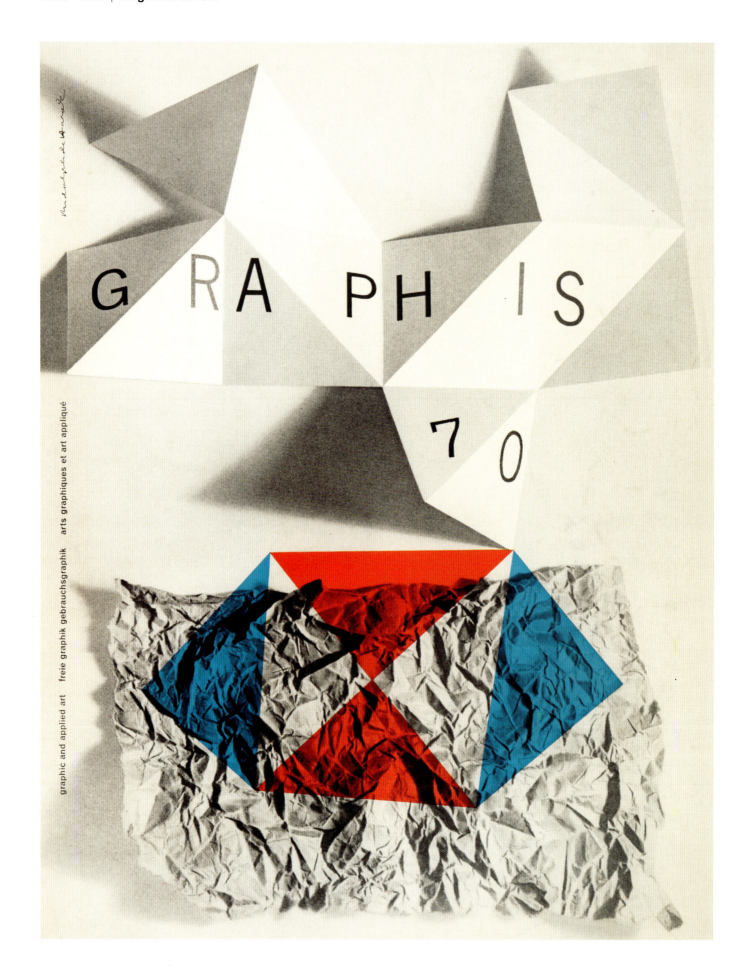

< Magazine cover,
Graphis, vol. 13, no. 70,
Graphis, Inc., 1957.
Rudolph de Harak,
photographer.

∨ Magazine cover, *Print,*
vol. 11, no. 3, William
Edwin Rudge, Publisher,
Inc., April/May 1957.
De Harak's second
cover for *Print* magazine
reflected his early
responses to a rational
Modernist approach to
graphic design. He based

this design concept on
the theme of the Seventh
International Design
Conference in Aspen,
'Design and Human Values.'

Magazine cover, *Print,* vol. 11,
no. 2, William Edwin Rudge,
Publisher, Inc., February/
March 1957.

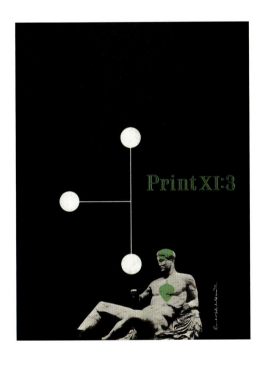

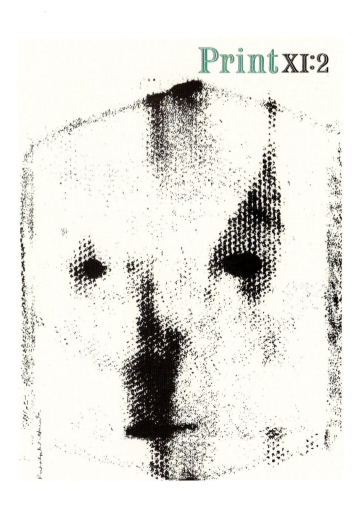

∨ Book jacket, *The Wild Honey,* by Victoria Lincoln, Rinehart & Co., 1953.

Book jacket, *The Time Cheaters,* by Wilson Tucker, Rinehart & Co., 1953.

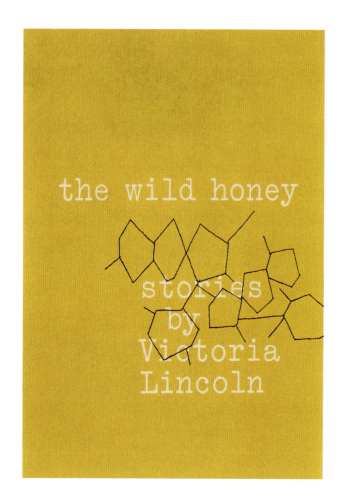

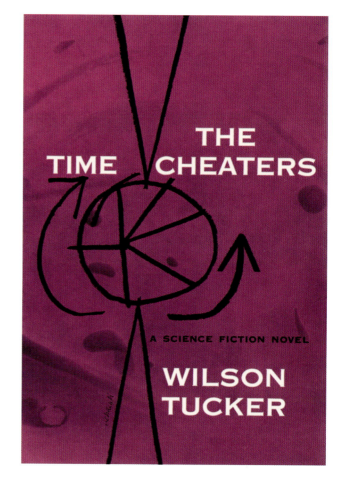

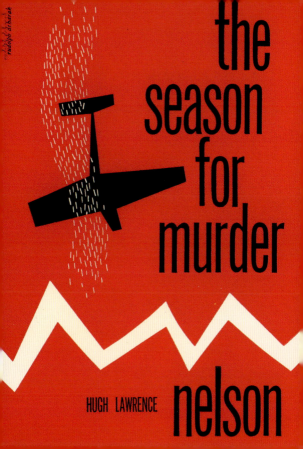

the
season
for
murder

nelson

HUGH LAWRENCE

∨ Book jacket, *Fifteen Short*
Stories by R. V. Cassill,
Herbert Gold, and James
B. Hall, New Directions
Publishing Corporation,
1957. Rudolph de Harak,
photographer.

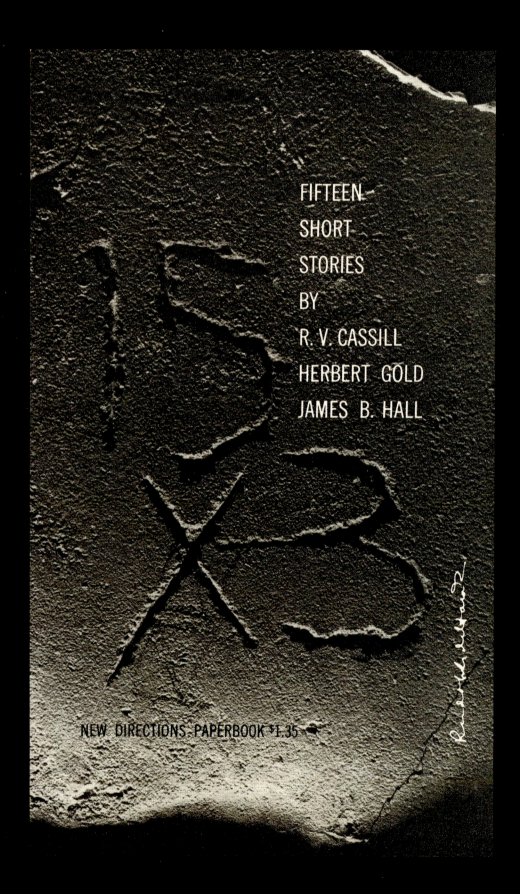

ND15

in prose and poetry

NEW DIRECTIONS 15

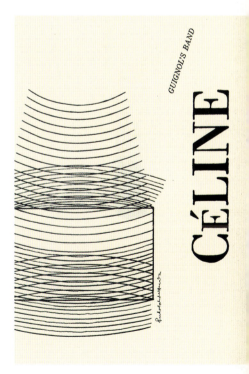

GUIGNOL'S BAND

CÉLINE

< Book jacket,
*New Directions 15:
An Anthology of New
Directions in Prose and
Poetry,* New Directions
Publishing Corporation,
1955.

∨ Book jacket, *Guignol's
Band,* by Louis-Ferdinand
Céline, New Directions
Publishing Corporation,
1954.

∨ Symbol, Kurt Versen
Lighting Company, 1957.

> Packaging pattern (detail),
Kurt Versen Lighting
Company, 1957. This bold
black banding pattern was
utilized on corrugated
kraft board material to
suggest the optical effects
of light. Selected for

The Package exhibition and
catalog in 1959. The Museum
of Modern Art (MoMA)
Design Collection, New York,
New York, USA.

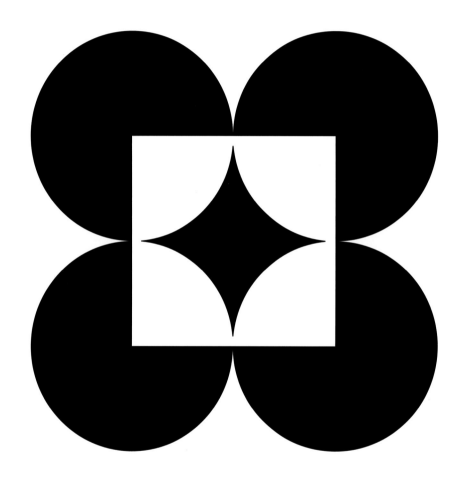

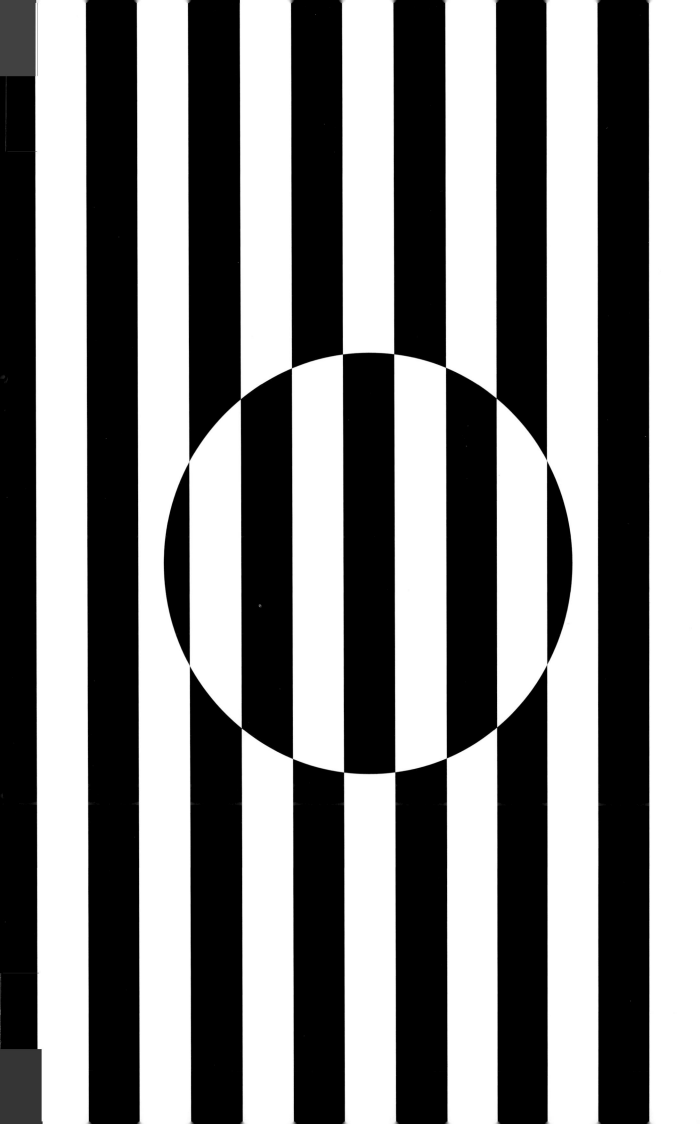

< Magazine cover (detail), *Print,* vol. 15, no. 3, Kaye-Cadel Publishing Corp., May/June 1961. Rudolph de Harak, photographer.

The Sixties: 1960–1969

The 1960s was a tumultuous decade in the United States, especially for its major cities, and an unforgettable one for those who lived through it. It was a study in contrasts in human imperfection, and unrest, new ideas, and drastic changes were ever-present. As the Vietnam War continued, protests spread throughout the country, not just about the war itself but also about morality and personal freedoms. Ironically, the New York World's Fair, with its theme of 'Peace Through Understanding', hosted over 51 million visitors during its eighteen-month run from April 1964 to October 1965. A few months before it opened, the Beatles — aka the 'Fab Four' — took their first steps on American soil, marking the beginning of a cultural revolution throughout the country. Over the course of the decade, New York City was hit with numerous strikes, including a seven-month teachers' strike, a lengthy newspaper strike, and a nine-day sanitation strike. Race riots occurred from coast to coast, including such cities as Chicago, Los Angeles, Washington, DC, and New York City, following the assassinations of Dr Martin Luther King and Robert F. Kennedy in 1968. The next year, over a half a million people descended upon a three-hundred-acre farm in upstate New York to attend what was billed as 'three days of peace, love, and music' at the Woodstock Music Festival. That same summer, the Stonewall Riots stood up against police oppression, launching the modern gay rights movement as we know it today.

It was also a momentous time period for the graphic design profession in the United States, especially in New York City, where

∨ Rudolph de Harak,
c. 1962. Ann Schultheiss,
photographer.

Ivan Chermayeff and Tom Geismar established their namesake design consultancy in 1960. In London, Bob Gill joined Colin Forbes and Alan Fletcher to form Fletcher/Forbes/Gill in 1962, which ultimately became the world-renowned design firm Pentagram. By the end of the decade, the International Typographic Style had emerged as the dominant force in graphic design throughout the country, as well as the world.

The International Typographic Style, also known as Swiss Style, profoundly influenced a group of Modernist graphic designers during the 1960s, who began to practice objective, rational, and systematic design throughout the United States. These independently minded individuals included Jacqueline Casey in Cambridge, Massachusetts; John Massey in Chicago, Illinois; Massimo Vignelli in Chicago, Illinois; and de Harak in New York City. Fortunately for these graphic designers, as well as many other practitioners around the country, corporations and institutions also started to fully embrace this new visual language, and it would remain a dominant influence on corporate design for the next twenty-five years. Graphic design professionals were now being called upon to assist their business clients in expanding their national and global presence through visual communication. Not only were designers being commissioned to create a new symbol or logotype, but they were also now being sought out to develop comprehensive visual communication systems for their clients. These systems are still clearly evident today in the visual identities of companies and institutions such as CBS, Chase, IBM, MIT, and Mobil, among many others.

International design publications and periodicals began to convey this new movement throughout the world, as well as across the United States. Josef Müller-Brockmann, Richard Paul Lohse, Carlo Vivarelli, and Hans Neuburg published their first issue of *Neue Grafik (New Graphic Design)* in 1958, a trilingual periodical that presented the philosophy and accomplishments of the Swiss Style to an international audience. Its format and typography were a living expression of the visual order and refinement achieved by Mid-century Modernist Swiss designers. *Graphis*, a bi-monthly international journal of advertising art and graphic design, established by Swiss designer and publisher Walter Herdeg, as well as a group of influential books by such designers as Müller-Brockmann (*The Graphic Artist and his Design Problems*, Teufen: Verlag Niggli AG, 1961), Karl Gerstner (*Designing Programmes*, Teufen: Verlag Niggli AG, 1964), and Emil Ruder (*Typographie: A Manual of Design*, Teufen: Verlag Niggli AG, 1967), all became international messengers of this new Modernist visual language.

De Harak was one of the first American graphic designers to embrace the International Typographic Style, and eagerly assimilated the rigorous and rational ideas of Müller-Brockmann, Gerstner, and Ruder. He also drew from the art movements of the era, such as Abstract Expressionism, Op Art, and Pop Art, consciously and continuously looking for a more disciplined structure in his thinking and practice of graphic design. While the early 1960s was certainly one of his most productive and prolific periods, it was also a time in which he used his ever-expanding consultant work as a primary means for further exploration and experimentation, with a wide range of approaches, techniques, and media. This became apparent in the various photographic processes, distinct color palettes, neutral typography, geometric forms, and abstract shapes that he ultimately

developed in his groundbreaking work for Westminster Records and
McGraw-Hill Paperbacks.

Creative Breakthroughs

Westminster Records was an American classical-music record label
that issued original recordings until it was sold to ABC-Paramount
Records in 1965. The label was founded in 1949 by Michael 'Mischa'
Naida, James Grayson, conductor Henry Swoboda, and Henry Cage.
From the start, the record label was known for its technically superior
recordings, which became extremely popular among a growing
community of audiophiles, especially when the company began
issuing stereophonic recordings in the late 1950s.

The Westminster commission led to one of de Harak's major
creative breakthroughs in his career. As he recalled to renowned
American author Steven Heller in a 1987 interview, 'this really was
the first time that I think everything was starting to come together
in terms of the way I wanted to work — simple image, strong clean
typography.' [1] From 1960 to 1962, he designed approximately
fifty album covers for the label. During this major undertaking, he
allowed himself the opportunity to seriously consider the diverse
and contrasting worlds of hard, delineated geometry and the soft,
hand-drawn lines of ethereal forms. To de Harak, Modernist graphic
design was not only about forms that 'were impeccable in their sense
of order, but also about forms that covered the entire emotional
spectrum'. [2] He further explained, 'I was always looking for the
hidden order, trying to somehow either develop new forms or
manipulate existing forms ... I wanted to create constellations so
rich that they could communicate content.' [3]

This would be the first of many times in his career that he
methodically and successfully revealed the 'hidden order' that he
was always searching for within his design solutions. In this case,

he produced a series of album covers
in which he developed conceptual
minimalistic imagery that interpreted
various music genres as well as evoking
the music's emotional structure and
style. For example, with his design
solution for *Sounds from the Alps* he
created three bold, black brushstrokes
that immediately convey melodic
sound waves while simultaneously
representing the Swiss Alps. These
reductive, evocative forms were
framed on a white background
and asymmetrically balanced with
typography hand-set in upper- and
lower-case Akzidenz-Grotesk located
at the cover's upper-left corner. The
Westminster symbol and logotype,
which he also designed, were visible at
the cover's upper-right corner.

De Harak thought that this was a
pivotal design solution for him because
it relied upon, as he said, 'a great

∨ Photograph for *A Preface to History*, 1963. Rudolph de Harak, photographer.

economy in its simplicity because it is saying as much as it can with as little as you can.' [4] It was also one of the first album covers he designed for Westminster in which he used only one typeface — the neutral, sans-serif Akzidenz-Grotesk — which he felt anchored the composition. This was a watershed moment, and one in which he gained a great insight into a refined methodology for working — a rational simplicity that would be his guiding light for the remainder of his career. The extensive exploration of visual forms and neutral typography for Westminster Records was his testing ground for subsequent book jackets and covers he designed during this time period for several publishers. However, de Harak's innovative thinking and approach grew exponentially with new meaning and direction with his landmark work for McGraw-Hill Paperbacks.

A Landmark Collaboration

In the early 1960s, American book publishers and graphic designers started working together for the first time with a collective, creative objective. At the forefront of this new collaborative movement was a group of visual pioneers and graphic designers, including Ivan Chermayeff, Tom Geismar, George Giusti, Roy Kuhlman, Alvin Lustig, Paul Rand, Fred Troller, and de Harak, who pushed the boundaries of Modernism to new heights within the publishing world.

One of the most prolific and influential collaborations between a graphic designer and client in Mid-century Modernist graphic design was the one shared by de Harak and the New York publisher McGraw-Hill in the 1960s. It started with a commission to design a new trademark for their paperback division. At that time, Dick Fisher was an editor at McGraw-Hill and contacted de Harak to see if he was interested in the new commission. De Harak recalled, 'So I did the trademark, but I wanted to show it in application…Dick sent me, I guess, half a dozen books that they were intending to reprint. And so, I took those covers, redesigned them, and applied the new trademark to them. And when he saw them, he said that he loved the trademark.' [5] Fisher also loved the new book covers and asked de Harak if he could use them; he agreed and negotiated a price per cover. In retrospect, de Harak saw his work for McGraw-Hill Paperbacks as a direct outgrowth and natural progression of his album cover work for Westminster Records a year earlier. Over a period of five years, he would design approximately four-hundred covers for the publisher. 'I would do anywhere between ten and twenty book covers in a month, … it was really wonderful,' [6] he later recalled. 'And if one were to ask me what was really the most satisfying time of my rather lengthy career, I would say the period from 1960 to 1965…I somehow touched the skirt of God, in terms of my enthusiasm and opening myself up in a very, very rich way.' [7]

At this point in his career, he clearly understood the fundamental visual principles of graphic design, even if he was self-taught. Each of these groundbreaking covers shares a common compositional system that applies the basic tenets of the International Typographic Style, with the use of a mathematically-constructed page grid, uniform sans-serif typography (Akzidenz-Grotesk) set flush left and ragged right, and an asymmetrical composition. De Harak's reliance upon these visual principles further enhanced and increased the viewer's ability to organize, differentiate, and most

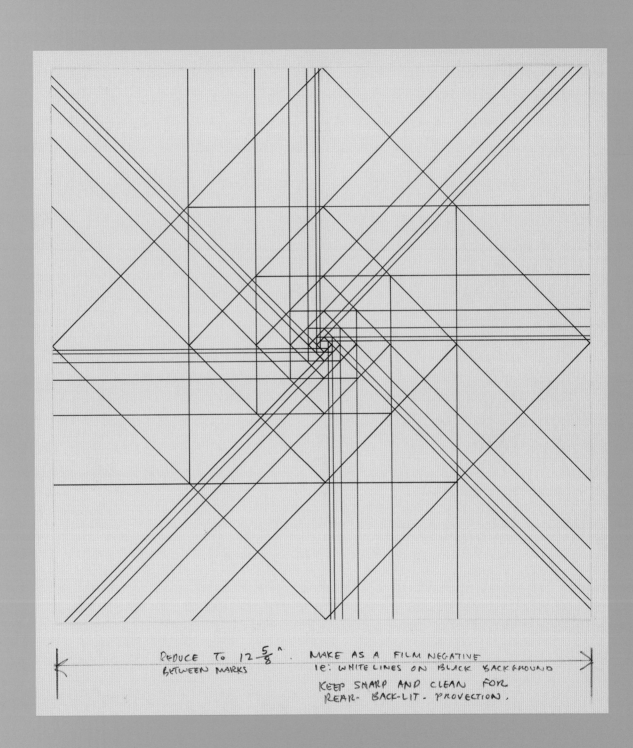

Original ink line drawing for *Technique of Executive Control,* 1960. Rudolph de Harak, illustrator.

∨ Photographic studies of
the American flag, c. 1961.
Rudolph de Harak,
photographer.

importantly, interact with the cover's visual content. One of his approaches relied upon using immediately recognizable objects to reinforce a book's theme. For example, he used an image of a knotted rope for Hans Selye's *The Stress of Life,* and an image of an old wheel suggesting the passage of time for Carl G. Gustavson's *A Preface to History*, both of which were photographed in high contrast by de Harak. For other titles, his solutions sometimes relied upon pure graphic elements, such as four right-angled arrows that resolve themselves into both a swastika and converging movement at the same time for Leon Gouré's *The Siege of Leningrad*. In 1993, Steven Heller reflected: 'The McGraw-Hill covers were paradigms of purist visual communication. Each element was fundamental since de Harak did not allow for the extraneous.

Yet, as economical as they were, each was also a marriage of expressionistic or illusionistic imagery and systematic typography, the same repertoire of elements that he would later use in other graphic work. De Harak became known for simplifying the complex without lessening meaning.' [8]

When undertaking the act and process of image making, whether glyph, pictogram, symbol, sign, drawing, illustration, painting, photography or typography, de Harak always considered numerous forms and methodologies. While these all possessed their own distinct and varied visual characteristics and functions, de Harak also understood their value and potential as meaningful and obvious visual counterpoints to narrative form. Each image represented an emotional experience that could be immediately understood and embraced by the viewer. The broad range of images he created for his McGraw-Hill book covers spanned a full spectrum that was defined at one end by realism and at the other by abstraction. Between these two visual extremes were a myriad of possibilities for him to choose from: the more realistic, the more direct and immediate the image; the more abstract, the more restrained and interpretive the image. His innovative approach to a book cover's visual content, as well as its compositional layout, ultimately gave the entire range of McGraw-Hill Paperbacks a distinctive visual brand that remained effective and unique for decades to come, as well as influencing future generations of graphic designers.

During the 1960s, de Harak used the Westminster and McGraw-Hill commissions to further hone his skills as a graphic designer and visual storyteller by considering these projects' limitations as a series of meaningful and insightful learning experiences. He explained these limitations as: 'a common size with a common medium, and that is the book cover medium or the record cover medium, but relative to McGraw-Hill, the books, so that I had basically all of the limitations as a continuum…as a constant. Even three colors. I couldn't go more than three colors. The sizes never changes. And it meant that I could, while working within the limitations, continue to try to hone my skills and make them even sharper, to better understand the type and so on.' [9] Both of these experiences, and the limitations they imposed, played a critical role in his creative growth and development.

De Harak's design consultancy, which was now located on East 19th Street in the Gramercy Park area of New York City, also grew exponentially, with an ever-expanding roster of new clients and opportunities. In addition to his extensive work for McGraw-Hill Paperbacks, he continued to design numerous book covers and jackets throughout the 1960s for other publishers, including Doubleday & Company, Harper & Brothers, Holt Rinehart & Winston, J.B. Lippincott Co., The Macmillan Company, Meridian Books, New Directions Publishing Corporation, Reinhold Publishing, and Vintage Books. Based on his earlier identity work for Kurt Versen Lighting Company, he also attracted new companies with similar visual communication needs such as Cumberland Furniture, Racine Press, and the American Federation of the Arts. In the world of editorial, he continued to design covers for such magazines as *Holiday*, *Esquire*, and *Dance*, but one of his most memorable design solutions was for *Print* in 1961. In the spring of that year, the editors invited him to be the magazine's guest editor for its May/June issue. Always wanting to expand his knowledge of and experience with new visual forms and approaches, he experimented with distorting and manipulating high-contrast Kodalith* films of photographs that he had taken of an American flag to emphasize its undulating waves. In keeping with his Modernist visual principles, he decided not to use the magazine's recently commissioned logotype and typographic standards, instead using Akzidenz-Grotesk for the entire issue. He proudly recalled, 'I took a photograph of the American flag which I then converted into a Kodalith and then had it printed in flat color. I still feel today it is one of the best things that I have done.' [10]

In February 1963, de Harak married Orietta Giardino in New York City. He and Orietta had their first child, a son Bruno, in June 1964 and lived at 113 East 60th Street on the Upper East Side of Manhattan. In 1966 they separated, divorcing two years later in 1968. Orietta de Harak died in 2015. In 1966, de Harak met his future wife Carol Godshalk Sylbert, a photographer, at an art gallery opening in New York City. In June 1969, they were married and were together for thirty-five years until his death in 2002.

As with his teaching at Cooper Union, now in its second decade, de Harak also continued with his involvement and enthusiastic support of the American Institute of Graphic Arts (AIGA) and its

*A Kodalith is a type of photographic printing film with an orthochromatic emulsion that gives a high-contrast result, with very dense and even blacks.

mission. He served as its vice president from 1967 to 1968, and was on the organization's board of directors from 1969 to 1970. In 1966, it celebrated its fiftieth anniversary with an exhibition and commemorative publication entitled *Fifty Years of Graphic Arts in America.* As chairman of the project, de Harak invited Will Burtin to write the introduction — nineteen years earlier, in Los Angeles, de Harak had been in the audience when Burtin presented his influential lecture 'Integration: The New Discipline in Design' at the Art Center School.

Expo 67 Montreal

Following in the footsteps of Will Burtin, who he had idolized from the moment he heard him speak in Los Angeles in 1947, de Harak set himself on a new and broader career path, one that expanded from the printed page to the three-dimensional world of environments and exhibitions. In 1965, he was awarded his first major exhibition commission for the Canadian Pavilion's 'Man, His Planet, and Space' exhibition at Expo 67 in Montreal. Earlier that year, Nicholas Chaparos, a professor of design at the University of Waterloo in Ontario, recommended him to design the pavilion, which was part of the 'Man the Explorer' theme pavilion group. Little did he know at the time that he started this intensive, two-year project that this type of work would become one of the cornerstones of his evolving design consultant practice, which would eventually encompass environmental graphics, wayfinding, and exhibition design. It also would lead him to becoming one of the leading exhibition and museum designers of the Mid-century Modernist era.

Expo 67, which ran from April through October of that year, featured ninety pavilions representing sixty countries and celebrated the theme of 'Man and His World', but it is best known today for introducing the world to new and innovative architecture such as the US Pavilion's geodesic dome, designed by American architect and futurist R. Buckminster Fuller, and the Habitat 67 modular-housing complex designed by Israeli-American architect Moshe Safdie. Being the sole exhibition designer of the Canadian Pavilion at Expo 67 was an eye-opening, challenging, and career-changing experience for de Harak. The Canadian Pavilion complex itself included a distinctive main building which was in the form of a large, inverted pyramid or 'Katimavik' (an Inuit word for 'gathering place') and three smaller linked theme pavilions located at ground level.

It was also during this time period that he finally had an opportunity to meet Burtin, one of his idols and influences. De Harak recalled that, 'Will had hired several people who were students of mine. And so, these students were always talking about me and he wanted to know who I was ... So, I called Will, and we went and had lunch. And what followed was a wonderful relationship ... I always thought of him as kind of my surrogate father.' [11] Years later, after becoming colleagues and friends, Burtin recommended de Harak for membership in the Alliance Graphique Internationale (AGI), the prestigious member-based association of professionals drawn from across the globe, united by working in the field of graphic design.

After their initial meeting, Burtin introduced de Harak to one of his staff industrial designers, David Sutton, who had started his career at the Burtin office. Sutton had gained extensive experience

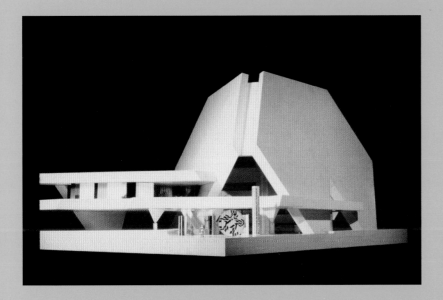

∨ Exterior study model
of Canadian Pavilion's
'Man, His Planet, and
Space' at Expo 67.

working with Burtin on three major exhibitions for the 1964 New York World's Fair, including the Kodak Pavilion, and would now work for de Harak as his design manager on the Canadian Pavilion. Years later, Sutton described his experience as one of the most exciting of his career and the beginning of a lifelong friendship with and mentorship by de Harak: 'My first experience with Rudy showed how he approached design problems differently. The entrance to the pavilion was going to be a long winding path, which meant lines of visitors. Rudy's first question was what do we do for people standing in line. His idea was to find out by observation. The 1964 New York World's Fair was still going on, and we spent many days photographing visitors standing in line and conducting interviews at the various pavilions. That information resulted in Rudy designing an entrance path to the pavilion that took the visitor past panels depicting aspects of 'Man, His Planet, and Space' and asking questions about things they would see inside the pavilion. It was very successful.' [12]

De Harak created a visitor experience and exhibition for 'Man, His Planet, and Space', totaling approximately 1,490 sq m (16,000 sq ft), that examined how far man had come as an explorer; man in his environment and his relationship to nature; the earth and its minerals and natural resources extracted from it; and beyond earth, which focused on the solar system and space. For example, at the pavilion's entrance a symbol of man was painted in green, red, blue, and black on a set of concentric aluminum circles. These rotated at different speeds, confusing and abstracting the image. At specific time intervals, the concentric circles stopped to form the image of man once again. Along the entrance path to the pavilion, a series of vertical entrance panels was placed at intervals to keep visitors engaged as they queued up for the exhibition proper. Each panel visually introduced and oriented visitors to specific areas and themes of the exhibition: in, on, and above the earth. 'In the Earth' utilized 3.65 m (12 ft) high mirror-polished chrome cylinders displaying various rare minerals found in locations around the earth. For 'On the Earth', a display of the faces of man was used to communicate the extent and variety of the races of the world and their environments. On another wall, the population explosion was communicated in 'real time' from the macro to the micro. Illuminated numerals flashed increasing totals as births took place in the world, in Canada, in Montreal, as well as in ten other international cities.

In his extensive research for 'Man, His Planet, and Space' over a two-year period, de Harak determined that exhibitions 'should be fundamentally quick, penetrating, emotional, visual experiences.' His ultimate goal was to capture the emotional involvement of the viewer. He succeeded in doing so by, as he said, 'clothing potentially drab and obscure facts in the exciting dress of inventive design solutions, and thereby giving these facts some human meaning ... my intention was to show geology, geography, and space science in unexpectedly beautiful ways in unexpected relationships to daily life.' [13] While the most popular visitor experience at Expo 67 was the USSR Pavilion, the Canadian Pavilion was the second most popular, with eleven million visitors during the exposition's six-month run.

In the summer of 1967, the short-lived if influential quarterly design publication *Dot Zero* published an interview with de Harak in which he discussed his experiences in designing the exhibition and interiors of 'Man, His Planet, and Space'.

Creating Emotional Involvement in Geography, Geology, and Space Science: An Interview with Rudolph de Harak

DZ: *How did it happen that you, an American were chosen to design one of the theme pavilion exhibitions 'Man, His Planet, and Space', for the Canadian government?*
RdH: Actually, there were a few Americans as well as designers of other nationalities working for the Canadians. Originally I was hired as a consultant-designer by the University of Waterloo in Ontario to work on this theme. Later, I worked directly with the CCWE (Canadian Corporation for the World Exposition).

DZ: *How close was your working relationship with CCWE?*
RdH: It was a rather typical design-client relationship. In certain areas of the project, we worked together very closely, and work went well. Other areas were not as easy. I feel that as a client they were very demanding. This would seem natural though. It was a very big project for CCWE to oversee and control. It was mostly helpful to me that my office was in New York and not Montreal.

DZ: *Did the pavilion for your exhibition limit, in a negative sense, the possibilities for designing the exhibition, or did it enhance and relate to them?*
RdH: The architecture of the building in which we were to install our exhibits was a great limitation. It would seem logical to me that the general idea or content of an exhibit should dictate, to a large extent at least, the form that the building takes, and this of course was not the case. Unfortunately, the buildings were designed well before the exhibition, perhaps indicating that the Canadians were more interested in an external showplace than in meaningful communicative information. (As a matter of fact, on the whole it would seem that the fair became an excuse for one great architectural competition.) A major problem that resulted from a lack of coordination between pavilion and exhibit was that although it was a massive exterior it was nevertheless strange in its stinginess in amount of usable, workable space. This made it extremely difficult to establish spatial exhibit areas with a logical sequencing of subject matter. As far as I am concerned the building was designed for no purpose other than attraction. And even here it was unsuccessful.

DZ: *What material were you originally given to work on? Were many limitations imposed on you, or did you have considerable freedom to choose what to say and how to work it out?*
RdH: Originally I was given a rough story outline by the University of Waterloo which I was asked to refine and expand upon in exhibition form. To accomplish this, it was necessary to organize a small, efficient design team. It was made up of myself as head designer, George McCue, a science writer whose background was

mainly with Time Inc. working as editor of the Time-Life Science series, and David Sutton as project designer and a chief draftsman-engineer. With this team I was able to develop an informative story that contained scientific fact, design an exhibition based on information, construct a model and gain approval from CCWE and the ACSM, a group of Canadian scientists organized for the purpose of maintaining scientific integrity throughout the fair. The limitations, naturally, were many. And they are always the challenge. Personalities were a strong consideration. Some people like blue, some like red. What I specifically mean is that not all scientists agree with each other concerning the same subject. Frequently, an element of the exhibition that was acceptable to one scientist was later, after being built, objected to and criticized for its scientific content or approach by another. In general however, the science committee was extremely helpful. Other limitations were the inabilities of some of the exhibit fabricators to translate working drawings into sensitive functioning reality.

DZ: *What did you understand to be your overall responsibilities to CCWE?*
RdH: There were too many to elaborate on. The key responsibility as far as I was concerned was to design and supervise the fabrication of the finest exhibition, the most creative and inspiring exhibition that I could possibly conceive within the framework of time (a critical path network), unique personalities and bad architecture.

DZ: *What do you mean by the 'finest exhibition, the most creative and inspiring exhibition'?*
RdH: I mean working in a visual communications situation where I can express ideas through words and forms that are satisfying and exciting to me and still basically comprehensible to people, that are common to their understanding, but seen from a point of view that has never before been experienced. What I am trying to say is that a proposition such as that of designing an exhibition for a world's fair should not be a safe one from a designer's standpoint. That is, he should not be content with doing what he already knows, but work towards solutions, even though they may be foreign to him, which are compatible to the particular problem. In other words, the problem he is working on should precipitate the design systems. This is always precarious because he isn't content to reach into the back of his head to pull forth some pat, ready-made solution. Working close to time, budget and many other limitations he can easily misjudge and make mistakes. Nevertheless, a creative designer must work in the most positive and meaningful manner for himself. If the designer is dedicated, I would suggest that his every singular creative effort has a greater potential for failure than it has for success. In the specific case of my project 'Man, His Planet and Space', I felt that the material with which it was necessary to work had seldom been displayed with the intention of involving the public emotionally. The first purpose of this exhibition from my point of view was to capture the emotional involvement of the viewer. This means that I tried to clothe potentially drab and obscure facts in the exciting dress of inventive design solutions, and thereby give these facts some human meaning. Thus, broadly speaking, my intention was to show geology, geography, and space science in unexpectedly beautiful ways in unexpected relationships to daily life.

⌄ Outline Venn diagram of
the organizational content
of the Canadian Pavilion's
exhibition and visitor
experience, 1965.

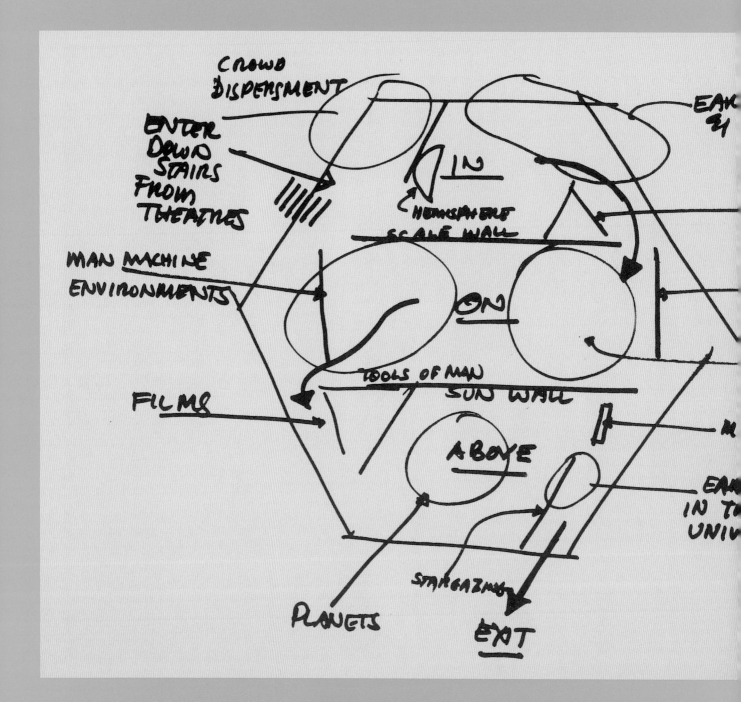

WAKES
CANOES

- MINERALS

POPULATION
EXPLOSION
WALL

FACES OF MAN
AREA

IS OF THE EARTH

e

DZ: *Now, after working on this project for almost two years, are you satisfied with the results of your efforts?*

RdH: All things considered, yes. This, however, needs some qualifying. To begin with, I don't think any creative person is totally happy with the outcome of his efforts, nor does he think these efforts are beyond improvement or further development. In this particular case, the biggest problem was that of too many words. And this problem was at least doubled because all the information was bilingual (French and English). The consultant scientists generally insisted on including a considerable amount of information which could only be communicated with words. Although I'm sure they feel otherwise, this attitude indicates that for them a fair is a reading, not a seeing, emotional experience. When this attitude manifests itself I think that any exhibition will fail. This does not mean that I haven't worked visually, but there are great globs of supportive texts which are very disconcerting and difficult for the visitors. The nature of the material was very broad, and was adaptable to many exhibition techniques, but the ground rules were such that to a large extent I had to work verbally.

The chief characteristic of fairs is that they are tailored for great quantities of people. Huge crowds. In fact, a fair is unsuccessful if it doesn't draw many visitors. This means that very rarely will the successful exhibition be seen and studied intimately by just a few at a time. Therefore, too many facts, too many images and too many words will just not be seen. There isn't just the time for the viewer. Fair exhibitions should be fundamentally quick, penetrating, emotional, visual experiences. Although it is true that some useful information is put forth in world's fairs, that some extraordinary, creative paths are formed in which to tell people about many things, that forecasts are made of our living future and that some of the prophesies even come true, I nevertheless hope that one fine morning we wake up and there will be no more world's fairs. As a designer, I am concerned with the meaningfulness of what I do. I am concerned about waste. Therefore, I center a proposition such as a fair with great ambivalence. I look for the opportunities that a fair can offer, but I may recoil at the lack of meaningfulness and permanence of my efforts. Certainly, emotional experiences, including those that are visual, neither must be of permanent physical things in order that they have meaning, nor must the experiences themselves be forever memorable. Nevertheless, six months from now, when the fair is over, even though I have gained experience, the evidence of my efforts will have disappeared. In terms of time, effort or money expended by me and by others involved in creating exhibitions, as well as by the viewers who saw it, I will ask myself whether there was a better way. [14]

127 John Street

In the 1960s, the practice of modern graphic design also expanded beyond the printed page to environmental graphics and wayfinding systems. Collaborations between architects and graphic designers became more of a norm, as a more holistic approach to design emerged between like-minded professionals. De Harak was one of the first in his profession to spearhead this collaborative effort. By the end of the decade, bold, geometric shapes and bright

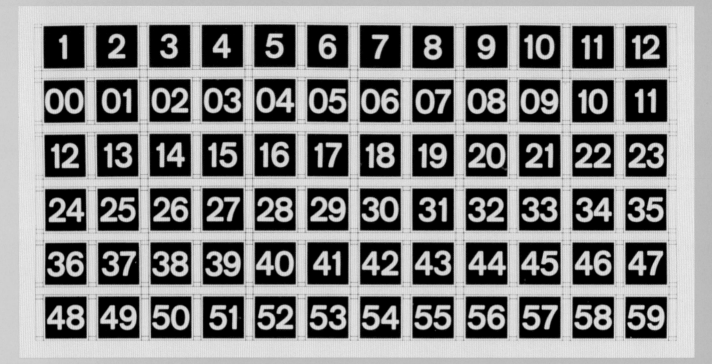

colors ruled the day from corporate high-rises to subterranean parking garages.

127 John Street was one of de Harak's first large-scale, multidisciplinary projects where he literally transformed the identity of a cold, sterile, and faceless building into an unforgettable visual experience filled with an 'atmosphere of pleasure, humor, and excitement for people'. [15] Built by Mel Kaufman of the William Kaufman Organization and designed by architects Emery Roth & Sons in 1968, 127 John Street was a 32-story, 98 m (320 ft) high, multi-tenant commercial office building located in New York City's financial district. As head of the William Kaufman Organization, one of city's most prominent family-owned real estate development firms, Kaufman was responsible for multiple buildings in Midtown Manhattan as well as in the financial district of Lower Manhattan. For more than fifty years, he was a visionary developer who helped redefine the Mid-century Modernist urban landscape of Manhattan with his unconventional and whimsical approach to commercial real estate projects. Two of those projects were designed by de Harak: 127 John Street (completed in 1968) and 77 Water Street (completed in 1970).

After its completion, 127 John Street became known as one of New York City's most exciting urban spaces of the decade, and one of de Harak's most popular and recognizable projects, due to the innovative and transformative contributions he made to the property. Its architecture was characteristic of the Modernist style of the period: a generic building mass, clad in a curtain wall of alternating horizontal bands of aluminum and tinted glass, with an open-floored structure to give maximum flexibility for tenant build-out. Even before entering the building, visitors were greeted by de Harak's enormous, three-story high digital clock — the world's largest at the time of its completion — which measured 12.2 m (40 ft) high by 15.2 m (50 ft) wide, and covered the Water Street façade. This kinetic, numerical supergraphic marked time by a series of rear-illuminated light boxes organized in a grid and composed of seventy-two squares,

< Graphic elevation of
three-story-high digital
clock at 127 John Street,
New York City, 1968.

∨ Detail of construction
drawing of typical
folded-steel love seat at
127 John Street, New York
City, 1968.

each measuring 1.2m (4 ft) square: twelve for hours, sixty for minutes and seconds. The clock face was arranged in six horizontal rows and twelve vertical columns, the top row with the numbers 1 through 12 for each hour, and the lower five rows with 00 through 59 for minutes and seconds. Each light box contained large-scale numerals set in the seminal sans-serif grotesque typeface, Akzidenz-Grotesk (Berthold Type Foundry, 1896). The current time was displayed in different colors: red for hours, blue for minutes, and yellow for seconds. The clock's rigorous composition and imposing scale captured de Harak's Modernist principles for the first time in an architectural context, yet shared many of the qualities that made his smaller-scale, print-related commissions so memorable. Still standing today, this unusual and imposing timepiece remains perhaps the ultimate reflection of a design ideology that was so emblematic of the era.

The entrance to 127 John Street itself was provocatively framed and enlivened by a structure comprised of tubular stainless-steel scaffolding supporting brightly-colored stretched-canvas squares and multi-leveled platforms, which served as both protection from the weather and sun decks for building tenants and passers-by. At street level, love seats of welded, folded steel painted in bright, primary colors provided respite for pedestrians. A 3.7 m (12 ft) long de Harak sculpture of an oversized fishing lure was suspended above a small pond-like pool of water located in the building plaza. The plaza's water theme was further enhanced with a large-scale mural entitled *Merman's Mermaid* by artist Forrest Wilson, located on a wall just north of this sculpture. This unusual mural paired a typical bare-breasted mermaid — half fish, half woman — with a 'reverse merman', half legs, half fish head. Paving in the plaza was of hexagonal asphalt tiles, similar to those used in Central Park. De Harak also had the opportunity to reinvent other street furniture for the building's vibrant and engaging public plaza, including trash receptacles, bicycle racks, and a red telephone booth.

Entering the building from Fulton Street, visitors encountered a 76.2 m (250 ft) long galvanized, corrugated-steel tunnel, illuminated by multiple rings of blue argon-gas-filled tubes, which guided them to the low- and high-rise elevators. Rudi Stern, neon artist extraordinaire and author of *Let There Be Neon* (New York: Harry N. Abrams, 1979), described the building's unorthodox entrance as 'an interesting integration of form and light. In an entryway with primary use in the daytime, the neon serves to draw in people; its

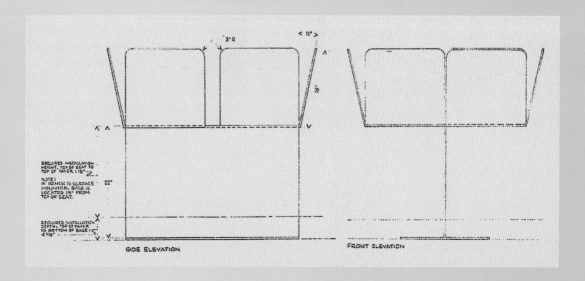

SIDE ELEVATION   FRONT ELEVATION

blue lines become a spiral of light through which one passes. It is an architectural use of the medium that has many implications for the future.' [16] In fact, the tunnel became so popular during the 1970s that it became a go-to location for fashion photographers, and provided a unique background (yet one that was used repeatedly) for album covers by such rock stars as Pat Benatar, Blondie, Genesis, Hall & Oates, and Kiss. The interior walls of the elevator cabs were clad in porcelain-enameled steel panels, illuminated from above and glowing bright blue for the low-rise floors and bright red for the high-rise floors. All building signs throughout the public areas of the building were set in Helvetica Medium (designed by Max Miedinger in 1957), with the exception of the building's exterior identification lettering and elevator lobby numbering. Here, '127 John Street' was composed of custom letterforms designed by de Harak (reminiscent of the typeface Microgramma, designed by Aldo Novarese and Alessandro Butti in 1952) and made up of individual 10 cm (4 in)-diameter pin-mounted chrome spheres. It was the only instance of a sleek glossy material used in contrast to the flat-finished steel, textured canvas, and raw concrete evident throughout the public space's exterior architecture.

At its completion, Ada Louise Huxtable, the first architecture critic of *The New York Times*, described de Harak's contributions to the project as a 'quasi-carnival of sometimes corny delights'. [17] The end result was one of de Harak's most humanistic projects — a veritable visual playground that entertained pedestrians, enlivened a faceless street, greatly enhanced the building's architecture, and ultimately redefined what a modern-day street-level entrance could be for a speculative office building.

Clocks and Timepieces

De Harak was always interested in experimenting with new ways in which to design clocks and timepieces, as was clearly evident in his tour de force, the three-story digital clock at 127 John Street. However, equally inventive and unique were the three Modernist wall clocks he created in 1966, as well as his sculptural Aurora Clock of 1969, all of which are part of the permanent design collection of New York's Museum of Modern Art (MoMA).

Designed in 1969 with manufacturer Kirsch/Hamilton, the Aurora Clock quickly became a Mid-century Modernist classic due to its distinctive color spectrum illumination and tubular housing, constructed of highly polished aluminum. The clock's internal illumination was created with a patented system of polarizing filters that separated white light into component spectrum colors, which then illuminate the clock face. The light source is a single, readily available No. 93, 120 volt/60 Hz bulb. The clock's hour and minutes hands, as well as its seconds disc, are all made of the same optically active filters and go through their own program of color changes. The clock's color-spectrum cycle repeats twice every minute, starting from red, then to orange through green to indigo and violet and back again.

In his book *Top Graphic Design* (Zurich: ABC Verlag, 1983), lifelong friend and renowned British graphic designer FHK Henrion used one of de Harak's timepieces, Clock (Model 103), to describe the power and resonance that his American colleague brought to his body of work: 'Rudolph de Harak is a problem solver. This can be said of all designers in varying degrees but some of his achievements are perfect examples of this most essential design function. I think particularly of his clock design. His clock dial I consider the definitive solution where simplicity and clarity form a perfect equation to show the figures in a combination of twice three vertical and twice three horizontal parallel lines. It is aesthetically highly satisfactory through its simple symmetry and perceptually optimal configuration: three lines symbolizing three numerals can be best taken in and easily differentiated at one glance.' [18]

1. Rudolph de Harak, interview by Steven Heller, February 1987 (transcript), in New York City. Steven Heller Collection, School of Visual Arts Archives, New York.
2. Rudolph de Harak, 'Oral History Interview with Rudolph de Harak', interview by Susan Larsen on 27 April 2000 (transcript), in Ellsworth, Maine. Archives of American Art, Smithsonian Institution, Washington, DC.
3. Ibid.
4. Ibid.
5. Ibid.
6. Ibid.
7. Ibid.
8. Steven Heller, '1992 AIGA Medalist: Rudolph de Harak', AIGA, 02 September 1992, https://epi.aiga.org/medalist-rudolphdeharak
9. Rudolph de Harak, interview by Steven Heller, February 1987 (transcript), in New York City. Steven Heller Collection, School of Visual Arts Archives, New York.
10. Ibid.
11. Rudolph de Harak, 'Oral History Interview with Rudolph de Harak', interview by Susan Larsen on 27 April 2000 (transcript), in Ellsworth, Maine. Archives of American Art, Smithsonian Institution, Washington, DC.
12. Richard Poulin, Interview with David Sutton, 26 April 2021.
13. Pamela Johnson, ed., 'Creating Emotional Involvement in Geography, Geology, and Space Science: An Interview with Rudolph de Harak', special issue on world's fairs, *Dot Zero*, no. 4, Summer 1967, pp. 24–29.
14. Ibid.
15. Richard Poulin, *Graphic Design and Architecture: A 20th-Century Design History*, Beverly: Rockport Publishers Inc., 2014, p. 161.
16. Rudi Stern, *Let There be Neon*, New York: Harry N. Abrams, Inc., 1979, p. 110.
17. Bill Shaffer, 'Modern Survivor', *Design Observer*, 23 August 2017, https://designobserver.com/feature/modern-survivor/39644
18. FHK Henrion, *Top Graphic Design*, Zurich: ABC Verlag, 1983, p. 79.
19. Rudolph de Harak, interview by Steven Heller, February 1987 (transcript), in New York City. Steven Heller Collection, School of Visual Arts Archives, New York.
20. Ibid.
21. Ibid.
22. Ibid.

∨ Album cover, *Lalo: Symphonie Espagnole, Wieniawski: Violin Concerto No. 2*, Westminster Recording Company, 1960.

SHOSTAKOVITCH
Piano Concerto No.1 opus 35
& No.2 opus 102
Eugene List, Piano

WESTMINSTER

∨ Album cover, *Vivaldi Gloria*, Westminster Recording Company, 1961.

Album cover, *Respighi: Fountains of Rome, Feste Romane,* Westminster Recording Company, *c.* 1960.

Album cover, *Introducing Fou Ts'ong, Piano, Mozart Piano Concerti,* Westminster Recording Company, 1960.

> Album cover, *Hermann Scherchen Conducts Trumpet Concerti, Haydn Vivaldi Handel Torelli,* Westminster Recording Company, 1961.

HERMANN SCHERCHEN
Conducts
TRUMPET CONCERTI
HAYDN/Vivaldi
Handel/Torelli

S·T·E·R·E·O

WESTMINSTER

< Album cover, *Ralph
Vaughan Williams: Fantasia
on 'Greensleeves,' English
Folk Song Suite, Fantasia
on a Theme by Thomas
Tallis*, Westminster
Recording Company,
1960.

∨ Album cover, *Beethoven:
Quartet Opus 59, No. 2,
Janacek Quartet*,
Westminster Recording
Company, c. 1961.

Album cover, *A Spanish
Guitar, John Williams/
Classical Guitar*,
Westminster Recording
Company, 1961.

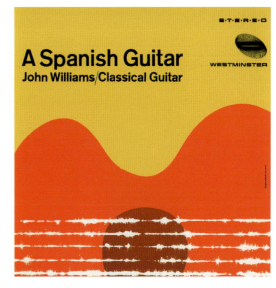

ˇ Album cover, *Ivor Novello's
Music Hall Songs,*
Westminster Recording
Company, 1960.

Album cover, *High Fidelity
Brass Ancient & Modern,*
Westminster Recording
Company, 1960.

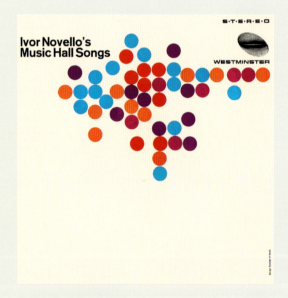

> Album covers, *Rossini
Overtures, Volume 1;
Rossini Overtures, Volume
2*, Westminster Recording
Company, *c*. 1961.
De Harak always
described these design
solutions for *Rossini
Overtures, Volumes 1*
and *2* as 'very crystalline,
colorful, and pure'.[19]

∨ Album cover, *Franz Liszt: The Two Piano Concerti, Vienna State Opera Orchestra, Edith Farnadi, Pianist,* Westminster Recording Company, 1960. Selected for 'Word and Image: Posters and Typography from the Graphic Design Collection of the Museum of Modern Art, 1879–1967,' Museum of Modern Art (MoMA), 25 January–10 March 1968. The Museum of Modern Art (MoMA) Design Collection, New York, New York, USA.

Franz Liszt:
The Two Piano Concerti
Sir Adrian Boult, Conductor
Vienna State Opera Orchestra
Edith Farnadi, Pianist

MS-192 STEREO

∨ Album cover, *While Making Love . . .*, *Eric Johnson and His Orchestra*, Westminster Recording Company, c. 1961.

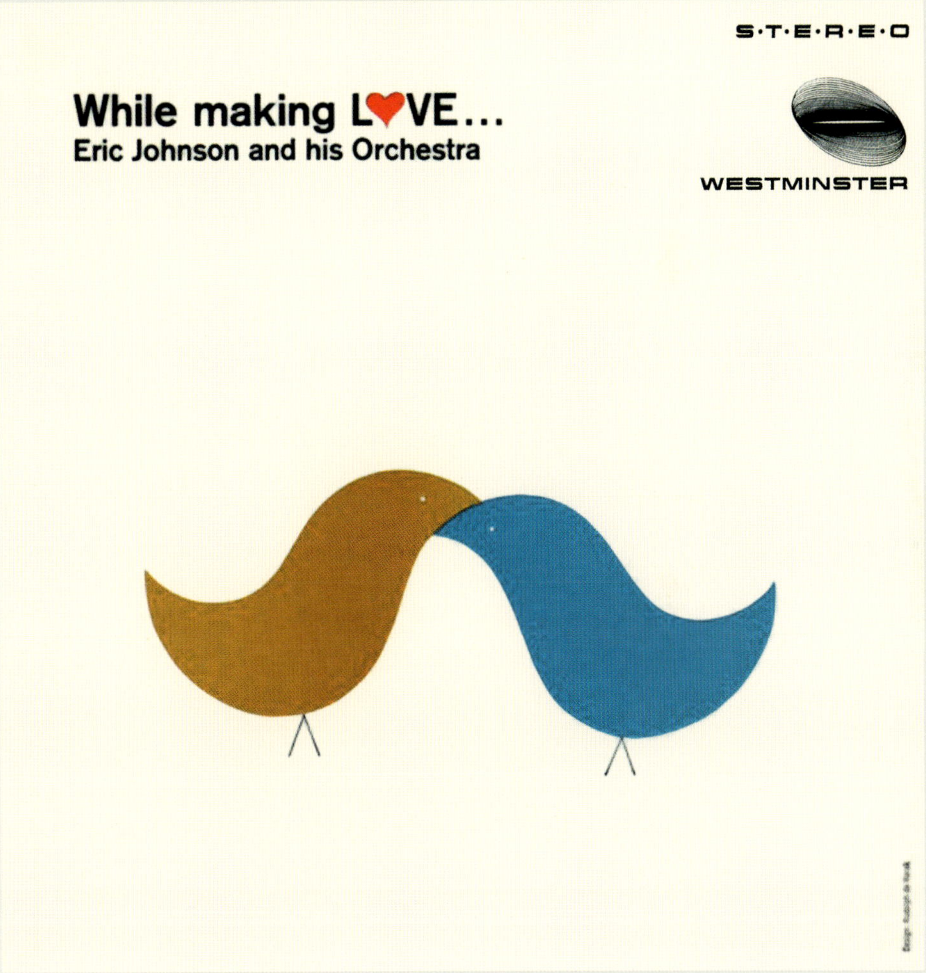

While making L♥VE...
Eric Johnson and his Orchestra

S·T·E·R·E·O

WESTMINSTER

TESTINGTESTINGTESTING
A Comprehensive Tool for Testing Equipment

WESTMINSTER

Design: Rudolph de Harak

∨ Album covers, *Scherchen Conducts the Bach Brandenburg Concertos Nos. 1 to 6; Scherchen Conducts the Bach Brandenburg Concertos Nos. 3 & 4; Scherchen Conducts the Bach Brandenburg Concertos Nos. 5 & 6,* Westminster Recording Company, 1960.

⌄ Album cover, *Bizet:*
   Carmen & L'Arlésienne,
   Westminster Recording
   Company, c. 1961.

Album cover, *A Dry Martini*
Please, Cy Walter,
Westminster Recording
Company, 1960.

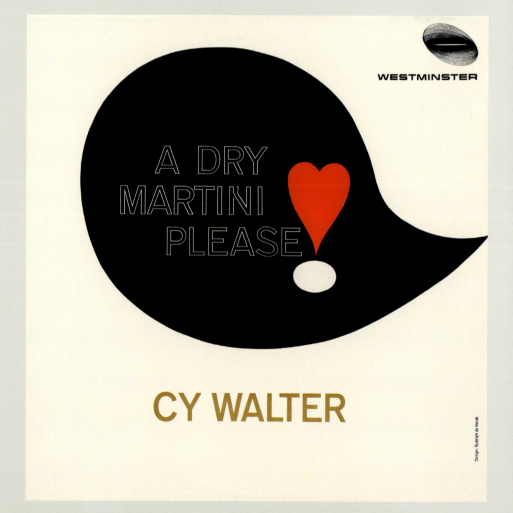

∨ Album cover, *Eric Coates/ London Suite & London Again Suite,* Westminster Recording Company, 1961. Rudolph de Harak, illustrator.

Album cover, *Gilbert & Sullivan for Orchestra, HMS Pinafore, Mikado, Pirates of Penzance, The Yeomen of the Guard, Patience, The Gondoliers,* Westminster Recording Company, 1961. Rudolph de Harak, illustrator.

Album cover, *Mozart: Eine Kleine Nachtmusik, Symphony No. 40 in G Minor,* Westminster Recording Company, 1960. Rudolph de Harak, illustrator.

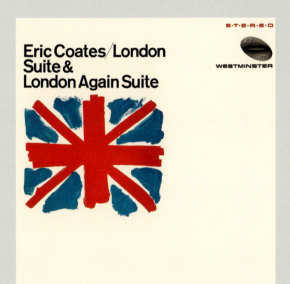

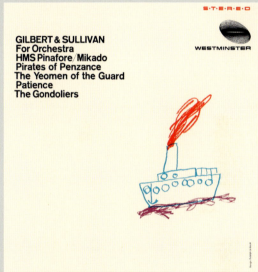

Nothingbut percussion vol.1

WESTMINSTER

Nothingbut percussion vol.2

WESTMINSTER

WESTMINSTER

Sounds from the Alps

Design: Rudolph de Harak

∨ Book cover, *Portrait
of André Gide, A Critical
Biography,* by Justin
O'Brien, McGraw-Hill
Paperbacks, 1964.

⌄ Book cover, *Monsieur Teste,* by Paul Valéry, McGraw-Hill Paperbacks, 1964. Rudolph de Harak, photographer. Having taken a photographic portrait of fellow graphic designer Jerome Kuhl, de Harak then sandwiched two negatives together to create this cover composition, a technique he used several times in his work.

⌄ Book cover, *Techniques of Leadership,* by Auren Uris, McGraw-Hill Paperbacks, 1964.

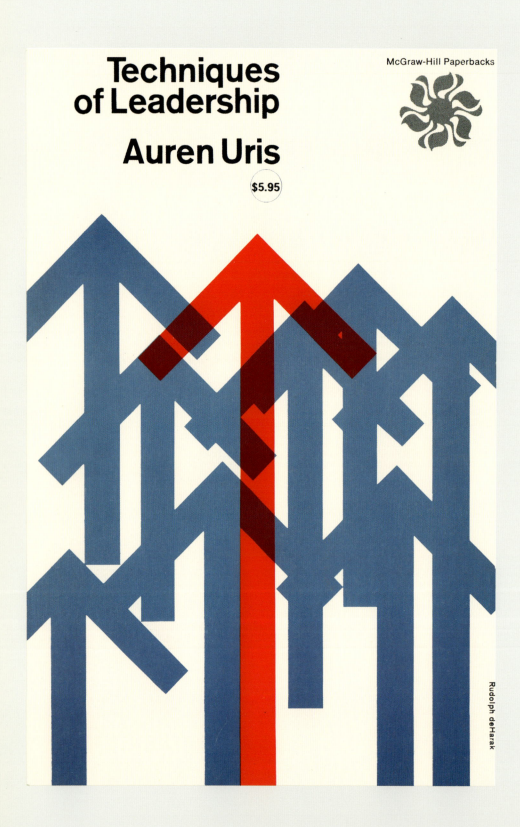

∨ Book cover, *The Stress of Life,* by Hans Selye, M.D., McGraw-Hill Paperbacks, 1963. Rudolph de Harak, photographer.

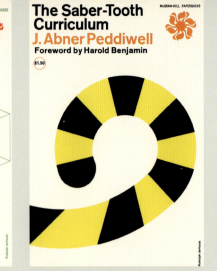

The Saber-Tooth Curriculum
J. Abner Peddiwell
Foreword by Harold Benjamin
$1.50

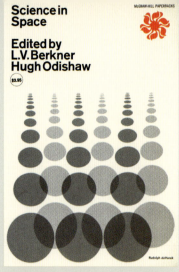

Science in Space
Edited by
L.V. Berkner
Hugh Odishaw
$3.95

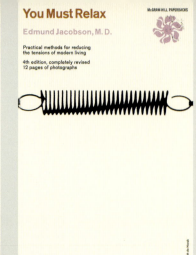

You Must Relax
Edmund Jacobson, M.D.
Practical methods for reducing the tensions of modern living
4th edition, completely revised
12 pages of photographs

Approach Archaeol
Stuart Piggott
Illustrated with photographs
$1.95

al illustrations.

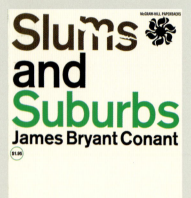

Slums and Suburbs
James Bryant Conant
$1.95

The Siege of Leningrad
Leon Goure
Foreword by Merle Fainsod
Stanford University Press
$2.95

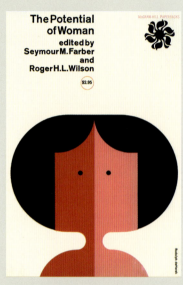

The Potential of Woman
edited by
Seymour M. Farber
and
Roger H.L. Wilson
$2.95

The M of Dr Calvi
$2.45
with a new introduction by

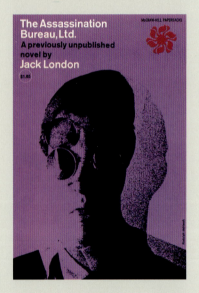

The Assassination Bureau, Ltd.
A previously unpublished novel by
Jack London
$1.65

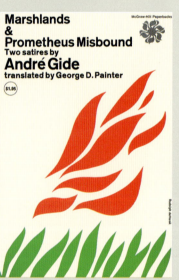

Marshlands & Prometheus Misbound
Two satires by
André Gide
translated by George D. Painter
$1.95

A Preface to History
Carl G. Gustavson
$2.50

Computers an
John A. Postle
How the new field of data pro serves modern business
$2.45

nality

Control of the Mind
Part 1
edited by
Seymour M. Farber
Roger H.L. Wilson
$2.95

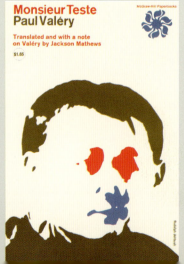

Monsieur Teste
Paul Valéry
Translated and with a note on Valéry by Jackson Mathews
$1.65

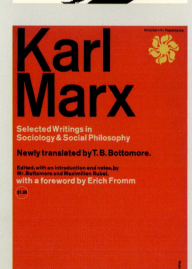

Karl Marx
Selected Writings in Sociology & Social Philosophy
Newly translated by T. B. Bottomore.
Edited, with an introduction and notes, by Mr. Bottomore and Maximilien Rubel, with a foreword by Erich Fromm
$1.95

Hebrew M The Book of C
Robert Grave
Raphael Pata
$2.75

Technique of
Executive Control
Erwin Haskell Schell

$2.95

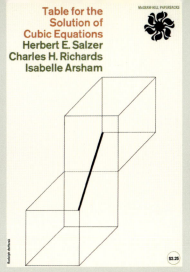

Table for the
Solution of
Cubic Equations
Herbert E. Salzer
Charles H. Richards
Isabelle Arsham

$2.25

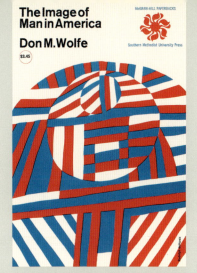

The Image of
Man in America
Don M. Wolfe

Southern Methodist University Press

$3.45

Political Thought
in Perspective
William Ebenstein
Essays on the great politi
theorists by their success

$3.75

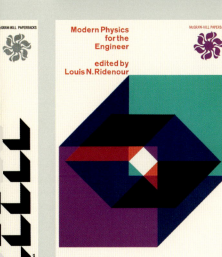

Modern Physics
for the
Engineer
edited by
Louis N. Ridenour

McGRAW-HILL PAPERBACKS

$3.95

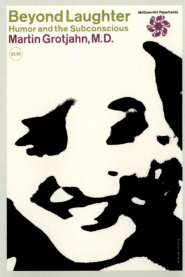

Beyond Laughter
Humor and the Subconscious
Martin Grotjahn, M.D.

McGraw-Hill Paperbacks

$2.95

The World of Geology
edited by
L. Don Leet
Florence J. Leet

McGRAW-HILL PAPERBACKS

$2.75

Jazz: A Histo
Winthrop Sargea
(Original title: Jazz: Hot and Hybrid)
New, revised and enlarged edition with mu

$2.95

An introduction to
Scientific Research
E. Bright Wilson, Jr.
University of Pittsburgh Press

$2.95

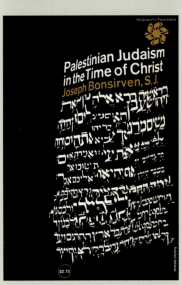

Palestinian Judaism
in the Time of Christ
Joseph Bonsirven, S.J.

McGraw-Hill Paperbacks

$2.75

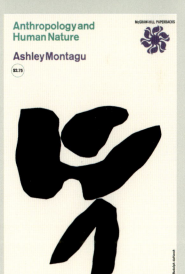

Anthropology and
Human Nature
Ashley Montagu

McGRAW-HILL PAPERBACKS

$2.75

The Nature of
Physical Reality
A Philosophy of Modern Phy
Henry Margenau

McGRAW-HILL PAPERBACKS

$3.95

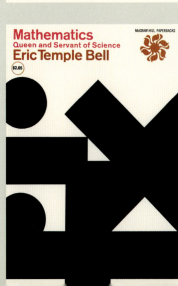

Mathematics
Queen and Servant of Science
Eric Temple Bell

McGraw-Hill Paperbacks

$2.65

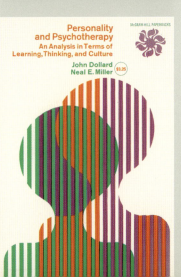

Personality
and Psychotherapy
An Analysis in Terms of
Learning, Thinking, and Culture
John Dollard
Neal E. Miller

McGraw-Hill Paperbacks

$3.25

The Crisis We Face
Automation and the Cold War
George Steele
Paul Kircher

McGRAW-HILL PAPERBACKS

$2.65

Psychoanalytic
Theories of Perso
Gerald S. Blum

$2.45

Book cover, *An Introduction to Scientific Research,* by E. Bright Wilson Jr, McGraw-Hill Paperbacks, *c.* 1962.

∨ Book cover, *Brains, Machines and Mathematics,* by Michael A. Arbib, McGraw-Hill Paperbacks, 1965. Rudolph de Harak, photographer.

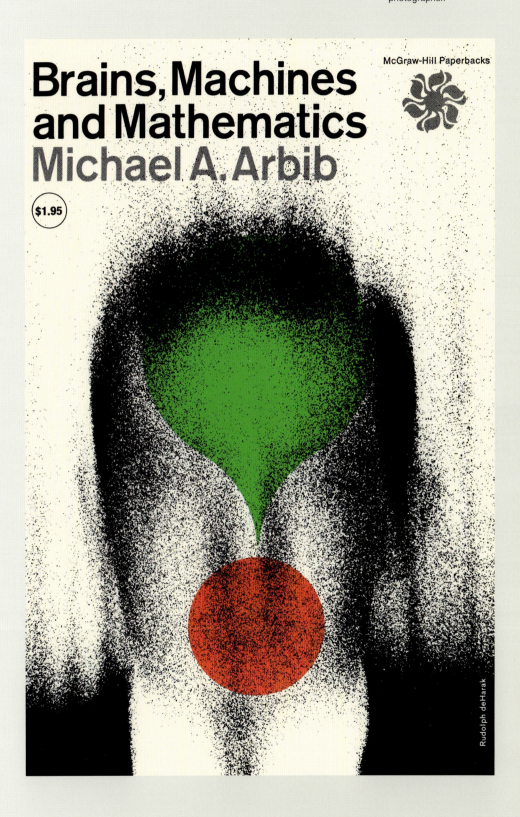

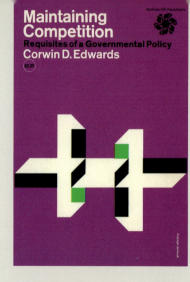
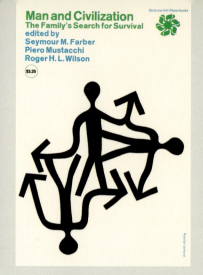

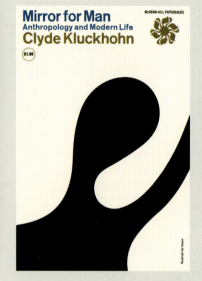

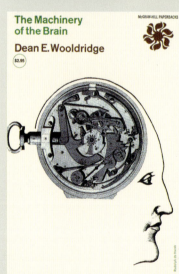

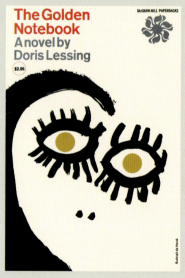

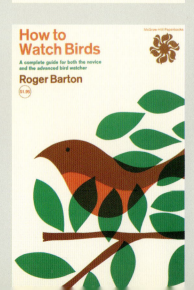

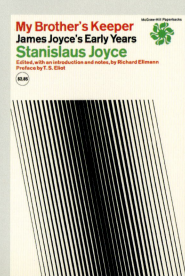

A Moral Philosophy for Management
Benjamin M. Selekman

Harvard University Press

$2.25

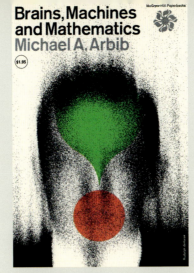

Brains, Machines and Mathematics
Michael A. Arbib

McGraw-Hill Paperbacks

$1.95

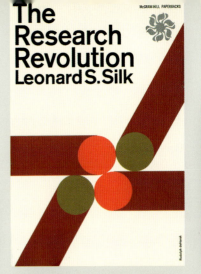

The Research Revolution
Leonard S. Silk

McGraw-Hill Paperbacks

Men Unde
Roy R. Grin
John P. Spie

$2.65

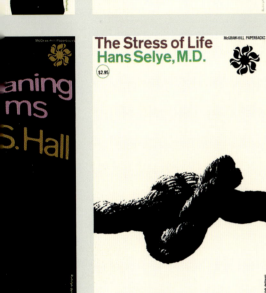

McGraw-Hill Paperbacks

aning
ms
S. Hall

The Stress of Life
Hans Selye, M.D.

McGraw-Hill Paperbacks

$2.95

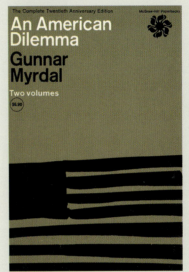

Statistical Treatment of Experimental Data
Hugh D. Young

McGraw-Hill Paperbacks

$2.95

The Complete Twentieth Anniversary Edition

An American Dilemma
Gunnar Myrdal

Two volumes

$6.90

McGraw-Hill Paperbacks

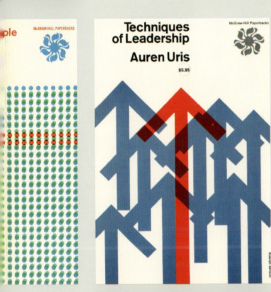

Portrait of
A Critical B
Justin O'Br

$2.95

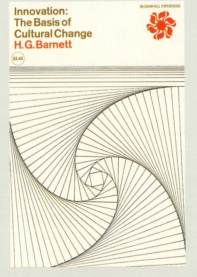

ple

McGraw-Hill Paperbacks

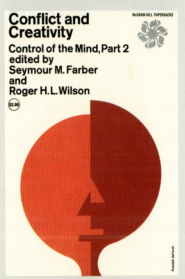

Techniques of Leadership
Auren Uris

$5.95

McGraw-Hill Paperbacks

Innovation: The Basis of Cultural Change
H.G. Barnett

$3.45

McGraw-Hill Paperbacks

Conflict and Creativity
Control of the Mind, Part 2
edited by
Seymour M. Farber
and
Roger H.L. Wilson

$2.95

McGraw-Hill Paperbacks

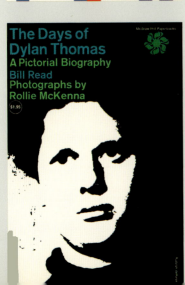

Units, Dimens and Dimensionles
D.C. Ipsen

$2.65

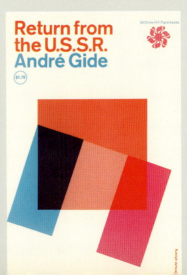

ns:
sis
d

McGraw-Hill Paperbacks

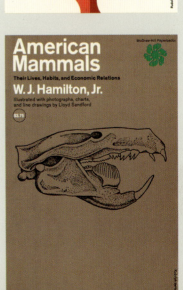

The Days of Dylan Thomas
A Pictorial Biography
Bill Read
Photographs by
Rollie McKenna

$1.95

McGraw-Hill Paperbacks

Return from the U.S.S.R.
André Gide

$1.75

McGraw-Hill Paperbacks

American Mammals
Their Lives, Habits, and Economic Relations
W.J. Hamilton, Jr.

Illustrated with photographs, charts, and line drawings by Lloyd Sandford

$3.75

McGraw-Hill Paperbacks

Late-Bloomin
and Other Storie
Anton Chekh
Newly translated
I.C. Chertok and

$1.95

∨ Book cover, *The
Saber-Tooth Curriculum,*
by J. Abner Peddiwell,
McGraw-Hill Paperbacks,
c. 1960.

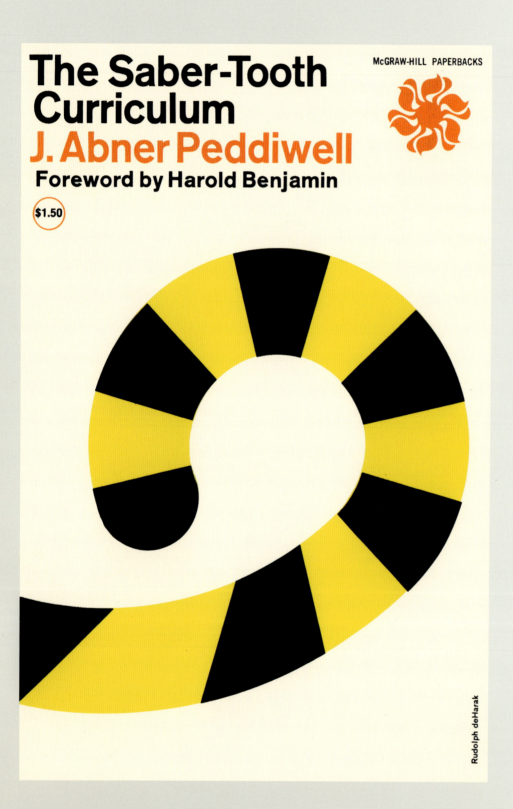

Book cover, *Computers and People,* by John A. Postley, McGraw-Hill Paperbacks, 1963. Throughout his career, de Harak was intrigued by and continually experimented with moiré and dot patterns, as well as optical illusions in his work. 'I love the ambivalence of what happens visually when you see something and you're not sure what you see, and then all of a sudden to start to see it.' [20]

∨ Book cover, *Technique of Executive Control,* by Erwin Haskell Schell, McGraw-Hill Paperbacks, *c.* 1960. The original artwork for this book cover was hand-drawn by de Harak, 400% larger than final size, with a 1/0.50 mm nib Rapidograph and black ink on acetate. This image was also used by him, approximately thirty years later, for the cover of *Print* magazine, May/June 1989, and reproduced in four, flat process colors — cyan, yellow, magenta, and black.

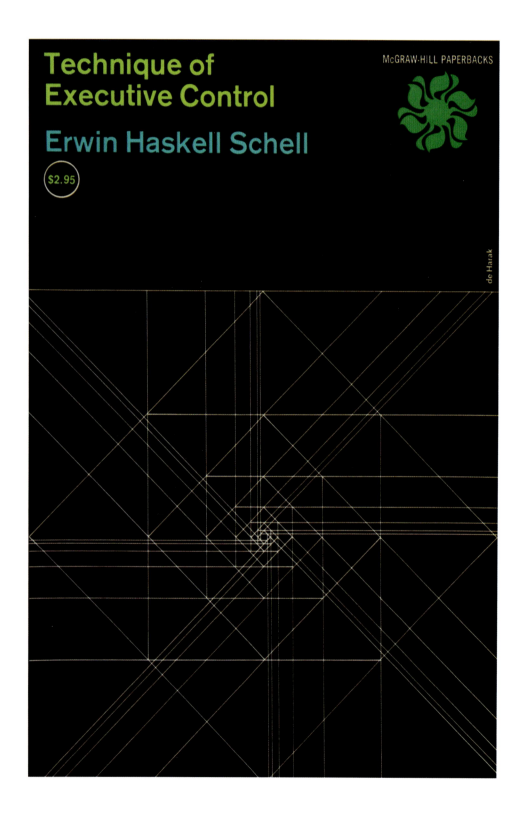

∨ Book cover, *Modern
Physics for the Engineer,*
edited by Louis N.
Ridenour, McGraw-Hill
Paperbacks, 1961.

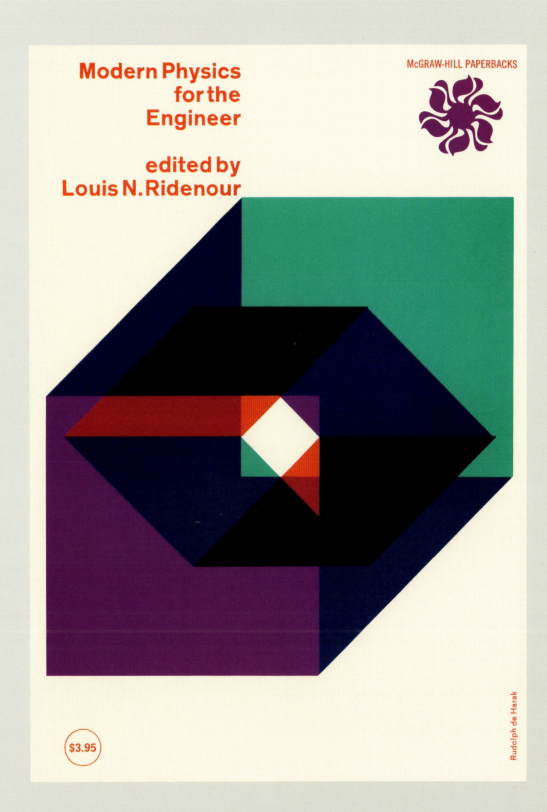

Modern Physics
for the
Engineer

edited by
Louis N. Ridenour

McGRAW-HILL PAPERBACKS

$3.95

Rudolph de Harak

˅ Book cover, *The Siege of Leningrad,* by Leon Gouré, McGraw-Hill Paperbacks, 1962.

∨ Book cover, *The Assassination Bureau, Ltd.*, by Jack London, McGraw-Hill Paperbacks, 1963. Rudolph de Harak, photographer. De Harak was an avid photographer and experimented with many image-generating techniques throughout his career. For this cover, he photographed his former student and fellow graphic designer John Condon in a series of double exposures.

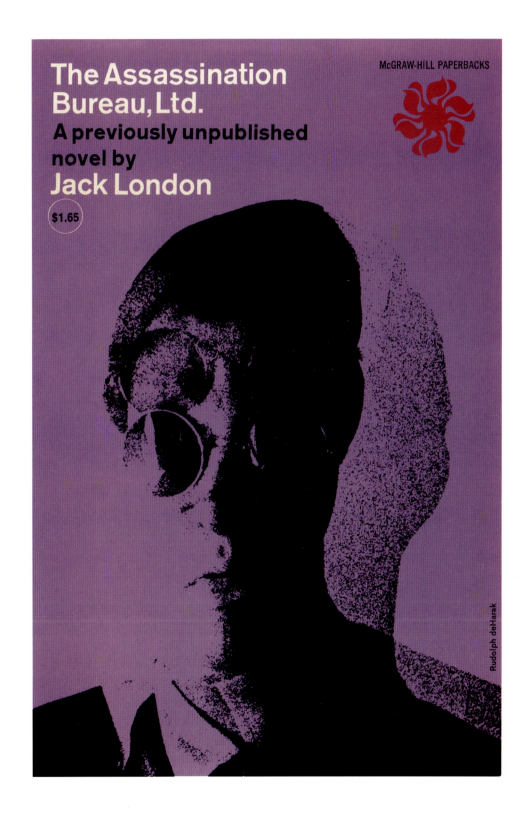

McGRAW-HILL PAPERBACKS

The Assassination Bureau, Ltd.
A previously unpublished novel by
Jack London
$1.65

Rudolph deHarak

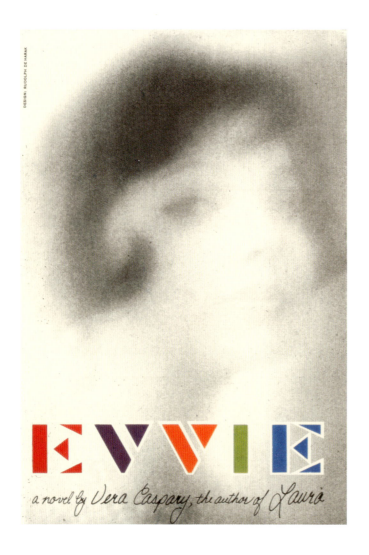

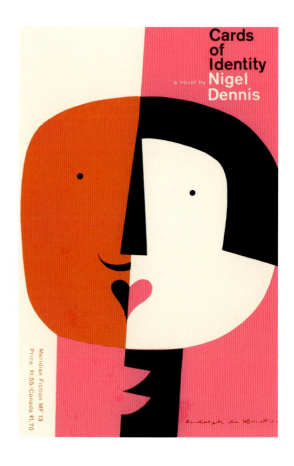

<	Book cover, *Evvie,*
	by Vera Caspary, Harper
	& Brothers, 1960.

	Book cover, *Cards of
	Identity,* by Nigel Dennis,
	Meridian Books, 1960.

∨	Book cover, *The Lime
	Twig,* by John Hawkes,
	New Directions Publishing
	Corporation, 1961.
	De Harak intentionally
	used a decorative typeface not necessarily
	associated with him and his
	typographic sensibility. The
	image is a collage he created
	and then rephotographed
	through Vaseline.

Book jacket, *The Drill is Death,* by Frances and Richard Lockridge, J.B. Lippincott Co., 1961. This book jacket reveals the influence of Saul Bass more than any other work by de Harak from the early 1960s. The purely graphic figurative image is reminiscent of Bass's 1959 poster for the Otto Preminger film *Anatomy of a Murder.*

Book jacket, *Candela, The Shell Builder: Works 1949–1961,* by Colin Faber, Reinhold Publishing, 1963.

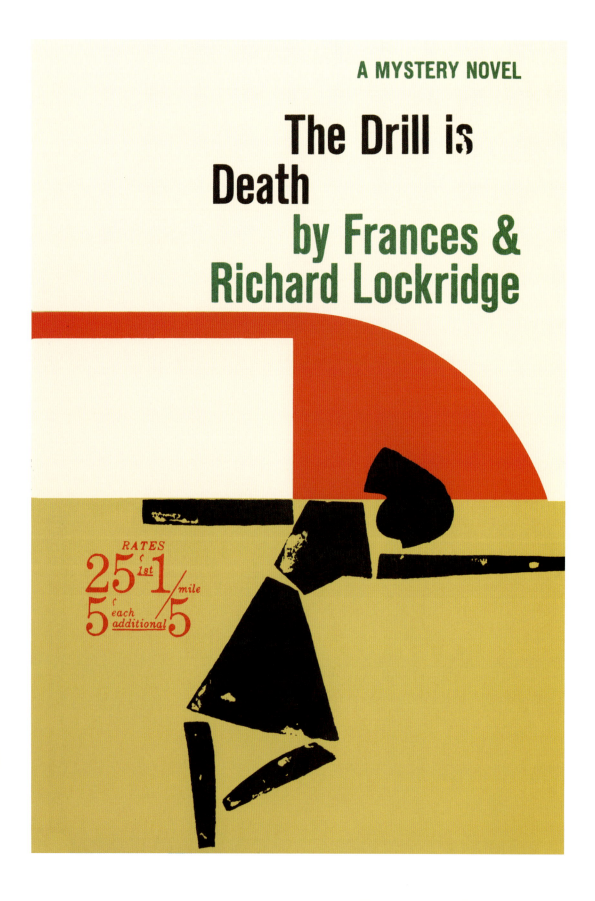

A MYSTERY NOVEL

The Drill is Death
by Frances &
Richard Lockridge

RATES
25¢ 1st 1/mile
5¢ each additional /5

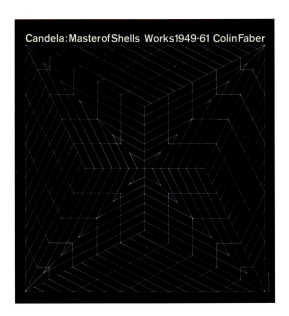

∨ Book jacket, *Of Time and Space and Other Things: Seventeen Essays on Science,* by Isaac Asimov, Doubleday & Company, 1965.

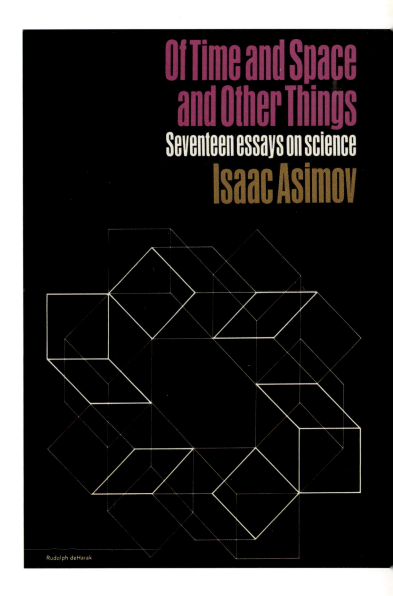

⌄ Book jacket, *Varieties of Mystic Experience,* by Elmer O'Brien, Holt Rinehart & Winston, 1964. Rudolph de Harak, photographer.

A prime example of de Harak photographing a typographic composition in Akzidenz-Grotesk through Vaseline to achieve his final design solution.

Varieties of Mystic Experience

Elmer O'Brien, S.J.

Rudolph deHarak

∨ Book cover, *Discrepancies and Apparitions: A Collection of Poems*, by Diane Wakoski, Doubleday & Company, 1966.

A collection of poems

Discrepancies and Apparitions
Diane Wakoski

⌄ Book jacket, *The Chameleons*, by John Broderick, Ivan Obolensky, 1961. Rudolph de Harak, photographer.

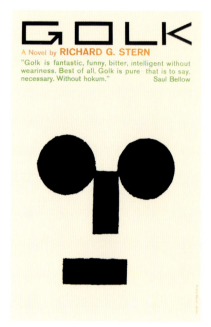

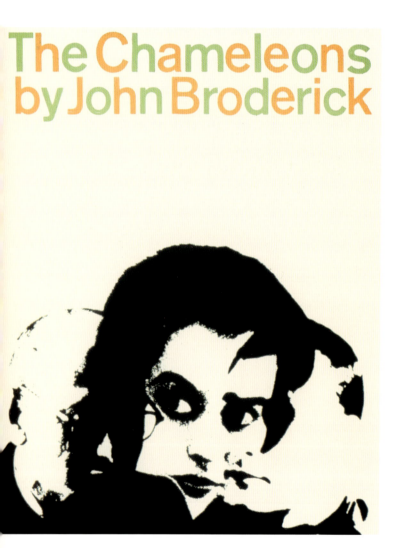

< Book cover, *Golk,*
by Richard G. Stern,
Meridian Books, 1960.

∨ Promotional poster,
Merle Marsicano, Merle
Marsicano Dance
Company, 1962. Rudolph
de Harak, photographer.
The Museum of Modern
Art (MoMA) Design
Collection, New York,
New York, USA.

> Promotional poster,
Images: Illusional, No. 2,
Rudolph de Harak Inc.,
c. 1969. De Harak always
felt that this poster was
one of the best concepts
he had ever created.
He recalled that the line
drawing took days

because it had to be
executed without a mistake,
only using a straightedge and
a ruling pen.

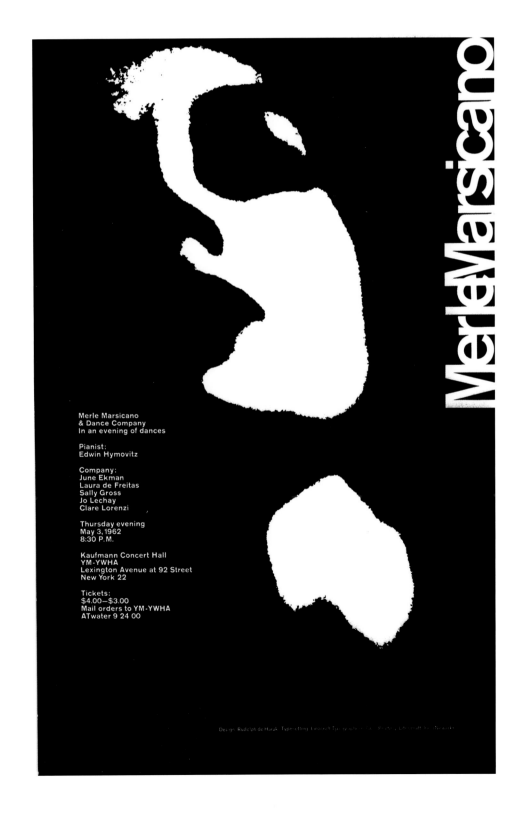

Merle Marsicano
& Dance Company
In an evening of dances

Pianist:
Edwin Hymovitz

Company:
June Ekman
Laura de Freitas
Sally Gross
Jo Lechay
Clare Lorenzi

Thursday evening
May 3, 1962
8:30 P.M.

Kaufmann Concert Hall
YM-YWHA
Lexington Avenue at 92 Street
New York 22

Tickets:
$4.00–$3.00
Mail orders to YM-YWHA
ATwater 9 24 00

Rudolph de Harak Inc 795 Lexington Avenue New York 21 N Y TEmpleton 2 9420

2 **Images: illusional**

Design: Rudolph de Harak   Printed by Photogravure and Color Company

Rudolph de Harak Inc   Graphic and Industrial Design   795 Lexington Avenue New York 21 New York Templeton 2-9420

4 **Images:** homologous

Design Rudolph de Harak Printed by Lithocraft, Inc. New Jersey

4 **Images:** homologous

< Promotional poster,
Images: illusional, No. 4,
Rudolph de Harak Inc.,
c. 1969. Leonardo da
Vinci's 'Vitruvian Man' was
a continuing inspiration
for de Harak in exploring
variations on how this
symbol could be
composed and what it
could communicate as
a visual icon.

∨ Magazine cover, *Dance
Magazine,* vol. 34, no. 6,
Dance Magazine, Inc.,
June 1960.

Magazine cover, *Dance
Magazine,* vol. 34, no. 12,
Dance Magazine, Inc.,
December 1960.

∨ Magazine cover, *Dance
Magazine,* vol. 36, no. 12,
Dance Magazine, Inc.,
December 1962.

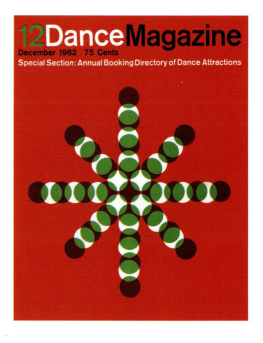

⌄ Magazine cover, *Print,*
vol. 15, no. 3, Kaye-Cadel
Publishing Corp., May/
June 1961. Rudolph
de Harak, photographer.

⌄ Magazine cover, *Esquire*,
vol. 57, no. 2, Esquire Inc.,
February 1962.

FEBRUARY, 1962
PRICE 60c

Esquire

THE MAGAZINE FOR MEN

The Entrenchment of the American Witch   Tennessee Williams' New Play "Night of the Iguana"   Europe for Sophisticates: A 20-Page Section ▽ ⊘ ⊖ William Styron on Death as a 💀 Penalty 🙂 A Quiet Day with Mr. Hemingway 🙂 Three Fast New Boats Designed Especially for Esquire   The Mad Humor of Zero Mostel

DESIGN: RUDOLPH DE HARAK

Magazine cover, *Esquire,*
Xmas Issue, vol. 56, no. 6,
Esquire Inc., December
1961.

Magazine cover, *Esquire,*
vol. 57, no. 5, Esquire Inc.,
May 1962.

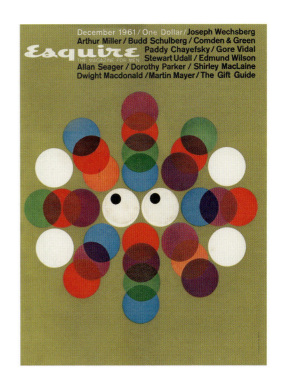

HOLIDAY

JULY 1963 · 60c

Travel U.S.A. 1963

∨ Information graphic, *Holiday,* 'Israel: A Special Issue.' vol. 42, no. 6, Curtis Publishing Company, December 1967. This illustration and information graphic, a map of Israel showing the consequences of the 1967 Six-Day War, were commissioned by Frank Zachary, art director of *Holiday* magazine. De Harak described his mindset while doing this project as 'all about a reliance on "systems". What I was trying to do was to take the arbitrariness out of design. And if one could set up a grid or a system to do something, a lot of decisions were being made for you … in other words, you didn't say, "Gee, should it move a quarter of an inch this way or a quarter of an inch that way."' [21]

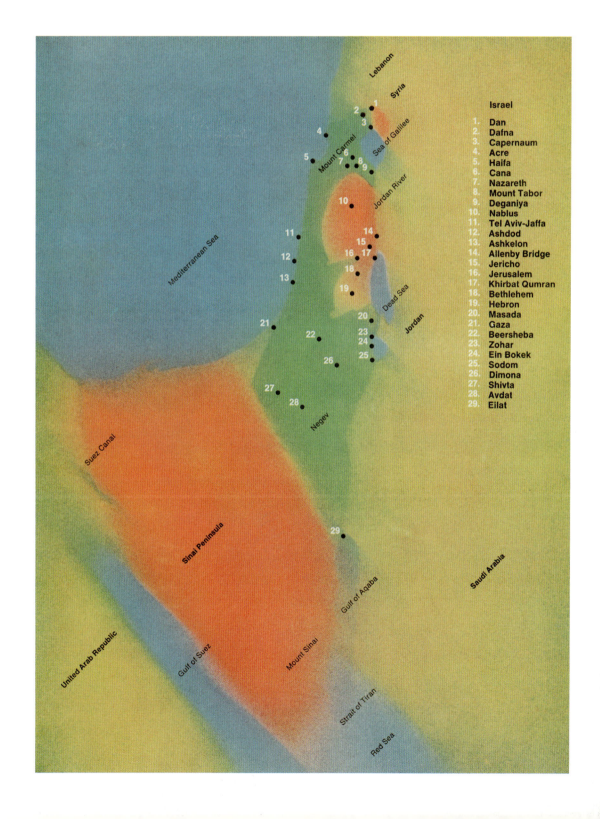

Israel

1. Dan
2. Dafna
3. Capernaum
4. Acre
5. Haifa
6. Cana
7. Nazareth
8. Mount Tabor
9. Deganiya
10. Nablus
11. Tel Aviv-Jaffa
12. Ashdod
13. Ashkelon
14. Allenby Bridge
15. Jericho
16. Jerusalem
17. Khirbat Qumran
18. Bethlehem
19. Hebron
20. Masada
21. Gaza
22. Beersheba
23. Zohar
24. Ein Bokek
25. Sodom
26. Dimona
27. Shivta
28. Avdat
29. Eilat

∨ Symbol, Racine Press,
  1960.

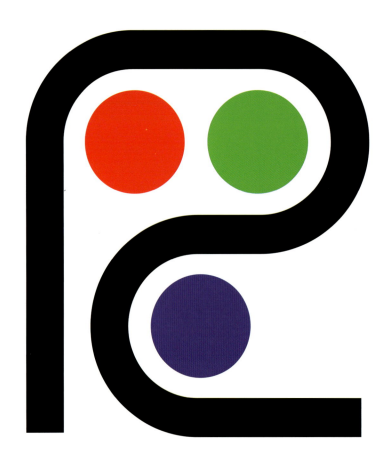

∨ Symbol, Cumberland
Furniture Corporation,
1960.

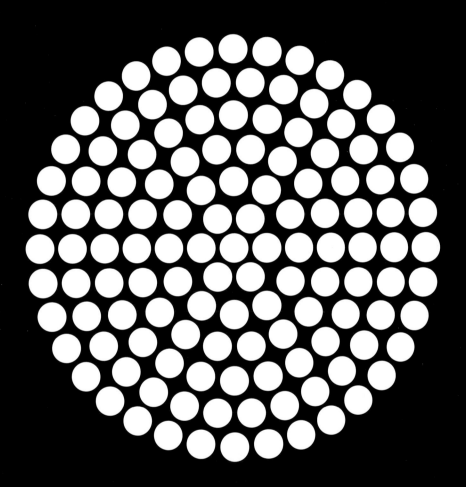

∨ Symbol, McGraw-Hill
Paperbacks, 1962.
De Harak thought the
symbol should be based
on 'a flower and a sun …
it's growth; it's an active
form'. [22]

↗ Symbol, American
Federation of the Arts
Traveling Exhibition
Program, American
Federation of the
Arts, 1967

Traveling exhibition,
International Trademarks,
American Institute of Graphic
Arts (AIGA), 1965.

Exhibition research,
planning, programming,
and design; environmental
and interpretive graphics,
'Man, His Planet, and Space'
exhibition at Expo 67,
Montreal, Quebec, Canada,
The Government of Canada,
1967.

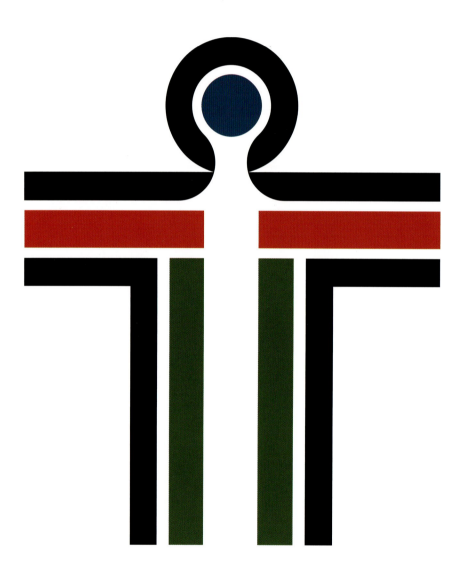

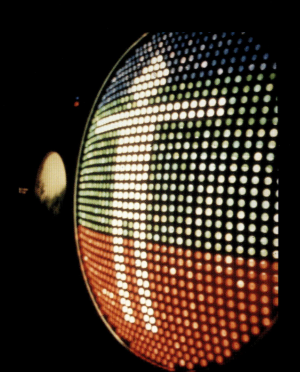

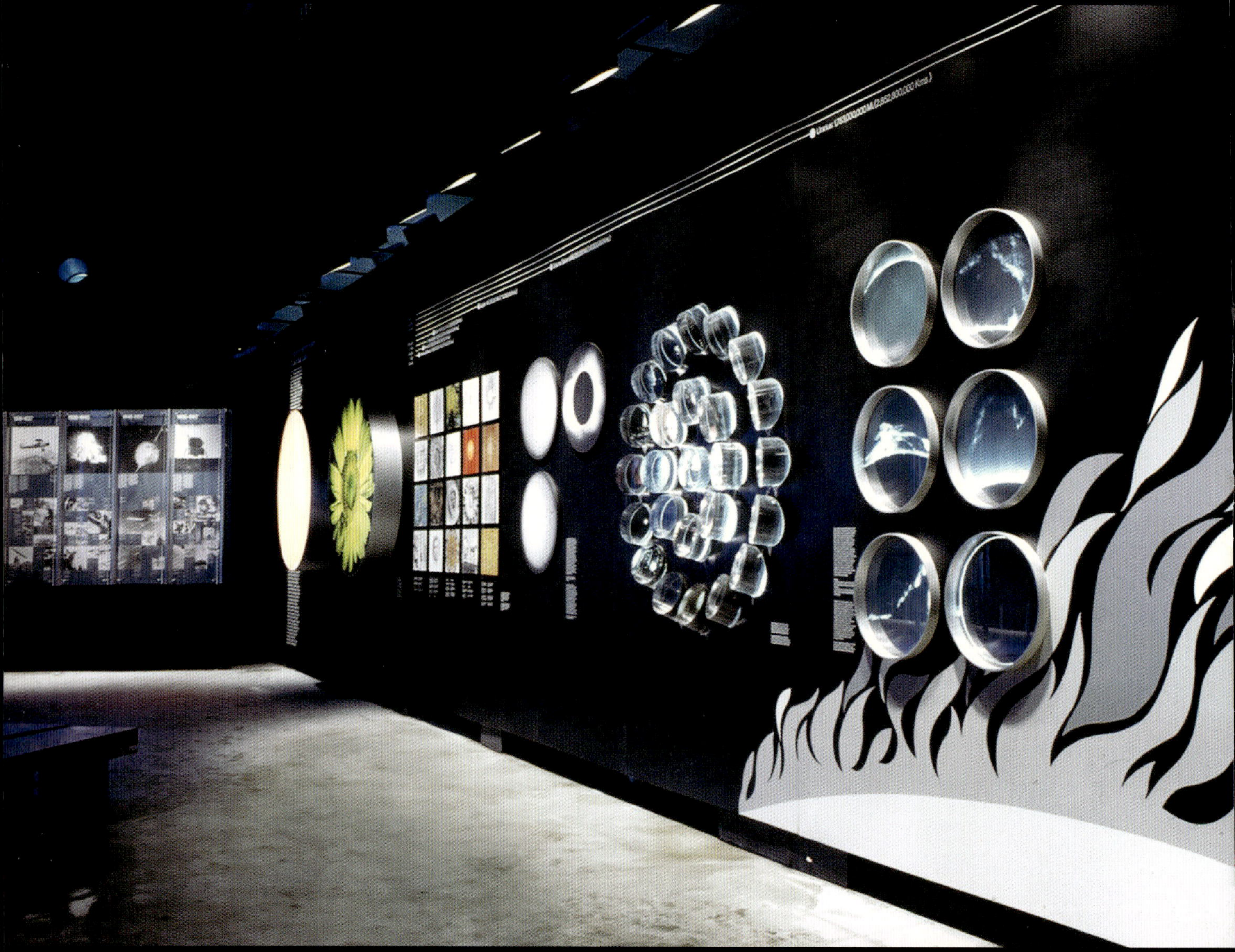

Logotype, Gallagher's 33,
New York City. The Brody
Organization, 1968. De Harak
created a playful '33' with
slightly distorted numerals
that suggested movement

on an athletic uniform.
Accompanied by the
Gallagher's signature, the
logotype appears in large
scale on the exterior façade
of the restaurant.

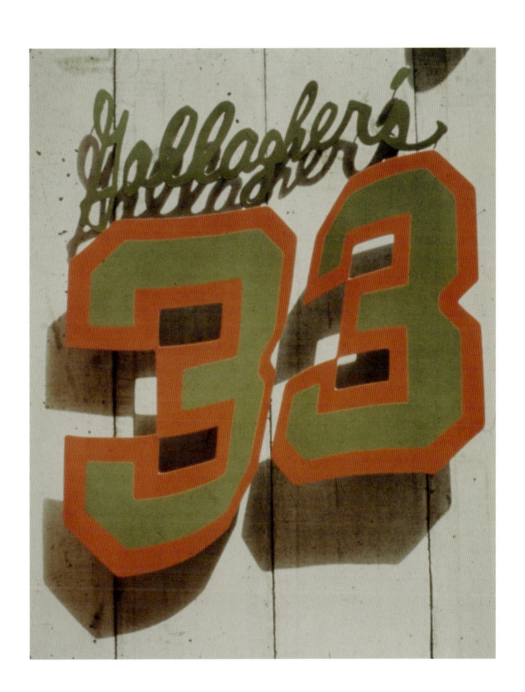

Interior design and environmental graphics, Gallagher's 33, New York City, The Brody Organization, 1968. This commission from The Brody Organization was for a fully-integrated corporate identity and interior design program designed for a sports-oriented restaurant and bar located directly across from Madison Square Garden. The sports theme was established through the use of both concrete support columns, which were exposed and sandblasted to suggest surfaces found in athletic areas, and of wall surfaces that were tongue-and-groove wood strips, painted green to simulate old bleacher walls at sports parks. Action sequences of sporting events and high-contrast photographic portraits of sports personalities were displayed through large, rear-illuminated, acrylic-faced transparencies, silk-screened illustrations, diagrammatic panels, and sculpture.

TOTAL

0 3

0 6

BULOVA SPORTS TIM

8:59

Environmental graphics,
wayfinding, furniture,
sculpture, and typography,
127 John Street, New York
City, William Kaufman
Organization, 1968.
Nathaniel 'Thorney'
Lieberman, photographer.

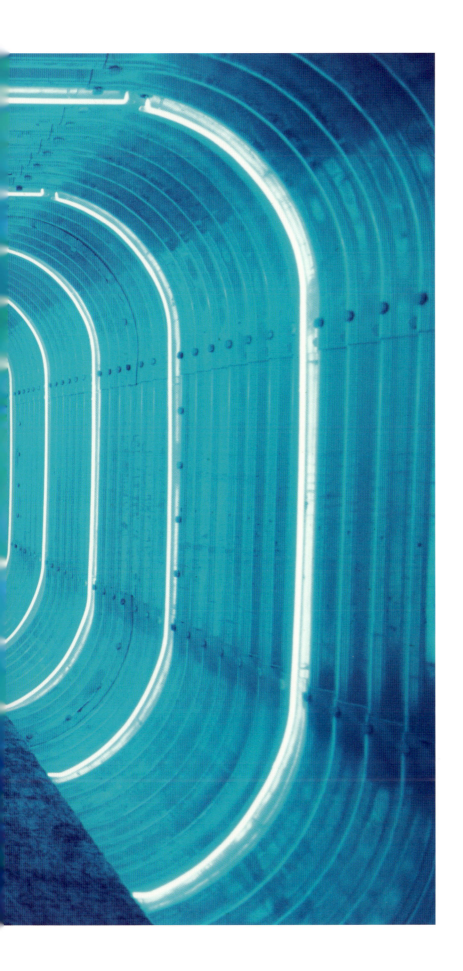

< Clock (Model 103), 1966
8.9 x 30.5 cm (3.5 x 12 in)
Chrome-plated metal and
plastic

Clock (Model 102), 1966
8.3 x 22.9 cm (3.25 x 9 in)
Chrome-plated metal and
plastic

Clock (Model 101), 1966
8.3 x 22.9 cm (3.25 x 9 in)
Chrome-plated metal and
plastic

The Museum of Modern Art
(MoMA) Design Collection,
New York, New York, USA
In 1967–1968, these
clocks were featured at
the Museum of Modern
Art's 'Recent Acquisitions,
Design Collection' exhibition
organized by Arthur Drexler,
Director, Department of
Architecture and Design.

∨ Aurora Clock, 1969
20.3 x 20.3 x 12.7 cm
(8 x 8 x 5 in)
Polished aluminum,
acrylic, polarizing filters
Hirsch/Hamilton
the Museum of Modern
Art (MoMA) Design
Collection, New York,
New York, USA.

Symbol Signs

The American Institute of Graphic Arts, under a contract from the United States Department of Transportation, Office of Facilitation, has created 34 passenger and pedestrian oriented symbols for use in airports, rail terminals and other travel facilities.

The intent of the project is to forestall the proliferation of symbol systems being developed for individual facilities throughout the country. After testing at selected Bicentennial sites, the designs will be evaluated, redesigned as necessary, and then recommended as a national standard.

To produce a consistent and inter-related group of symbols that could bridge the language barrier and simplify the identification of services, concessions and processing activities, the AIGA attempted to take full advantage of strong and widely recognized existing symbol concepts. While all symbols have been re-drawn, new concepts have been introduced only where no satisfactory ones already existed.

A comprehensive report prepared by the AIGA includes a detailed description of the process employed to create the symbols as well as guidelines for their use as part of a rational sign system. The document is available to the public through the National Technical Information Service, Springfield, Virginia 22151.

This program was undertaken by direction of the Secretary of Transportation. An Advisory Committee, comprised of government and industry representatives, was formed to make recommendations to the Secretary. The Committee is sponsored by the Assistant Secretary for Environment, Safety and Consumer Affairs, and coordinated by the Office of Facilitation.

U.S. Department of Transportation Advisory Committee on Transportation-Related Signs and Symbols:
William R. Myers, Executive Director
Thomas H. Geismar, Chairman

The American Institute of Graphic Arts
1059 Third Avenue, New York, NY 10021
Karl Fink, President
Edward M. Gottschall, Executive Director

AIGA Committee on Signs and Symbols:
Thomas H. Geismar, Chairman
Seymour Chwast
Rudolph deHarak
John Lees
Massimo Vignelli

Graphic design of all symbols:
Cook and Shanosky Associates Inc.

Guidelines for use of the symbols:
Page, Arbitrio and Resen Ltd.

Project coordination:
Don and Karen Moyer

Telephone / Mail / Currency Exchange / First Aid / Lost and Found				

Baggage Lockers / Elevator / Toilets, Men / Toilets, Women / Toilets				

Information / Hotel Information / / Ground Transportation				

Rail Transportation / Air Transportation / Heliport / Water Transportation				

Car Rental / Restaurant / Coffee Shop / Bar / Shops				

Ticket Purchase / Baggage Check-in / Baggage Claim / Customs / Immigration				

< Promotional poster (detail), *AIGA Symbol Signs*, 1975. Cook & Shanosky Associates, designers.

In clear contrast to the previous decade, the 1970s was referred to by many as the 'Me Decade', a phrase coined by American novelist Tom Wolfe in an essay for *New York* magazine in August 1976. Most Americans turned inward and seemed to be focused on their own individual well-being rather than on the social and political issues that had been so much a part of their lives in the 1960s. It was also a time period of great upheaval throughout the United States, including New York City. The Watergate scandal turned the country upside down early in the decade, leading to Richard Nixon's resignation from the presidency in 1974. The Vietnam War ended in 1975 after more than twenty years of fighting, protests, and violence at home and abroad. New York City gained notoriety for its high crime rates, the filthy conditions of its streets, and a subway system in disrepair. Times Square was overrun by prostitutes, pimps, and drug dealers. The New York Police Department (NYPD) came under scrutiny for corruption, thanks to the revelations of the infamous whistle-blower Frank Serpico, a NYPD cop. And, in October 1975, the *Daily News* reported on its front page that President Gerald Ford told New York City to 'drop dead'.

A new era in graphic design also began to take form in the 1970s, with the exploration of new theories, tenets, and practices. At the onset of the worldwide information age and the digital revolution, Modernism and the International Typographic Style began to wane in popularity in favor of the Postmodernist movement, which began to show its influence in many design disciplines.

Postmodernism brought focus and value to freedom of expression and individualism. It represented the rejection of what was deemed 'modern' for a more individualized approach to style, aesthetics, and design. Its stylistic conventions ranged from an amalgamation of diverse motifs; the use of unconventional historicist references; and a freedom of expression that was not possible or acceptable within Modernist tenets. Early supporters of this movement included American writer and activist Jane Jacobs, who criticized the soullessness of the urban environment in her 1961 book, *The Death and Life of Great American Cities* (New York: Random House, 1961), and renowned American architect Robert Venturi, whose 1966 dictum 'less is a bore' from his treatise *Complexity and Contradiction in Architecture* (New York: the Museum of Modern Art, 1966) became a mantra for future generations of graphic designers and architects. Pop Art and popular culture were also major influences on Postmodernism, and functioned as counterpoints to the now familiar world of Modernism and objective rationalism.

During the 1970s, de Harak's design consultant practice began to build momentum, primarily due to major commissions he had completed in the late 1960s, specifically the Canadian Pavilion at Expo 67 in Montreal, and 127 John Street, and Gallagher's 33 in New York City. His increasing interest in multidisciplinary work led him to pursue diverse projects in the two-dimensional as well as the three-dimensional worlds, much like one of his early idols and influences, Alvin Lustig, who always maintained that 'a true designer should not limit his or her activities to the printed page'. [1] De Harak came to believe that a Modernist's foundation and philosophy provided creative freedom to practice and move from one design discipline to another. Whether designing a poster, a book, an exhibition, or a house, the creative process and approach were always the same; it was a shared process and approach. This was the basis for de Harak's newfound success with multidisciplinary work. He didn't find it intimidating nor beyond his capabilities to continually cross lines within disciplines. It was also the reason why the editors of *Print* magazine featured de Harak (and a few of his design colleagues) as exemplifying the 'New Type of Design Professional' in their November/December 1970 issue.

The start of the 1970s was a pivotal time for de Harak and his design practice. Within the first few years of the new decade, he received commissions that would become the largest projects of his career to date, namely 77 Water Street; the US Pavilion at Expo 70 in Osaka; the AIGA (American Institute of Graphic Arts) Symbol Signs; the United Nations Plaza Hotel; and The Metropolitan Museum of Art. All of these projects would inevitably alter not only his reputation and standing within the graphic design profession, but also throughout the wider design world, and even beyond.

77 Water Street

Designed by architects Emery Roth & Sons, 77 Water Street is a 26-story, 80 m (262.5 ft) tall, multi-tenant commercial office building located in New York City's financial district. As with 127 John Street, its architecture was characteristic of the Mid-century Modernist style of the period, with a standard glass and aluminum curtain wall. At the time of its completion in 1970, 77 Water Street was described by

∨ Typographic treatment
of rear-illuminated,
acrylic-paneled elevator
cab interiors at 77 Water
Street, New York City,
1970.

Ada Louise Huxtable, the highly respected architecture critic of *The New York Times*, as 'a small gem with a sleek glass and aluminum "skin" structure of considerable finesse'. [2]

Despite its generic exterior, the building became to be known as one of the most exciting projects of the early 1970s due to the innovative and transformative contributions of the independent-minded de Harak. Unexpected yet humorous special effects located at street level included a series of stepped water pools crossed by footbridges; illuminated metal umbrellas, or 'heat trees', that rendered the plaza's open spaces more usable during colder months; and a replica of a turn-of-the-century, wood-framed candy store that provided a fully functioning symbol of an earlier, more personable time. The store also featured nostalgic signs from early-twentieth-century brands on its exterior, as well as a striped awning. Conventional lobby elements, namely the building directory and telephone booths, were transformed into graphic and sculptural objects for the outdoor plaza. De Harak devised a sign program for the commercial office building based on Akzidenz-Grotesk (Berthold Type Foundry, 1896), which he used for the exterior building address, interior signs, and tenant directories, as well as on the building management office's stationery and related print materials. Rear-illuminated acrylic panels for the elevator cab interiors featured bitmap-like numerals, suggesting the business function of the commercial building. De Harak was also given the opportunity to create one of his first sculptures for the building's exterior public space, Bennett Plaza. Here, he conceptualized a three-dimensional symbol for the plaza comprised of 120 stacked, 2.54 cm (1 in) thick, square stainless-steel plates placed together in an upward spiral to create a three-dimensional, rotated helix rising 4.26 m (14 ft) above the ground.

77 Water Street also introduced a notable departure for a commercial office building, as de Harak was asked to create an unusual and one-of-a-kind self-contained recreational environment on the building's rooftop, twenty-six floors above street level. While de Harak was not shy about pushing boundaries — as was evident with his recently completed work for Mel Kaufman at 127 John Street — it was Kaufman himself who suggested that he 'put something on the roof because people fly over it'. [3] Kaufman wanted to humanize the structure and give its neighbors a more pleasant view than boring air-conditioning equipment. De Harak noted: 'Usually roofs wind up with a cooling plant, some elevator machinery, and a water tower — all of which look terrible. We were asked to bring the rooftop to life — to make it an enjoyable experience both for people who go out upon it as well as for those who can see it from adjoining buildings.' [4]

A replica of a famous British World War 1 biplane, the Sopwith Camel, was installed on the roof of the building at one-to-one scale on a landing strip, set against a brightly painted background of mechanical equipment — it remains an unexpected sight for those working in neighboring skyscrapers. Sarasota-based sculptor William Tarr constructed the 9.75 m (32 ft) long welded-steel 1916 biplane fighter based on drawings and specifications produced by de Harak. The aircraft was originally constructed on the streets of Lower Manhattan, then cranes hoisted it up to its final location on the landing strip, which was carpeted in AstroTurf. The runway is complete with landing lights and windsock. 'We picked the World War I theme,' de Harak further explained, 'because of the romance and the nostalgia associated with that period. We also felt that the 'nuts and bolts' quality of the old biplane was more interesting than the more contemporary aircraft.' [5] He firmly believed that his plans for the roof were concerned with more than aesthetics: 'Architecture — especially the urban kind — is meaningless unless it involves people. This rooftop is meant to be a place where people can go out and utilize the space, with room to move about freely. In this sense, I feel our solution is as functional as it is aesthetically interesting.' [6]

De Harak always described Kaufman as 'a terrific client. He may have definite ideas about what he wants, but you can contribute to and embellish them ... Most of his ideas are very good anyway. He is not concerned with architecture and design per se, but as it relates to an organic environment.' [7] During their first collaboration on 127 John Street, de Harak had found that Kaufman had three overriding interests — people, humor, and design. All were certainly evident with their collaboration on 77 Water Street.

Expo 70 Osaka

In 1967, in an effort to attract the most talented architects and exhibition designers in the country, the United States Information Agency (USIA) organized a competition to design the US Pavilion at Expo 70 in Osaka, Japan. The winning entry, which prevailed unanimously over submissions by eleven design teams (including leading American architects and artists such as Isamu Noguchi, George Nelson, Minoru Yamasaki, James Stewart Polshek, and Paul Rudolph, among others) was the New York City partnership of architects Davis Brody and Associates (now Davis Brody Bond), in collaboration with exhibition designers Ivan Chermayeff, Tom Geismar, and Rudolph de Harak. The winning submission became legendary as one of the most noted and technically advanced buildings at the world exposition, as well as for its innovative architectural experimentation.

Originally founded in 1952 by Lewis Davis, Samuel Brody, and Chester Wisniewski as Davis Brody & Wisniewski, the firm gained a reputation for social engagement and technical innovation, the latter of which was conspicuous in their competition entry for Expo 70. This was the first building of its kind to include an air-encapsulated structure reinforced by steel cable, and was a forerunner of many covered stadiums that employed the same technology. When completed, it was described by Peter Blake in *Architectural Forum* as 'a master work of structural elegance and ... technological advances'. [8] Unlike most comparable projects, the US Pavilion at Expo 70 was designed inside and out by a unified, collaborative team operating on a single budget. The architects gave input and advice on the exhibitions, and the exhibition designers participated in architectural

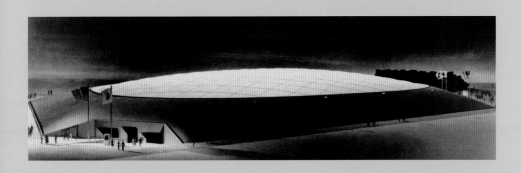

∨ Exterior model of
US Pavilion at Expo 70.

decisions, thereby guaranteeing that, unlike the Canadian Pavilion's 'Man, His Planet, and Space' exhibition at Expo 67 in Montreal, the final design solution for the building and the exhibition would be one and the same — an integral cohesive visitor experience.

Expo 70 ran for a period of six months and was the first world exposition to be staged in Japan. Seventy-nine nations were represented — more than any other world exposition of the era — with an estimated 67 million visitors touring the 85-acre site between March and September 1970. The US Pavilion was almost invisible when seen from the outside, but unforgettable once you entered. An enormous elliptical crater the size of two football fields was dug on the six-acre site, and its edges built up with excavated soil to create a perimeter berm. It was then covered by what remains the largest, lightest, clear-span air-supported cable roof ever built, with a clear span of 84 m (274 ft) by 142 m (465 ft). Super-elliptical in shape, this domed roof was made of translucent, vinyl-coated fiberglass, which filtered natural light in during the day and radiated light out at night, and was supported by four blowers that maintained a constant air pressure inside the building. A steel net that employed cables 6 m (20 ft) on center and arranged in a diamond pattern provided a construction armature and secondary support, without the need for pillars or foundation. With no central tension ring, the roof cables were anchored to a concrete compression ring resting on, but not anchored to, the earth berm.

Inside, the surface of the excavated berm was lined with mirrored mylar, creating eye-popping light effects and kinetic reflections very much in the spirit of the era. The resulting space reached a height of 18 m (60 ft) and contained 9,290 sq m (100,000 sq ft) of floor area over two levels. The structure accommodated up to 10,000 visitors an hour, twice the number of visitors accommodated at Buckminster Fuller's US Pavilion at Expo 67.

The pavilion contained seven major exhibitions celebrating the theme of 'Images of America' past and present: photography, painting, sports, space exploration, architecture, folk arts, and experimental arts. The organization of the interior spaces and visitor paths provided the public with numerous vantage points, giving them views through and over railings, as well as views above, below, and at eye level. Exhibitions floated from the building's roof grid, emerged dramatically from the mylar-covered berm, and appeared on monumental display panels. For example, a visitor could be looking at a display of American sports, but at the same time could also see portrait paintings from colonial times, the Lunar Module, and dramatic photographs from New York City's East Harlem, giving them a diverse and complex view of life in America.

One of the two featured exhibitions designed by de Harak at the US Pavilion was a photographic exhibition titled 'Ten Photographers'. Curated by John Szarkowski, director of photography for the Museum of Modern Art (MoMA) in New York City, the exhibition consisted of one hundred over-scaled

black-and-white transparencies, ranging in size all the way from
60 cm (2 ft) to 609 cm (20 ft). The photographs depicted America as
seen through the eyes of ten outstanding American photographers,
including William Garrett with his aerial views of the American
landscape, Diane Arbus with her portraits of anonymous Americans,
Bruce Davidson with his photographs made in one block of African-
American and Puerto Rican East Harlem, Lee Friedlander with his
photographs of characteristic fragments of the man-made
environment, and Paul Vanderbilt with his images of the farm-
lands and villages of the upper Midwest. Also represented was the
photographic work of André Kertész, Garry Winogrand, Duane
Michals, Joel Meyrowitz, and Ansel Adams. De Harak devised a
wall-panel system for displaying these over-scaled, rear-illuminated
transparencies, which provided an accessible, engaging, and
panoramic view of American landscapes, lifestyles, and portraiture.
All one-hundred photographs were intentionally displayed in
monochromatic black-and-white to reinforce and emphasize their
documentary quality.

The second exhibition designed by de Harak celebrated sports
in America and provided viewers with a dynamic overview of the
subject. De Harak's reliance on action-film footage, actual sports
equipment, and memorabilia from world-famous sports stars and
personalities made the exhibition one of the major highlights of the
pavilion. Iconic moments in the history of a wide range of American
sports such as baseball, football, basketball, auto racing, golf, and
surfing were presented by rear-view projections, accompanied by
their equipment, highlighting the interests, history, and regions of the
country. Baseball — perhaps the most popular sport in Japan — was
represented by the actual lockers, uniforms, and accessories used
by such greats as Babe Ruth, Walter Johnson, Joe Di Maggio, and
Ty Cobb. Visitors witnessed the chronological development of the
baseball glove, early catchers' masks, and shin-guards, as well as the

original bats used by many of America's baseball heroes. Football, as well as golf and fishing, was also celebrated with a display of helmets and shoulder pads, and golf clubs, rods, and reels. Another area was devoted to the automobile in sports. Here, a battery of sports cars was on display, including a Granatelli Turbocar, an Indy 500 Championship racing car, and dune buggies, as well as a fully accessorized Harley-Davidson motorcycle and a motorized one-person gyrocopter. Also included were a variety of sailboats, sunfish, surfboards, and snowmobiles that floated slightly above the mylar-covered berm.

The most popular display of the entire Expo 70 Osaka was a moon rock brought back to earth by the Apollo 12 mission, which was located in the 'Space Exploration' exhibition of the pavilion, attracting 16.2 million visitors. Other highlights included the 'American Painting' exhibition representing the best of American realists from colonial times onwards; an exhibition of American architecture that juxtaposed indigenous buildings with noteworthy Modernist architecture of the twentieth century; an exhibition on American folk art; and a 'New Artists' exhibition that resulted from twenty-four young artists participating in residencies at forty large American corporations.

The US Pavilion was one of the very few buildings at Expo 70 that embodied major technical and architectural innovation, yet it was also built on time and under budget. Peter Blake even predicted that this innovative building would ultimately be seen as 'one of the few manifestations at Osaka that truly advanced the art of structure in the twentieth century'. [9] It was not only a masterwork of structural elegance and technological advances, but also proof of the extraordinary collaboration between its design team, which along with Davis Brody and Associates, Chermayeff & Geismar, and Rudolph de Harak, included the USIA's chief engineer, Jack Masey, and the structural engineer David Geiger.

Friends and Collaborators

In 1979, Ivan Chermayeff and Tom Geismar were awarded the graphic design profession's highest honor — the AIGA Gold Medal. De Harak introduced both designers at the awards presentation and recalled the period when all of them first met and were starting their young careers: 'In graphic design, the establishment designers were Will Burtin, Alvin Lustig, Paul Rand, Lester Beall and Saul Bass. Art Kane was seriously contemplating leaving the drawing board for his cameras, Jay Maisel had just started on his career as a photographer. And Henry Wolf was turning the magazine industry on its ear with his fresh concepts of design at *Esquire*. Lou Dorfsman was already almost legendary at CBS.' [10] He continued to talk about the pair's shared philosophy and approach to work, as well as their contributions to the profession. 'Most of us in the design profession are indebted to Chermayeff and Geismar,' de Harak pointed out, 'so much of what they did was new. It was conspicuous, and it has influenced us all. Also, through their efforts, good design has become more acceptable, thus making it more possible for all of us to do better work.' [11]

Often referred as one of America's most influential graphic design partnerships, Ivan Chermayeff and Tom Geismar have

created some of the most memorable and recognizable images and identities of the mid-twentieth century. Among their corporate identity programs were Mobil, Xerox, PBS, NBC, Univision, Viacom, TimeWarner, the Smithsonian, National Geographic, and Chase Manhattan Bank, and they also worked on the US Pavilions for Expo 58 in Brussels, Expo 67 in Montreal, and Expo 70 in Osaka, the latter in collaboration with de Harak.

AIGA Symbol Signs

In the 1970s a committee of American graphic designers, under the auspices of the American Institute of Graphic Arts (AIGA), developed an extensive system of pictograms for the US Department of Transportation called 'symbol signs'. This set of passenger- and pedestrian-oriented pictograms became the first federal symbol standards for airports, train stations, and other public-transit facilities throughout the United States. To encourage widespread adoption, the symbols were offered free of charge to any qualified users. This landmark achievement represented the first time a cohesive and universal system of pictograms had been designed that communicated essential information across language barriers to international travelers in all bus stations, airports, railways, and ship terminals throughout the country. It was also the first time that a government agency (US Department of Transportation's Office of Facilitation) and a professional organization (AIGA) had collaborated on a comprehensive design effort for the public good. Prior to this effort, numerous civic and public organizations such as railways, airlines, and Olympic Games committees had developed sets of pictograms for use in guiding the public to transportation venues and international events. These efforts resulted in numerous, well-designed graphic programs; however, none of them was suitable for the needs of federal travel facilities, nor did they address the needs of a diverse public made up of different ages and cultures.

Tom Geismar was invited to lead the project, and started by organizing a five-member committee of graphic designers, all with extensive experience in the design of symbols and signing. The group was comprised of Massimo Vignelli, Seymour Chwast, John Lees, and de Harak. Initially, a thorough and extensive process was undertaken to ensure further optimum results. Committee members agreed that they would base their evaluations on semiotics, a philosophical and behavioral theory of signs and symbols developed by philosopher and semiotician Charles Morris in the 1930s. Morris believed that the study and analysis of signs and symbols could result in a more definitive and effective means of visual and verbal communication. The committee's reliance on this theory was an invaluable tool that provided scientific foundation to its findings. It also demonstrated the members' commitment to the Modernist design principle of developing a rational, universal visual language for the public good. The Office of Facilitation and the AIGA committee ultimately agreed upon an initial list of thirty-four messages they wanted graphically represented. Simultaneously, AIGA compiled an extensive inventory of existing transportation-related symbols used throughout the United States and abroad for further visual reference and evaluation. Early iterations of the committee's work were tested at selected attractions for the United States Bicentennial

> Cover for *Symbol Signs Repro Art*, reproduction art and guidelines for the system of symbol signs developed for the US Department of Transportation by the American Institute of Graphic Arts (AIGA), 1974.

celebration and related transportation facilities — the cooperating cities were Boston, New York City, Philadelphia, Washington, DC, and Williamsburg, Virginia. Following the committee's evaluation for clarity and effectiveness, a final selection of pictograms was then made for further adapting or redesigning; and detailed design guidelines were established for their subsequent refinement.

The actual task of designing the final set of pictograms in a cohesive and unified graphic style of consistent line, shape, weight, and form, based on the committee's analysis, findings, and input, was completed by graphic designers Roger Cook and Don Shanosky of Cook & Shanosky Associates. Cook and Shanosky followed the committee's design guidelines and prepared drafts of each of the thirty-four symbol signs for testing, review, and approval. This final set of pictograms was released for public use in 1974; a supplemental set of sixteen pictograms was subsequently developed by the same committee members and designers in 1979. Page, Arbitrio and Resen designed the guidelines for usage that accompanied both releases. Both sets are still in use today, having been adopted by the US Department of Transportation and various governmental departments such as the Federal Aviation Administration, General Services Administration, US Department of Health Education and Welfare, Amtrak, and the Air Transport Association.

Both phases of the project, as well as its graphic designers, were recognized for 'Outstanding Achievement in Design for the Government of the United States of America' in 1985 by President Ronald Reagan with one of the first US Presidential Design Awards. Additionally, *AIGA Symbol Signs* are copyright-free and have become the standard for off-the-shelf symbols in the catalogs of most sign companies throughout the United States.

United Nations Plaza Hotel

One, Two, and Three United Nations Plaza — a combination office building, hotel, and luxury residential condominium designed by American architects Kevin Roche John Dinkeloo & Associates — was New York City's first mixed-use development. Paul Goldberger,

∨ One and Two United
Nations Plaza building
exterior, New York City,
1975. ESTO/Wolfgang
Hoyt, photographer.

architecture critic for *The New York Times*, praised the project as 'an exquisite minimalist sculpture' [12] when it first opened in 1975. The master plan for the new development was organized in three phases over a period of thirteen years (Phase 1 completion: 1975; Phase 2 completion: 1982; Phase 3 completion: 1988) and included three buildings: two forty-story towers connected by a common base totaling 67,540 sq m (727,000 sq ft), and a third building of fifteen stories totaling 19,045 sq m (205,000 sq ft) that serves as the headquarters for UNICEF. Each of the two towers contains office spaces, a restaurant, and a health club, but they shared a single hotel lobby for the United Nations Plaza Hotel, which spanned both towers. Separate entrances were provided for the office components.

In 1974, de Harak was commissioned by Roche, the building architect, along with the project developer, United Nations Development Corporation (UNDC), and the hotel's operator, Hyatt International, to develop a comprehensive environmental graphics and wayfinding sign program for the entire complex, as well as a branding, identity, and print amenities program for the hotel.

To fully integrate these programs with the architecture, one of the first tasks undertaken by de Harak was to design a custom typeface for the project that complemented the Modernist design vocabulary of the building's exterior. The resulting UNPH typeface was based on sans-serif geometric typefaces that reflected the simplicity of pure geometric form and were void of any obvious historical references, such as Morris Sans (designed by Morris Fuller Benton in 1930), Microgramma (designed by Aldo Novarese in 1952), and Eurostile (designed by Aldo Novarese in 1962). In many ways, this typeface was de Harak's response to Tschichold's influential book *Die neue Typographie* (Berlin: Verlag des Bildungsverbandes der Deutschen Buchdrucker, 1928) which praised the aesthetic qualities of 'anonymous' nineteenth-century sans-serif typefaces. The letterforms in UNPH are constructed from a pure geometric shape, solely based on a square module, and maintain a consistent monoline appearance as well as a strict reliance upon set criteria for letterspacing. The typeface, comprised of only capitals, an ampersand, and numerals, was primarily used for large-scale applications, for instance in the architectural and environmental graphics throughout the property, as well as for the hotel's logotype.

The promotional materials for the United Nations Plaza Hotel were also designed by de Harak to reinforce the Modernist character of the architecture and interior finishes, as well as highlight its services and amenities. For example, the embossed and debossed pattern on the cover of the menus for its Ambassador Grill restaurant were taken directly from the pattern of its floor tiles. The guest services directory and the promotional shopping bags utilized images of the many rare tapestries and textiles displayed throughout the hotel. De Harak and his staff were able to maintain a consistent design program for the United Nations Plaza Hotel for over twelve years.

The Metropolitan Museum of Art

From 1973 to 1983, New York's Metropolitan Museum of Art undertook a major redesign, renovation, expansion, and reinstallation program for the Lila Acheson Wallace Galleries of Egyptian Art.

> The Metropolitan Museum
of Art, Fifth Avenue
building façade and main
entrance, New York City,
c. 1980. Deborah Kushma,
photographer.

The Met's collection of Ancient Egyptian art, considered the finest and most comprehensive in the Western Hemisphere, consists of approximately 26,000 objects, including the exceptional Temple of Dendur, an ancient sandstone temple dismantled to save it from the rising waters of the Nile River when the Aswan High Dam was built, and reassembled at the museum in 1978.

This landmark project, organized in three phases and totaling 13,350 sq m (143,500 sq ft), provided for the display of the museum's entire ancient Egyptian art collection, arranged chronologically in thirty-two galleries so that all material of a particular period was integrated. De Harak and his staff worked closely with the museum's master plan architects — Kevin Roche John Dinkeloo & Associates once again — and its curatorial staff, and were responsible throughout

the three phases of the project for the design of all casework displays, interpretive graphics, didactic labels, and maps. Extensive educational and interpretive materials in the form of rear-illuminated information panels and tables, many incorporating extensive captions, were installed throughout the galleries to introduce basic concepts of Ancient Egyptian art and culture, as well as provide descriptions of individual exhibition areas. Both the information tables and the casework were constructed of polished stainless-steel and glass, with exhibition texts and captions silkscreened on the inside surface (aka second surface) of the glass, allowing for legible yet unobtrusive reading and simple maintenance. At the entrance to the galleries, a 7.6 m (25 ft)-long, rear-illuminated photographic timeline introduced two thousand years of Egyptian history and culture. De Harak subsequently developed this timeline into an accordion-fold book, which was published and distributed by the museum.

Since de Harak's work on 'Man, His Planet, and Space' at Montreal's Expo 67, he had always felt that designing exhibitions was an exciting, but challenging undertaking. He believed that the viewer should always be immediately aware of the exhibition's content and not of the design vocabulary displaying that content. Talking about his work at the Met, he further explained, 'It was a project requiring extreme discipline, terrific intensity, and continuity. What was decided in 1974 at the onset of this project had to have the same sense of ambience and consistency to last through to its completion. One could not simply change styles and concepts midstream, thereby sacrificing the overall look of the Wing. This took a great deal of restraint sticking with the original design. The project took twelve painstaking years to complete with very little, if anything, left to chance. When one walks through it, its splendor and all-important cohesiveness is omnipresent.' [13]

American author Steven Heller later described de Harak's involvement with this expansive undertaking in a 2004 article for *Baseline* magazine: 'When the Met's architect, Kevin Roche, invited de Harak to work on the new wing he wanted someone who would conform to the modern scheme of the new wing and its master plan, and yet be sympathetic to the Met's traditions. The project took ten years to complete — years that were devoted to exhaustive research of every nuance of the magnificent collection before the design process began. Deciding what and how to show the panorama of ancient history with enough entry-points to engage even the casual viewer was as difficult a challenge as de Harak had ever faced. How to identify the invaluable materials required a variety of inventive formats. Transparency was one of the keys. De Harak discretely printed captions on glass, which gave the viewer the option to learn about and/or see the treasured objects at the same time.' [14]

The completed project garnered critical praise from numerous scholars, critics, art historians, Egyptologists, architects, and designers, including John Russell, art critic of *The New York Times*, who described the overall installation as 'conversational', [15] and Ada Louise Huxtable, its architecture critic, who stated that it created 'an exemplary balance between art and information.' [16]

For over fifteen years, de Harak and his staff were also responsible for the design of the museum's exhibitions, its environmental and interpretive graphics, its donor recognition program, as well as the wayfinding sign programs used in other areas of the museum, including the Uris Center for Education, the André Meyer Galleries of Nineteenth-Century European Art, the Lila Acheson Wallace Wing for Twentieth-Century Art, and The Museum Bookstore. However, perhaps most famous is his work on the Met's highly visible shopping bag program. Talking about his iconic bags for the newly renovated bookstore, de Harak recalled that 'it took the powers that be at the Met quite a long time to accept the solution for the shopping bags. And then, of course, once they did accept it, it was all the rage. They hesitated because it was too modern…they would have preferred if it was marbleized paper or something to that effect. Kevin Roche was a strong advocate for this solution and that is why it was accepted. Once it was, they couldn't keep them in stock…people loved them!' [17]

His solution was emblematic of his desire to always explore contrasts and dualities in visual storytelling. In this case, a traditional typeface, namely Caslon 540, designed by William Caslon in 1725, was juxtaposed with three modern primary colors: yellow, blue, and red. He designed the bags so that the name of the museum wrapped around all four sides, with the front of the bag always reading 'Met'. They immediately became a powerful branding device for the museum's first-ever retail establishment, acting as an iconic memento that visitors could take away when they left. The shopping bags weren't just highly noticeable throughout New York City, they ended up in every major city throughout the world, becoming one of the most universally visible projects that de Harak created in his entire career. The Museum Bookstore used several million bags a year and, for over thirty years, they were printed exactly as de Harak as conceived them. In addition, the Met's own design department adopted Caslon 540 as the go-to typeface for almost every area of the museum.

The Metropolitan Museum of Art project solidified de Harak's relationship with the Pritzker Prize-winning architect Kevin Roche, who became one of his main collaborators and champions — the pair worked together for over twenty-five years on numerous corporate headquarters, cultural, and institutional projects. In 2017, the architect and author Robert A.M. Stern eloquently stated in a documentary on Roche: 'It would be impossible to write a history of twentieth-century architecture without Kevin Roche.' [18]

Continued Growth and Recognition

Due to these major multidisciplinary commissions, de Harak continued to expand his staff and office space. The beginning of the 1970s found him and his design consultancy, now known as Rudolph de Harak and Associates, located at 150 Fifth Avenue in the Flatiron District of Manhattan. He continued to design large- and small-scale branding and identity programs throughout the decade for a range of companies, organizations, and institutions, such as the Benrus Watch Company, Coral Harbour Resort, Alan Guttmacher Institute, Horizon Lighting, Illuminating Engineering Society of North America, National Association of Radio and Television Broadcasters, New York State Park Commission for the City of New York, the Grand Central Oyster Bar & Restaurant at Grand Central Station, Real Estate Mortgage Investment Conduit (REMIC), Symbiosis, and *The New York Times'* Information Bank. In publishing, he designed book covers and jackets for Doubleday & Company; publications for the National Endowment for the Arts and for Cooper Union's The Irwin S. Chanin School of Architecture; and magazines for *Linea Grafica, Perspectives*, and *Public Relations Journal*. He also designed album covers for Improv Records.

His passion for and commitment to the academic world, as well as the design community, also benefitted from his continued growth and experience. While de Harak continued to teach at Cooper Union during the 1970s, he also gave workshops, seminars, and lectures at numerous universities and design organizations throughout the United States and Europe, while serving on the American Institute of Graphic Arts' (AIGA) board of directors, and also as the US National President for the Alliance Graphique Internationale (AGI) from 1975 to 1977.

In 1971, a new trilingual book series — split by geography into *Graphic Designers in the U.S.A.* and *Graphic Designers in Europe* — was published by Universe Books. Edited by Henri Hillebrand, the intention of the eight-volume series was to provide readers interested in design with their first opportunity to study the work of twenty-four of the world's leading graphic designers. De Harak was one of the featured graphic designers. The text in each book was printed in three languages: French, English, and German. The individual design philosophies expressed within were as varied as the

∨ De Harak (*middle row, second fr right*) with AIGA committee members and staff, New York City, *c.* 1970.

designers' styles, and were often in direct opposition to each other. For example, French artist and illustrator Jean-Michel Folon, noted for his very stylized drawings and paintings for magazine covers and posters, believed that 'a design must be kept as imprecise as possible, because a design is an opportunity for the imagination of the viewer.' [19] In contrast, de Harak saw the designer as directed by self-imposed standards: 'He is bound by his refusal to accept the way things look simple because they have been acceptable. He cannot depend only on what he knows. His development, and the uniqueness of the solution must come from what he doesn't know. Thus, within the framework of this commitment there must exist the full realization that his every singular effort toward creativity has a greater chance of failure than it has for success.' [20] The first two published volumes of the eight-volume series included features on Louis Danziger, Herb Lubalin, Peter Max, and Henry Wolf; and R.O. Blechman, Chermayeff and Geismar, Paul Davis, and de Harak.

De Harak was also invited by David Sutton — his project manager for the Canadian Pavilion at Expo 67 in Montreal, and for the US Pavilion at Expo 70 in Osaka — to talk at 'The Art of Typeface Design and Visual Communications', an international typographic symposium held in Washington, DC in October 1974. Sutton was now working at the Federal Design Improvement Program and was co-chair of a symposium that had evolved from a need to teach approximately twenty attorneys of the copyright section of the Library of Congress how to distinguish between typefaces and their applications; about the problems faced by a designer of new typefaces; and about the relationship of technology to typeface design and use. He asked de Harak to join a panel of speakers that amounted to a who's who of distinguished typeface designers and typographic experts from around the world including Aaron Burns talking on 'Modern Typography and the New Technologies', Hermann Zapf on 'Design Problems', Matthew Carter on 'Typeface Design: Why and How Typefaces Differ', Thomas Geismar on 'Typography for Industry and the Corporation', and Herb Lubalin on 'Typo-Graphics: The Use of Letterforms for Total Communications'. De Harak tackled the subject of 'Typography of Signage, Architecture and Exhibitions'. Sutton recalled that 'Rudy got everyone's attention by showing creative uses of type beyond the printed page.' [21]

In 1977, de Harak was awarded a residency at the New Arts Program (NAP) at Kutztown State College in Pennsylvania. Founded in 1974, the NAP is a nonprofit library, museum, and exhibition space that provides a forum for the public to interact with major artists from the literary, visual, and performing arts. Its residencies include performances, exhibitions, and one-on-one conversations, cultivating direct dialogue between artists and audiences.

That same year, de Harak was invited by the National Endowment for the Arts to speak at its 'Studio Seminar for Federal Graphic Designers'. Nicholas Chaparos, Director, School of Design,

> Rudolph de Harak,
  New York City, c. 1978.
  Carol de Harak,
  photographer.

University of Cincinnati, and a close friend and colleague, attended the seminar and wrote: 'When Rudolph de Harak spoke... he chose as his theme "the designer's responsibility for content and meaning — and how it affects the images he creates". It was a subject which reflects his life-long concern for perfection and excellence. This was an appropriate subject to open a working seminar of US government designers, since their constraints in image-making are not dictated by the marketplace but rather by the laws, programs, and bureaucracy of one of the world's most complex democratic governments. Rudolph de Harak has achieved excellence as a designer who solves problems in both the government and the marketplace.

'In illustrating the theme, de Harak showed examples of his paperback covers done for McGraw Hill (approximately three-hundred fifty images), a body of work which clearly established a design idiom and changes the face of paperback cover design in the United States. One by one, he stated the problems and considerations that led him to the final design solution for these covers. Questions from the audience were far-ranging, asking for information about the methodologies embodied in his exhibition design work for governments (Canadian Pavilion at Expo 67 Montreal, Canada; US Pavilion at Expo 70 Osaka, Japan) and institutions (The Metropolitan Museum of Art). In replying to these questions, he candidly revealed his path to the solutions, the quick wit and intuition of some, the trial and error of others.

'As the morning concluded, the audience had had more than a glimpse into the mind of one of the world's leaders in graphic design. It was very appropriate that de Harak should have discussed the exploration of this basic area of graphic design, because his extensive career, from its very beginning, has had its hallmark in the uncompromising, often pragmatic, but always philosophical approach woven into the projects he has undertaken. The same uncompromising attitude prevails in his teaching. His students appreciate his enthusiasm and respect for each individual's sense of integrity, and many recall the times spent with him with deep feeling and emotion.

'To his peers, he is the designer's designer. By pointing the direction and sharing his resources, he has been able to effect significant changes in American professional graphic arts organizations, gaining new recognition for graphic designers and at the same time broadening their usefulness to the professions. But Rudolph de Harak is hardest on himself. He possesses great energy, which when combined with his design experience enables him to focus on a problem with immediacy and clarity. This has been seen consistently in his problem-solving activity in graphic, exhibition, and industrial design over the past thirty years.' [22]

> Environmental graphics,
wayfinding, and sculpture,
77 Water Street, New York
City, William Kaufman
Organization, 1970.
Nathaniel 'Thorney'
Lieberman, photographer.

1. Alvin Lustig, *The Collected Writings of Alvin Lustig*, New Haven: Holland R. Melson, Jr, 1958.
2. Ada Louise Huxtable, 'A New City is Emerging Downtown', *The New York Times*, 29 March 1970, p. 239.
3. Forrest Wilson, ed., '77 Water Street, New York', *Progressive Architecture*, March 1971, pp. 66–75.
4. Ibid.
5. Ibid.
6. Ibid.
7. Ibid.
8. Peter Blake, 'Biggest Big Top', *Architectural Forum*, vol. 131, no. 5, December 1969, pp. 68–69.
9. Ibid.
10. Rudolph de Harak, introduction at the presentation of the American Institute of Graphic Arts (AIGA) Gold Medal to Ivan Chermayeff and Tom Geismar, New York City, 16 October 1979.
11. Ibid.
12. Paul Goldberger, 'Kevin Roche Finishes a Trio and Changes His Tune', *The New York Times*, 29 November 1987, Section II: p. 42.
13. Rudolph de Harak, interview by Steven Heller, February 1987 (transcript), in New York City. Steven Heller Collection, School of Visual Arts Archives, New York.
14. Steven Heller, 'Rudolph de Harak: A Playful Modernist', *Baseline,* no. 45, 2004, pp. 25–32.
15. John Russell, ' Romance of Egyptology', *The New York Times,* 10 October 1976, Section II: pp. 1, 23.
16. Ada Louise Huxtable. 'Taking the Wraps Off Egypt', *The New York Times,* 10 October 1976, Section II: p. 18.
17. Rudolph de Harak, interview by Steven Heller, February 1987 (transcript), in New York City. Steven Heller Collection, School of Visual Arts Archives, New York.
18. Statement by Robert A.M. Stern in *Kevin Roche: The Quiet Architect*, directed by Mark Noonan, London: Wavelength Films, 2017.
19. Madeline R. Kraner, 'Graphic Artists Lauded in New Universe Series', *Publishers Weekly*, vol. 201, 7 February 1972.
20. Ibid.
21. Richard Poulin, Interview with David Sutton, 26 April 2021.
22. Nicholas J. Chaparos, 'Rudolph de Harak', *Graphis*, vol. 33, no. 193, 1977, pp. 444–445.
23. Rudolph de Harak, interview by Steven Heller, February 1987 (transcript), in New York City. Steven Heller Collection, School of Visual Arts Archives, New York.
24. Ibid.

∨ Sculpture, *Helix,* New York
City, William Kaufman
Organization, 1970
0.45 x 0.45 x 3.04 m
(1.5 x 1.5 x 10 ft)
Stainless-steel.
Nathaniel 'Thorney'
Lieberman, photographer.

Exhibition research,
planning, programming,
and design; environmental
and interpretive graphics,
US Pavilion, Expo 70,
Osaka, Japan, United States
Information Agency (USIA),
1970.

STP Turbocar

The first racing car to be designed around a turbine engine, the STP Turbocar touched off instant controversy when it was introduced at the 1967 Indianapolis "500" race. Its Pratt & Whitney engine, originally built for use in small aircraft, boats and helicopters, burns kerosene rather than the potentially explosive hot fuels used in conventional race cars, other special safety features include fuel tanks located deep inside a strong backbone frame. The Turbocar led the 1967 "500" until the 197th lap, when a gear case bearing failed. Subsequently, engine size restrictions barred the vehicle from U.S. racing competition.

Dr. Anthony ("Andy") Granatelli, STP Corporation

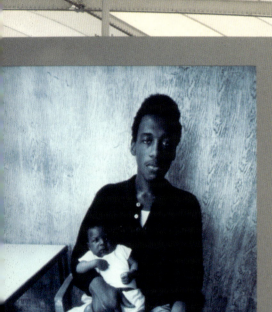

ブルース デービッドソン
Bruce Davidson

1970–1979 | Lila Acheson Wallace Galleries of Egyptian Art at The Metropolitan Museum of Art

Exhibition research, planning, programming, and design; environmental and interpretive graphics, Lila Acheson Wallace Galleries of Egyptian Art, New York City, The Metropolitan Museum of Art, 1972–1983. The Temple of Dendur is the centerpiece of the Lila Acheson Wallace Galleries of Egyptian Art at The Metropolitan Museum of Art. Built in BCE 15 as one of many Egyptian temples commissioned by Roman emperor Augustus (BCE 63–CE 14), it was removed from its original location in the 1960s and given to the museum in 1978.

The Genealogy
of Ancient Egypt

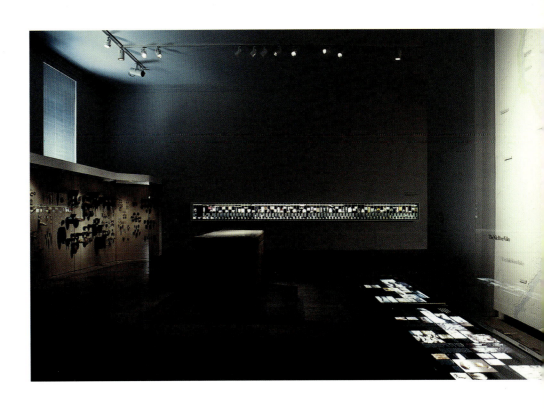

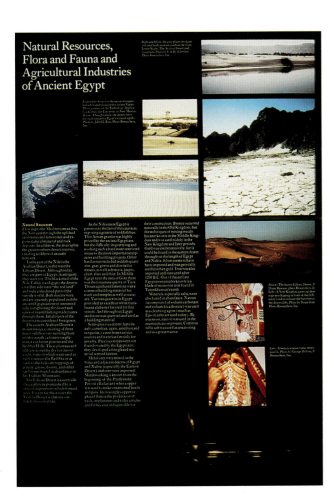

Natural Resources, Flora and Fauna and Agricultural Industries of Ancient Egypt

Natural Resources

Flowing to the Mediterranean Sea, the Nile cuts through the uplifted sandstone and limestone and deposits natural mineral and rock deposits. In addition, the river splits the great northern desert into two, creating a ribbon of an oasis between.

To the east of the Nile is the Arabian Desert, to the west the Libyan Desert. Although today they are part of Egypt, in antiquity they were not. The black mud of the Nile Valley was Egypt; the deserts on either side were "the red land" and were considered part of the outside world. Both deserts were, and are, sparsely populated and the ancient Egyptians were interested only in exploiting the desert and oases or in establishing trade routes through them. Inhabitants of the desert were considered foreigners.

The eastern Arabian Desert is mountainous, consisting of three major subdivisions running from north to south: a limestone plateau, a sandstone plateau and the Red Sea Hills. These plateaus and hills are scored by dry ravines or wadis, some of which were used as trade routes in the Red Sea or to roads to the rich outcroppings of granite, gneiss, diorite, and other hard stones found in abundance in the Arabian Mountains.

The Libyan Desert is essentially a large plateau punctuated by a series of depressions which formed oases. Except for the oases the Western Desert is almost continuously devoid of life.

As the Nile enters Egypt it passes over the last of the cataracts, exposing a granite of reddish hue. This Aswan granite was highly prized by the ancient Egyptians but the difficulty in quarrying and working such a hard stone restricted its use to the more important sculptures and building projects. Other hard stones included reddish quartzite, gray gneiss and diorite for statues, as well as breccia, jasper, chert, slate and shist. In Middle Egypt near the area of Giza there was the limestone quarry of Tura. This magnificent limestone was a common building material for tomb and temples as well as statuary. Various quarries in Egypt provided an excellent white translucent alabaster favored for fine vessels. And throughout Egypt sandstone was quarried and used as a building material.

Semi-precious stones (lapis lazuli, carnelian, agate, amethyst and turquoise), came from various sources and were used mainly for jewelry. Precious stones were not found or used by the Egyptians; they developed a fine glazed material termed faience.

Metal sites were mined in the Sinai and adjacent deserts of Egypt and Nubia (especially the Eastern Desert) and ores were imported. Metalworking is known from the beginning of the Predynastic Period (Badarian) when copper was used to make ornamental beads and pins. Increasingly copper replaced flint in the production of tools, implements and toilet articles until it became indispensable for their construction. Bronze occurred naturally in the Old Kingdom, but the techniques of mixing metals became known in the Middle Kingdom and was used widely in the New Kingdom and later periods. Gold was used extensively, for it could be found in the eastern desert throughout the length of Egypt and Nubia. Silver seems to have been imported and was generally used less than gold. Iron was also imported and rare until after 1200 B.C. One of the earliest Egyptian examples known is a blade of meteoritic iron found in Tutankhamun's tomb.

Minerals, especially salts, were also found in abundance. Natron (a compound of sodium carbonate and sodium bicarbonate) was used as a cleansing agent (much as Epsom salts are used today). By extension, natron was used in the mummification process. Common table salt was used as a seasoning and as a preservative.

Right and below: In some places the dunes cut sand banks even encroach on the river. Lower Right: The Arabian Desert and mountains. Photos by F. & B. Schneider, Photo Researchers, Inc.

Lower left: Sinai is a rich source of copper, malachite and turquoise for ancient Egypt. Photo courtesy of the Technology Application Center, the University of New Mexico. Below: Though barren, the deserts were the main source of Egypt's mineral supply. Photo by John G. Ross, Photo Researchers, Inc.

Above: The barren Libyan Desert. Photo by Diane Rawson, photo Researchers, Inc. Left: A New Kingdom painting shows eye make-up being in front of the eye; color is red to indicate the bitterness of the desert cliffs. Photo by Brian Brake, Photo-Researchers, Inc.

Left: A bedouin woman today wears wealth. Photo by George Holton, Photo Researchers, Inc.

...re slaughtered, women attendants—
...em carrying sunshades and
...ces—and cattle walk left.
...ld have faced them, her
name written...

26.3.353 H-I, K, O, W, X, Z, DD-EE,
OO, QQ; 31.3.1 J, M; 68.12

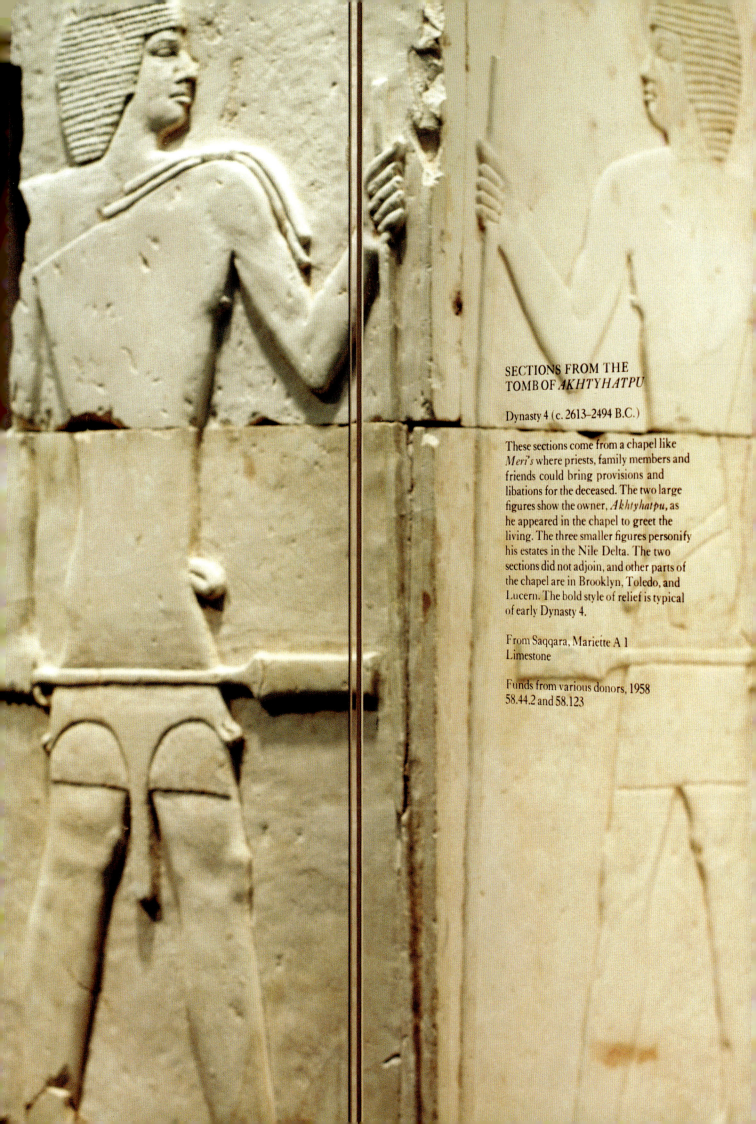

SECTIONS FROM THE TOMB OF *AKHTYHATPU*

Dynasty 4 (c. 2613–2494 B.C.)

These sections come from a chapel like *Meri's* where priests, family members and friends could bring provisions and libations for the deceased. The two large figures show the owner, *Akhtyhatpu*, as he appeared in the chapel to greet the living. The three smaller figures personify his estates in the Nile Delta. The two sections did not adjoin, and other parts of the chapel are in Brooklyn, Toledo, and Lucern. The bold style of relief is typical of early Dynasty 4.

From Saqqara, Mariette A 1
Limestone

Funds from various donors, 1958
58.44.2 and 58.123

∨ Accordion book, *Timeline of Culture in the Nile Valley and its Relationships to Other World Cultures,* The Metropolitan Museum of Art, 1979.

3300 Predynastic Period
Gerzean
Maadi

3200

3100 Archaic Period
Dynasty 0
Dynasty 1

2900 Dynastic Period
Archaic Period
Dynasty 2

The flint implements produced during the Gerzean Period are very beautiful. Mastery of flint-making techniques had been achieved and at this time was combined with an appreciation for the aesthetic qualities of the object. This wide, slightly curved knife has a very thin, sharp blade with a regular, rippled pattern produced by careful flaking. It is this type of blade which was fitted into the elaborately carved ivory handles of the period. Such knives were probably more than ordinary tools, perhaps used for some ceremonial purpose.

The typical painted pottery of the Gerzean Period was a red-on-buff ware, often decorated with many-oared boats as illustrated here. The female figures with long skirts cannot be identified with certainty, but they are probably goddesses or priestesses. Similar figures and boats appear in a unique wall-painting, the earliest known from Egypt, in a tomb at Hierakonpolis. An important feature of the Hierakonpolis tomb is the presence of mud brick. The use of mud brick later made possible fortifications and elaborate building structures in the rapidly evolving Egyptian civilization.

At the time this sculpture of a young lion was carved (c. 3200–3100 B.C.), all of Upper Egypt was unified under one ruler, but Lower Egypt remained a separate entity. Temples to the gods were being constructed. This lion cub, believed to have been found in a temple at Gebelein, is a representative example of the sophistication and refinement of the arts of the period. There was a major creative upsurge in the arts at this time. This upsurge is evidenced in the statuette illustrated here, carved in a very hard stone (quartz) not capturing the form and feeling of the subject with an economy of means.

This large, shield-shaped palette of King Narmer dates from the very end of Dynasty 0 or the beginning of Dynasty 1, c. 3100 B.C., and was found in the temple precinct at Hierakonpolis. Hierakonpolis was by this time an important political and religious center in Upper Egypt. The palette commemorates a victory, perhaps the final one, in the struggle for the unification of the entire Nile Valley. The largest and most important figure is the king wearing the crown of Upper Egypt. He brandishes a mace and is about to strike a Lower Egyptian enemy. The victory of Upper Egypt over Lower Egypt is shown again above the prisoner, where a falcon (representing the god Horus) grasps an emblem with papyrus branches, the symbol of Lower Egypt. The decision of the sculptor artist anticipates the classical relief style of the Dynastic Period.

There are some indications of political strife during Dynasty 2 (c. 2890–2686 B.C.), even though the historical records are very meager. There were two royal burial grounds, one at Abydos, the other at Saqqara, each containing tombs of different pharaohs. The above stela is from Saqqara and is the earliest known monument of this type from this cemetery. The falcon god Horus, the embodiment of the king, surmounted a paneled façade, or *serekh*, containing the hieroglyphs *Ra* and *nb*, meaning "Ra is (my) lord." Stelae of this type, usually erected in pairs, were the focal point of the royal mortuary cult.

Above: Flint knife blade; Metropolitan Museum of Art.
Left: An tapered and White Temple at Warka in southern Iraq.

Above: Painted pottery vessel; Metropolitan Museum of Art.
Left: Figure of a bearded man from Warka in southern Iraq; Iraq Museum, Baghdad.

Note: Lion cub; Metropolitan Museum of Art.
Left: Limestone stamp seal from Iraq or Iran; Metropolitan Museum of Art.

Above: Palette of King Narmer from Hierakonpolis; Egyptian Museum, Cairo.
Left: Proto-Elamite cast statuette from Iran; Metropolitan Museum of Art.

Above: Stela of Raneb from Saqqara; Metropolitan Museum of Art.
Upper left: Sumerian stela from Iraq; Metropolitan Museum of Art.
Left: Carved steatite vessel from Iran or Iraq; Metropolitan Museum of Art.

Visitor information guide, *A Plan of the Lila Acheson Wallace Galleries of Egyptian Art,* The Metropolitan Museum of Art, 1979.

The galleries of Egyptian Art are arranged in chronological order, beginning to the visitor's right as one enters the Wing, and continuing in a counterclockwise direction back to the starting point. Special collections (such as the models of Mekutra) are located off the main route, along with study areas. All objects in the Department are displayed, and there is a gallery for special exhibitions.

The galleries were reinstalled between 1972 and 1983, and funded by Lila Acheson Wallace.

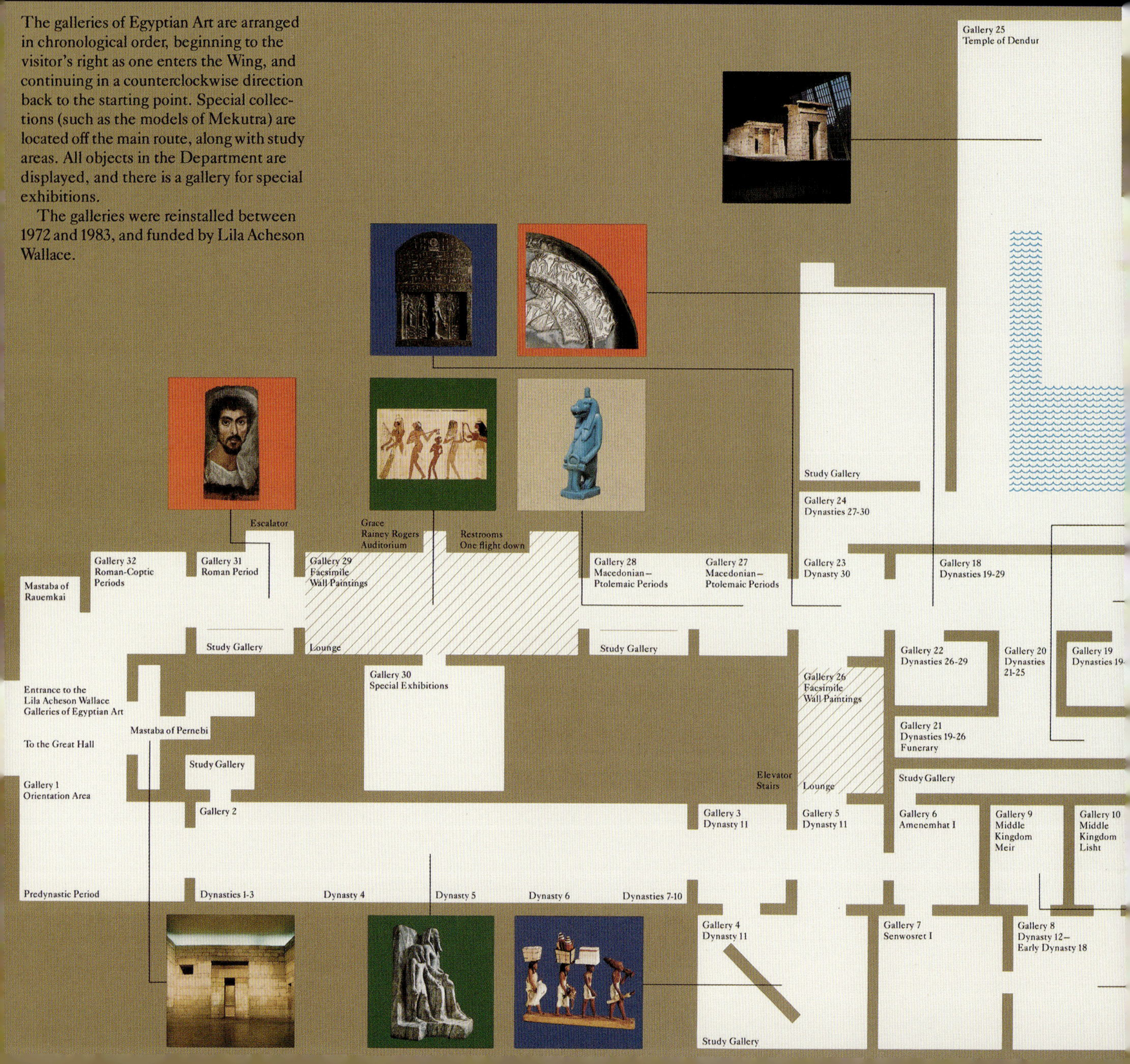

Gallery 25
Temple of Dendur

Study Gallery

Gallery 24
Dynasties 27-30

Gallery 23
Dynasty 30

Gallery 18
Dynasties 19-29

Escalator

Grace
Rainey Rogers
Auditorium

Restrooms
One flight down

Gallery 32
Roman-Coptic
Periods

Gallery 31
Roman Period

Gallery 29
Facsimile
Wall Paintings

Gallery 28
Macedonian–
Ptolemaic Periods

Gallery 27
Macedonian–
Ptolemaic Periods

Mastaba of
Rauemkai

Study Gallery

Lounge

Study Gallery

Gallery 22
Dynasties 26-29

Gallery 20
Dynasties
21-25

Gallery 19
Dynasties 19-

Gallery 30
Special Exhibitions

Gallery 26
Facsimile
Wall Paintings

Entrance to the
Lila Acheson Wallace
Galleries of Egyptian Art

Gallery 21
Dynasties 19-26
Funerary

Mastaba of Pernebi

To the Great Hall

Study Gallery

Study Gallery

Gallery 1
Orientation Area

Elevator
Stairs

Lounge

Gallery 2

Gallery 3
Dynasty 11

Gallery 5
Dynasty 11

Gallery 6
Amenemhat I

Gallery 9
Middle
Kingdom
Meir

Gallery 10
Middle
Kingdom
Lisht

Predynastic Period

Dynasties 1-3

Dynasty 4

Dynasty 5

Dynasty 6

Dynasties 7-10

Gallery 4
Dynasty 11

Gallery 7
Senwosret I

Gallery 8
Dynasty 12–
Early Dynasty 18

Study Gallery

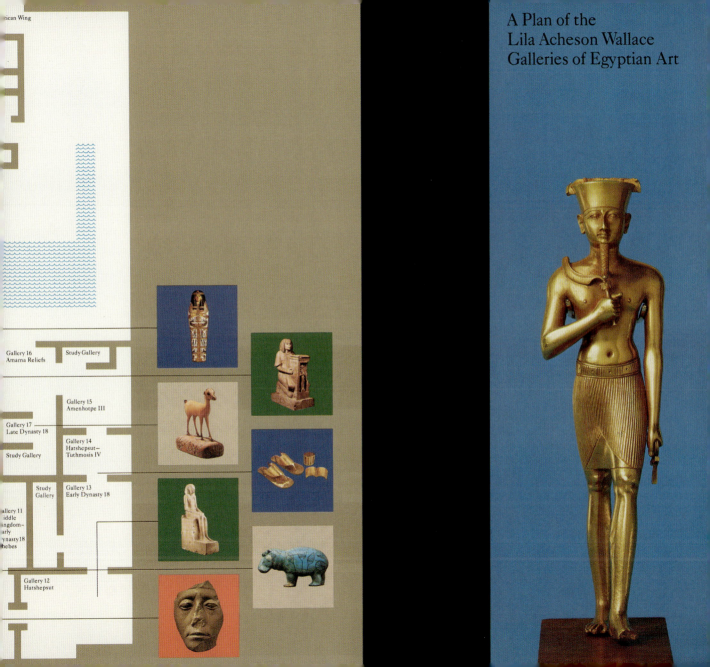

American Wing

A Plan of the
Lila Acheson Wallace
Galleries of Egyptian Art

Gallery 16
Amarna Reliefs

Study Gallery

Gallery 15
Amenhotpe III

Gallery 17
Late Dynasty 18

Gallery 14
Hatshepsut–
Tuthmosis IV

Study Gallery

Study
Gallery

Gallery 13
Early Dynasty 18

Gallery 11
Middle
Kingdom–
Early
Dynasty 18
Thebes

Gallery 12
Hatshepsut

Exhibition research,
planning, programming,
and design; environmental
and interpretive graphics,
André Meyer Galleries
of Nineteenth-Century
European Art, New York City,
The Metropolitan Museum
of Art, 1972–1983.

EDGAR DEGAS
French, 1834-1917

1. DANCER PUTTING ON HER STOCKING
   After 1890 (Millard) ; 1886-1911 (Rewald)
   Bronze cast no. 70/A
   Bequest of Mrs. H. O. Havemeyer, 1929.
   The H. O. Havemeyer Collection
   29.100.381

2. DANCER PUTTING ON HER STOCKING
   After 1890 (Millard) ; 1886-1911 (Rewald)
   Bronze cast no. 29/A
   Bequest of Mrs. H. O. Havemeyer, 1929.
   The H. O. Havemeyer Collection
   29.100.382

3. DANCER PUTTING ON HER STOCKING
   1900-12 (Millard) ; 1896-1911 (Rewald)
   Bronze cast no. 52/A
   Bequest of Mrs. H. O. Havemeyer, 1929.
   The H. O. Havemeyer Collection
   29.100.418

4. DANCER FASTENING THE STRING OF
   HER TIGHTS
   1885-1900 (Millard) ; 1900-05 (Beaulieu) ;
   1882-95 (Rewald)
   Bronze cast no. 33/A
   Bequest of Mrs. H. O. Havemeyer, 1929.
   The H. O. Havemeyer Collection
   29.100.405

5. THE BOW
   After 1890 (Millard) ; 1896-99 (Beaulieu) ;
   1896-1911 (Rewald)
   Bronze cast no. 24/A (actually no. 34 within the set)
   Bequest of Mrs. H. O. Havemeyer, 1929.
   The H. O. Havemeyer Collection
   29.100.410

6. DANCER LOOKING AT
   THE SOLE OF HER

Environmental graphics,
wayfinding, and retail displays,
The Museum Bookstore, New
York City, The Metropolitan
Museum of Art, 1972–1983.

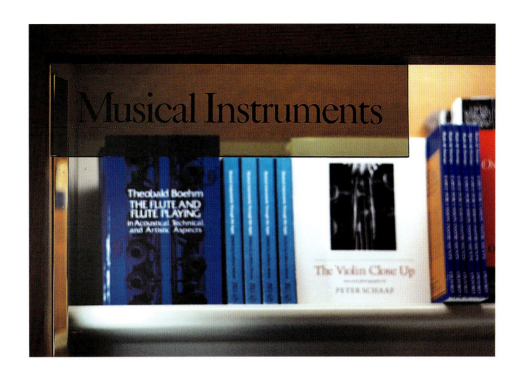

Shopping bag program, The Metropolitan Museum of Art, 1978. With over one million bags printed every year, these eye-catching, iconic shopping bags immediately became an instant success and one of the most visible symbols of 'The Met'. This award-winning solution — the perfect blending of classic typography with Modernist imagery in bright, primary colors — was first introduced with the opening of the renovated and rebranded 'the Bookstore' located off the Museum's Great Hall.

The Met
Museu
of Art

↙ Symbol, Horizon Lighting
Company, 1976

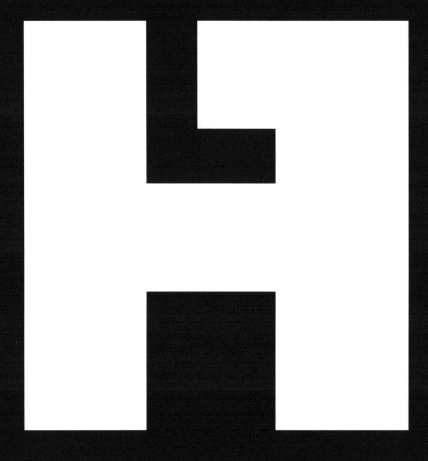

⌄ Symbol, National
Association of Radio and
Television Broadcasters,
c. 1972.

⌄ Symbol, Benrus Watch
 Company, *c.* 1970.

∨ Logotype and typeface,
Benrus Watch Company,
c. 1970.

BENRUS

ABCDE
FGHIJK
LMNOPQ
RSTUVW
XYZ
-123456
7890?&
$()/"",.;!

⌄ Symbol, New York State
Park Commission for the
City of New York, *c.* 1972.

Symbol, Coral Harbour
Resort, 1972.

Logotype, *The Information Bank,* The New York Times, 1972.

THE INFORMATION BANK

Logotype, *International Family Planning Perspectives and Digest*, Alan Guttmacher Institute, 1978.

INTERNATIONAL FAMILY PLANNING PERSPECTIVES AND DIGEST

Logotype, Oyster Bar & Restaurant at Grand Central Station, The Brody Organization, 1974.

Logotype, Commission for
Cultural Affairs of the City of
New York, c. 1973.

commission for
cultural affairs
of the
city of new york

Logotype, *Perspectives*,
Alan Guttmacher Institute,
c. 1973.

Perspectives

Logotype, *Public Relations
Journal*, Public Relations
Society of America, c. 1970.

PUBLIC
RELATIONS
JOURNAL

ˇ Logotype studies,
After Dark, Dance
Magazine, Inc., *c.* 1972.

⌄ Magazine cover,
After Dark, vol. 5, no. 6,
Dance Magazine, Inc.,
October 1972.

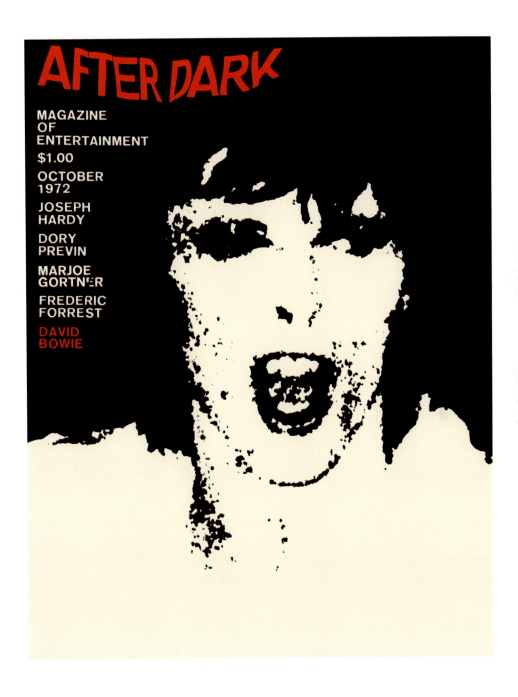

⌄ Magazine cover, *Linea Grafica,* no. 3, Officio Moderne, May/June 1974. For this cover solution, de Harak enlarged typewriter type from a vintage Remington typewriter into monumental, sculptural letterforms. He said that this cover was one of the most exciting solutions he created during the 1970s. He recalled, 'The thing that I loved the most about it is that it is really pure. Each one of those shapes in itself doesn't necessarily mean anything until you see it in relationship to an "n" or an "r". In other words, this doesn't necessarily mean an "a" unless you read the word "graphical"…I also love the fact that they are real loose forms but at the same time they are truly disciplined forms.' [23]

> Magazine cover (detail), *Public Relations Journal,* Public Relations Society of America, May 1977.

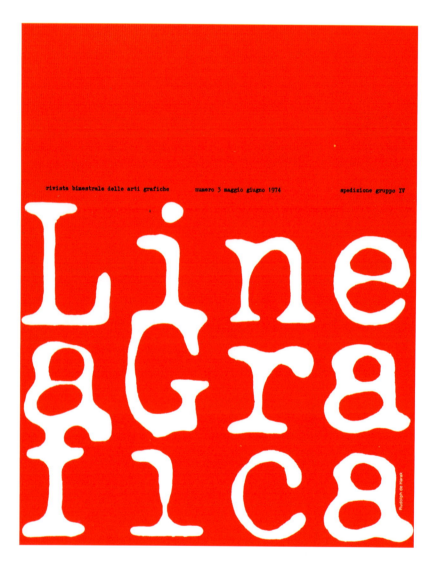

< Magazine cover (detail), *Linea Grafica,* no. 3, Officio Moderne, May/ June 1974.

∨ Magazine cover, *Public Relations Journal,* Public Relations Society of America, May 1977.

Magazine cover, *Public Relations Journal,* Public Relations Society of America, November 1977

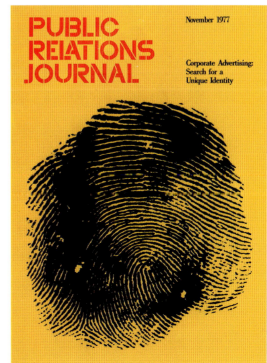

∨ Promotional poster,
AIGA Symbol Signs,
1975. Cook & Shanosky
Associates, designers.

> Research, analysis, and
iconography development,
AIGA Symbol Signs,
AIGA, US Department
of Transportation, 1974.

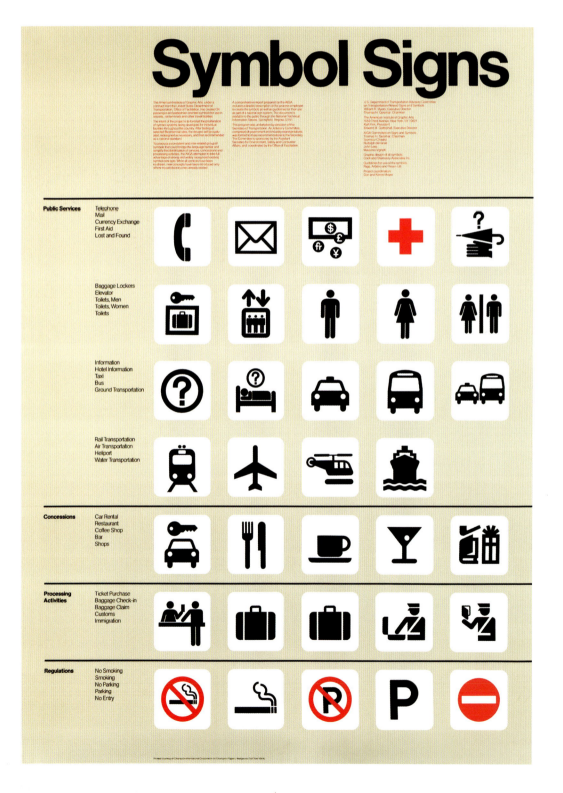

∨ Research, analysis, and
iconography development,
AIGA Symbol Signs,
AIGA, US Department
of Transportation, 1974.

264 | 265

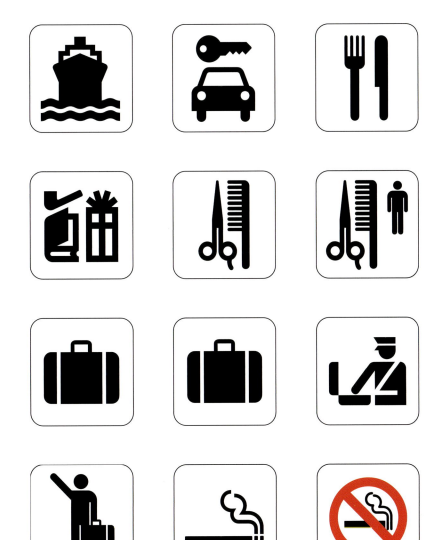
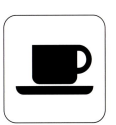
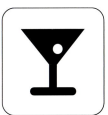
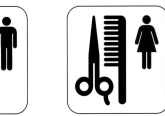
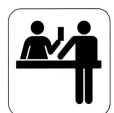
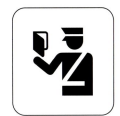
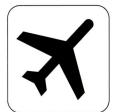
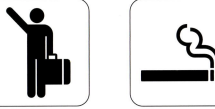
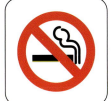
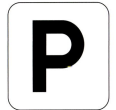
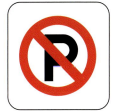
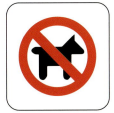
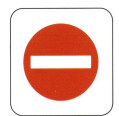
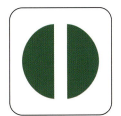
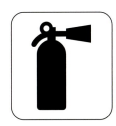
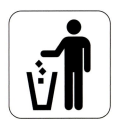

< Fleet graphics, *The New York Times*, 1975. De Harak expressed in a 1987 interview with Steven Heller that this commission was a thrill for him to do: 'Lou Silverstein gave me the assignment. I redrew each letterform and redid the letter spacing to work for this new composition and in a new context and scale.' [24]

∨ Symbol and typeface,
United Nations
Plaza Hotel, United
Nations Development
Corporation (UNDC),
Hyatt International, 1975.
The symbol, which is
suggestive of waving
flags, appeared on all
marketing, promotional,
and advertising print
media.

ABCDEF
GHIJKL
MNOPQR
STUVWX
YZ&

UNITED
NATIONS
PLAZA
HOTEL

One United Nations Plaza
New York, New York 10017
Telephone 212 355 3400
Telex 126803

Managed by Hyatt International Corporation

∨ Guest services brochure,
*United Nations Plaza
Hotel,* United Nations
Plaza Hotel, 1976. Peter
Fink, Charles Gatewood,
Carol Godshalk, James
Joern, photographers.

Recreational Facilities

Year-round swimming, sauna and exercise
facilities; indoor air-conditioned tennis.

Rent-a-Car

For Avis, Budget or Hertz, please call the
Concierge.

Reservation Manager   Dial 1060

Room Information

The United Nations Plaza Hotel has 289
luxury rooms and suites. All with color
television, AM-FM radio, and individually
controlled thermostats for regulating tempera-
ture. Interior design by Roche Dinkeloo and
Associates. Guestrooms and public areas
feature original works of textile art gathered
from all over the world... and a breathtaking
skyline view of Manhattan.

Room Service

From 7 A.M. to midnight. Dial 2.

Safety Deposit Boxes

Available for guests at the front desk.

Sales Office   Dial extension 1029; 1027.

Secretarial Help

Stenographers, typing, transcribing and
copying facilities can be arranged through
the Concierge.

Security Service

Additional personal security may be
arranged by calling the Assistant Manager.
Existing security measures in the house may
be explained in detail by calling the Chief of
Security. Extension 1003, 1004.

Shoe Shine

Overnight service; morning returns. Dial 5.

Shopping

You are not far from fashionable Fifth
Avenue or the marvelous boutiques of
Madison Avenue.

Sightseeing Tours

Individual and group tours, by foot, car, bus,
helicopter or yacht. Experienced guides
can show you through the United Nations,
the Empire State Building, Greenwich
Village, Chinatown, the Statue of Liberty,
Lincoln Center, Harlem, Wall Street, Radio
City, NBC Studios, Museums, and
Manhattan By Night. Special language tours
can be arranged with a seven-hour notice.
Call the Concierge.

Stock Exchange Quotations

Channel 10 on your room cable-television.
Daily quotes and business headlines are
teletyped from 10:15 A.M. to 4:15 P.M.

Tobacco Shop

Adjacent to main lobby. International
selection of cigars, cigarettes, candy,
magazines, toilet articles and newspapers.
Excellent variety of softcover books.

Translation Services   Call the Concierge.

Transportation

Information on local tours, airlines, bus and
train schedules and subway directions. Call
the Concierge.

Telecommunications

We are pleased to accommodate you with
facilities for Telex, Telegram and Mailgram
communications for a minimal fee. Call the
Assistant Manager. Dial 1.

Telex: 126803   Cable: UNPLAZATEL

Theatre Tickets   Call the Concierge.

Turtle Bay Tennis & Swim Club   Dial 18

Valet and Laundry

Same-day service, Monday through Friday.
In by 8:30 A.M. returned by 7:00 P.M. Dial.

Voltage: 110

Environmental graphics and
wayfinding, United Nations
Plaza Hotel, New York City,
United Nations Development
Corporation (UNDC),
Hyatt International, 1975.

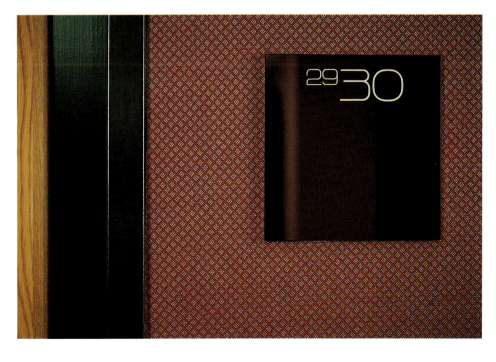

∨ Postage stamp and
envelope, *USA 2C
Authorized Non-Profit
Organization,* United
States Postal Service,
1976. This two-cent
envelope was designed
for use in bulk mailings by
non-profit organizations,
with an embossed stamp
of a stylized five-pointed
star on a pinwheel
background.

⌄ Symbol, Symbiosis, Inc.,
  1979.

SYMBIOSIS, INC.   Post Office Box 177M   Bay Shore, New York 11706   212 674 2332

SYMBIOSIS, INC.   Post Office Box 177M   Bay Shore, New York 11706

∨ Symbol, *Alan Guttmacher Institute*, 1973. Located in New York City and Washington, DC, the Alan Guttmacher Institute is a leading research and policy non-profit organization committed to advancing sexual and reproductive health and rights throughout the world, disseminating research across associated fields.

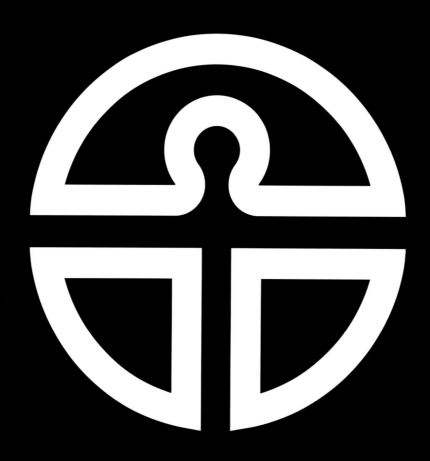

∨ Magazine cover,
Perspectives, vol. 8, no. 3,
Alan Guttmacher Institute,
May/June 1976.

Family Planning

Perspectives

Volume 8, Number 3, May/June 1976

Number and Timing Failures Among U.S. Legitimate Births, 1968-1972
Trends in Attitudes Toward Abortion, 1972-1975
The Bad Old Days: Clandestine Abortions Among New York's Poor

Family Planning Program Effects on the Fertility of Low-Income U.S. Women

⌄ Magazine cover,
Perspectives, vol. 8, no. 6,
Alan Guttmacher Institute,
November/December
1976.

Family Planning

Perspectives

Volume 8, Number 6, November/December 1976

Teenage Income and Clinic Fees
Organized Family Planning Services in the United States: FY 1975
The Specification of Fertility Planning Status
Women's Organizations: A Resource for Family Planning and Development

Abortion Utilization: Does Travel Distance Matter?

Magazine cover,
Perspectives, vol. 8, no. 4,
Alan Guttmacher Institute,
July/August 1976.

Magazine cover,
Perspectives, vol. 11, no. 3,
Alan Guttmacher Institute,
May/June 1979.

Magazine cover,
Perspectives, vol. 8, no. 1,
Alan Guttmacher Institute,
January/February 1976.

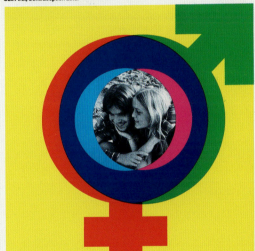

Family Planning
Perspectives
Volume 8, Number 4, July/August 1976

SPECIAL ISSUE: Teenagers USA

The Social and Economic Consequences of Teenage Childbearing
Contraception, Abortion, and Taking Chances
Fertility Control Services: Access and Use
Sex First, Contraception Later

Family Planning
Perspectives
Volume 11, Number 3, May/June 1979

Unintended Pregnancies in the United States, 1970-1972
Informed Consent for Fertility Control Services
Cigarette Smoking and Reproductive Health
Probabilities of Intercourse and Conception Among U.S. Teenagers

Sterilization in the United States

Family Planning
Perspectives
Volume 8, Number 1, January/February 1976

Pregnancy, Teenagers and the Law: 1976
Early Vacuum Aspiration: Minimizing Procedures to Nonpregnant Women
Expenditures for U.S. Family Planning Services
Abortion Referral in Federally Funded Family Planning Programs

Mortality Associated with the Control of Fertility

⌄ Magazine cover,
 Perspectives, vol. 10, no. 1,
 Alan Guttmacher Institute,
 January/February 1978.

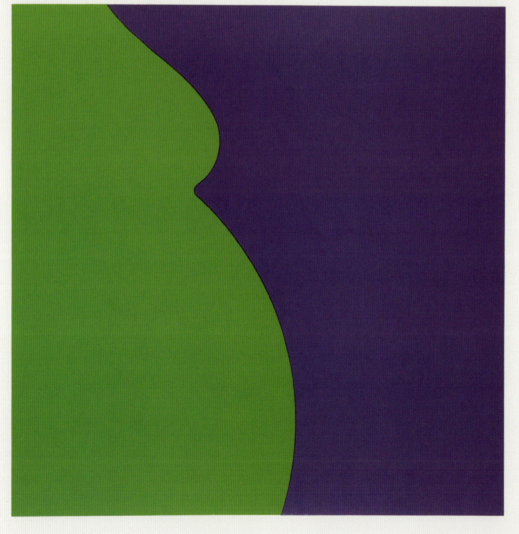

Illuminating Engineering Society
of North America

Howard Brandston
President
1983-84

141 West 24th Street
New York, New York 10011
212 924 4050

Illuminating Engineering Society
of North America

Howard Brandston
141 West 24th Street
New York, New York 10011

< Exploded engine (detail),
  Cummins Engine
  Corporate Museum,
  Columbus, Indiana,
  Cummins Engine Company,
  1983.

For many Americans, the 1980s symbolized a new beginning, epitomized by the election of Ronald Reagan as the fortieth President of the United States. It was also an era in which the majority of Americans were increasingly seen, even by themselves, as self-centered and materialistic. While Reagan, a former Hollywood actor with a reassuring disposition and optimistic style, appealed to most conservatives, his administration would become well-known for creating the worst recession since the Great Depression, and a federal government that accumulated more debt during his tenure than any other time in the twentieth century.

'Decades are like people,' wrote Frank Bruni, American journalist and op-ed columnist for *The New York Times*. 'Some take up more oxygen than others. The 1980s were that way, most notably at the start and especially in New York City ... People lived louder and larger than they had just years before.' [1] While the city slowly made its comeback from near financial disaster in the late 1970s, it also started to clean up its proverbial act. Gentrification and renewal were now seen as a means to improve lives throughout the city, yet they also deepened its inequalities, with an impact that would be felt for generations to come. New York City was also often seen as an epicenter for tragedy and social unrest during this time period. In December 1980, legendary British songwriter and activist John Lennon was assassinated, sending shock waves throughout the city and around the world. Grief-stricken New Yorkers stood vigil for days following the shooting, which took place in front of Lennon's place

∨ Rudolph de Harak &
Associates Inc. at
320 West 13th Street,
New York City, c. 1981.
Deborah Kushma,
photographer.

of residence, The Dakota, located on Manhattan's Upper West Side. By the end of the 1989, the AIDS crisis, which had largely been ignored by Reagan and his administration, reached new heights with approximately 100,000 deaths, many in New York City. In response, a multicultural group of New Yorkers created ACT UP (AIDS Coalition to Unleash Power) in 1987, a grassroots faction of political activists working to end the pandemic and to improve the lives of people with AIDS through direct action, medical research, treatment, and advocacy.

The decade also became known for 'style over substance' — not only in politics, but in popular culture and the design disciplines. Throughout the 1980s, European Modernism and the International Style continued to unravel, as its influence waned and its basic tenets came under scrutiny. Freed from its supposed confines, designers had the opportunity to forge radical new forms of visual expression and communication, many of which, perhaps ironically, incorporated visual elements and references culled from history. Under the banner of Postmodernism, an amalgamation of graphic styles, typefaces, visual clutter, and chaos abounded. In graphic design, the groundbreaking work of designers such as Edward Fella, Neville Brody, Dan Friedman, April Greiman, and Wolfgang Weingart now took center stage. In the built environment, American architects Michael Graves' Portland Building in Portland, Oregon and Philip Johnson and John Burgee's AT&T Building in New York City quickly became seminal examples of early Postmodernist architecture. New technologies also fueled this movement of freedom and self-expression, in particular the introduction of the Apple Macintosh computer in 1984, the success of which was accelerated by the advent of desktop-publishing software programs a year later. Coupled with the creative opportunities offered by Postmodernism, the creative possibilities for graphic designers now seemed limitless.

At the beginning of the 1980s, de Harak expanded and relocated his design consultancy to a renovated loft building in the West Village of Manhattan. American author Steven Heller, remembering his first visit to this new office space, described it as, 'bright, airy, and very spacious. What hits you immediately as you step in is that everything is white and uncluttered. Much like a blank sheet of paper on de Harak's desk, it is pristine and prepared to leap into the realm of creativity with one well-thought-out stroke of his pen.' [2] With more studio space and an increased number of staff designers, de Harak was now positioned to take on a more multifaceted set of new challenges and creative opportunities. Due to his extensive work and successful collaboration with Kevin Roche and the Roche Dinkeloo office on The Metropolitan Museum of Art's renovation and expansion during the 1970s, other world-renowned architects throughout the United States started to reach out to de Harak, looking to establish working relationships and offering him opportunities to join their design teams. Within a few years, he would be working with numerous offices, including Edward Larabee Barnes Associates; Beyer Blinder Belle; Davis Brody and Associates; Gruzen & Partners; Gwathmey Siegel & Associates Architects; Kohn Pedersen Fox Associates; Pei Cobb Freed & Partners; Cesar Pelli & Associates; James Stewart Polshek and Partners; John Portman & Associates; Skidmore, Owings & Merrill; Robert A.M. Stern Architects; and Edward Durrell Stone Jr and Associates.

The 1980s was to be a transitional period for de Harak. By the end of the decade, every major aspect of his professional and personal life would change — his practice, his teaching, his connection to graphic design, and his pursuit of self-expression and creative fulfillment.

Exhibitions and Museums

Within the first year of the new decade, de Harak received several commissions that added to his already extensive roster of exhibition and museum projects. The first was the temporary retrospective exhibition 'Rufus Porter Rediscovered: Artist, Inventor, Journalist 1792–1884', on view at the Hudson River Museum in Yonkers, New York, from April to July 1980. Porter was an early nineteenth-century American polymath — an inventor, folk artist, engineer, and journalist — who was known for airship designs, mechanical patents, and small watercolor portraits, and who, in 1845, founded *Scientific American*, America's oldest continuously published magazine.

De Harak's design solution for this 372 sq m (4,000 sq ft) temporary exhibition was a study in contrasts and scales. He chose to mount Porter's collection of miniature paintings, patent drawings, and technical writings in a series of small-scale, rear-illuminated display cubes located in the exhibition's entry gallery. In another gallery, one of Porter's few remaining fanciful panoramic rural landscape murals was photographed with a large-format camera, and the resulting image of a rural landscape was installed at full-size to evoke the period room in which it had originally been located. To further simulate the scale and architectural character of this room, de Harak introduced both a translucent, stretched fabric to lower the gallery's ceiling height, and line drawings of wood paneling and wainscoting, which were silkscreened onto the gallery walls to give the viewer a more intimate and realistic experience. Home furnishings and a camera obscura, which Porter had used to produce an accurate likeness of his subjects, were displayed in adjoining galleries. For the exhibition's promotional poster, de Harak used an image of a glass negative of a Rufus Porter photographic self-portrait from the early 1870s. This poster received several design awards and recognitions at the time, and is in the design collections of the Los Angeles County Museum of Art (LACMA) and the Museum of Modern Art (MoMA).

The following year, de Harak designed a temporary exhibition entitled 'A Romance With the City: Irwin S. Chanin', which celebrated the achievements of the New York City-based builder, developer, architect, engineer, financier, and philanthropist. The exhibition was organized by Cooper Union's The Irwin S. Chanin School of Architecture to honor one of its most distinguished graduates. Chanin's contributions to New York City were extraordinary. From the 1920s through the 1940s, he built eight Broadway theaters, as well as the Roxy and Beacon movie palaces and two twin-towered Art Moderne apartment houses — the Majestic and the Century, both on Central Park West. One of his most iconic buildings, the Chanin Building, still stands at the southwest corner of 42nd Street and Lexington Avenue in Midtown Manhattan and remains one of the preeminent examples of American Art Deco. Yet Chanin had more than just a financial interest in his real estate holdings. He played a significant role in all of his projects, and was intimately involved in every detail due to his architectural training, making him an anomaly amongst most real estate developers.

The 167 sq m (1,800 sq ft) exhibition, curated by architect and theorist Diana Agrest, was on view at the Arthur A. Houghton Jr Gallery at Cooper Union from November 1982 to January 1983. It was a memorable combination of retrospective materials, including sepia photographs and rear-illuminated transparencies of Chanin-designed buildings and interiors, mounted on display panels with clear acrylic facias. The largest element within the exhibition was a set of ornamental entrance gates from Chanin's Manhattan office, while ornate Art Deco radiator grilles from the Chanin Building were presented in a large display vitrine. Other displays included Chanin-designed furniture, including upholstered chairs and side tables, and personal memorabilia. A promotional poster and an accompanying 112-page catalog, both designed by de Harak, were produced to coincide with the exhibition, the latter including new contemporary color photography by renowned photographer Roberto Schezen.

That same year, de Harak was invited by The Government of the Philippines and New York City-based architects Beyer Blinder Belle to collaborate with them on the design of the Philippine Pavilion at the 1982 World's Fair, held from May to October in Knoxville, Tennessee. He actively participated in the curatorial selection of all exhibition material for the pavilion, including contemporary and traditional Philippine art and artifacts such as masks, grave markers, hats, hand-woven fabrics, and a large 'vinta' sailboat. The largest item displayed was a military transport vehicle-cum-taxi dating from World War II when these vehicles were still a typical sight on the streets of Manila. Alongside object and artifact-driven stories, de Harak developed visual stories on the history, geography, and people of the Philippines. These were depicted on rear-illuminated panels and wall-mounted displays that included photographs and interpretive text. The 1982 World's Fair, formally known as the Knoxville International Energy Exposition with the theme of 'Energy Turns the World', attracted over eleven million visitors to its 280,000 sq m (70-acre) site located between downtown Knoxville and the University of Tennessee campus. The fair's main structure, the Sunsphere — an 81 m (266 ft) high steel tower topped with a five-story gold globe — has become a symbol for the city.

All three of these exhibition projects further honed de Harak's storytelling skills, particularly when it came to bringing space, time, and sequence together in the built environment. These experiences also laid the conceptual groundwork for his next commissions, which were to change the trajectory of his career and enhance his stature as a designer — but, more importantly, confirm his mastery as a visual storyteller. In 1982, de Harak was asked by architect Kevin Roche to help develop corporate museums for three headquarters

⌄ Preliminary study model
   of General Foods
   Collection exhibition
   galleries, 1983.

projects that Roche Dinkeloo was currently designing for General Foods Corporation in Rye Brook, New York; Conoco Inc. in Houston, Texas; and Cummins Engine Company in Columbus, Indiana. These major commissions would ultimately advance not only de Harak's design consultancy, but more importantly, his legacy within the world of graphic design.

Master Visual Storyteller

The General Foods Corporate Museum, subsequently known as the General Foods Collection, was conceived and organized by de Harak as a timeless celebration of food, achieved through the interpretation and presentation of implements and objects related to four major food functions — processing, preparation, storage, and serving. Senior management at the company had initially conceived the museum as a collection of advertising and packaging memorabilia from their various brands, which ranged from Birds Eye Frozen Foods and Maxwell House Coffee to Jell-O and Log Cabin Syrup. De Harak, however, had an alternative vision for the 372 sq m (4,000 sq ft) space on the fourth floor of their new headquarters. He ultimately convinced them that a collection of food-related objects and implements would better celebrate not only their brands, but also, and more importantly, the intimate relationship that their customers had with these products.

Over one thousand food-related items were collected and catalogued — including baskets, plates, platters, grinders, scrapers, graters, churns, cups, and spoons — from across different cultures and periods. These were used to communicate the story of food throughout history, with their individual attributes or contrasts between them highlighted. De Harak and his designers were responsible for the initial research, concept development, curatorial and interpretive planning, collection acquisition, design, documentation, and installation of the project. The Collection's main exhibition gallery displayed objects and implements in linear floor-to-ceiling display casework that undulated 28.35 m (93 ft) along one wall. Sectioned, tempered glass panels, which fitted into floor and ceiling grooves, fronted this casework. This gallery also contained two large island glass cases, each 5.5 x 1.8 m (18 x 6 ft), one at either end of the space, which ran parallel to its central axis. Located in the center of the main exhibition gallery were eight pedestal-mounted vitrines, which displayed an evolving selection of material from the Collection. Angling off either end of the gallery were public corridors with wall-mounted casework for temporary exhibitions.

This temporary exhibition program changed on a biannual basis, and explored specific food themes, including 'Thought for Food', 'Food in Folk Art', and 'The Extension of the Hand'. Associated objects and implements highlighted particular attributes or contrasts relevant to the particular theme, and were accompanied by interpretive exhibition texts, imagery, and brochures. 'Thought for Food' was an exhibition of

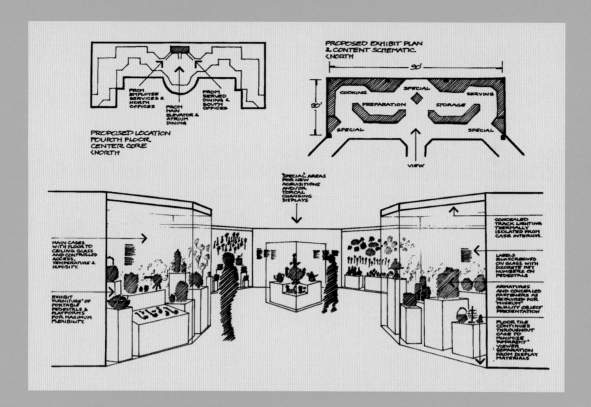

cookery books from Roman times to the present. 'Food in Folk Art' celebrated the decorative artistry inspired by foodstuffs. 'The Extension of the Hand' focused the viewer's attention on the many varieties of handheld utensils and objects used in the preparation and serving of food throughout history.

In addition to these exhibitions and their accompanying brochures, de Harak was also commissioned to design a comprehensive environmental graphics and wayfinding sign program for the General Foods Corporate Headquarters. Taken as a whole, de Harak's work for the company not only enriched its work environment, but also conveyed the universal and multifaceted relationship between food and world culture to those working in or visiting its headquarters building.

Located in its new Houston headquarters, the Conoco Corporate Museum was intended to celebrate the progressive nature of the company's attitude toward the technological, environmental, and human aspects of energy exploration and development. This 465 sq m (5,000 sq ft) permanent museum exhibition commemorated Conoco's one-hundred-year history, and illustrated the important role the company and its employees had played in the history and development of the petroleum industry in the United States and beyond. Sections were included on early advertising and marketing, exploration tools and measurement devices, the science and development of drill bits, and the history of the Ponca Native American tribe and its critical contributions to Conoco and its development. Exhibition content collected over the years by employees, business colleagues, and friends was used to further enhance the visitor experience. As at the General Foods Corporate Museum, de Harak and his designers were responsible for the initial research, thematic development, curatorial and interpretive planning, collection acquisition, design, documentation, artifact mounting, and installation at the museum, as well as the design of its museum catalog. Again, a comprehensive environmental graphics

< Preliminary interior
sketches of General
Foods Collection
exhibition galleries, 1983.

∨ De Harak's initial sketch
of the 'exploded engine',
1983.

and wayfinding sign program was also implemented throughout the new headquarters building.

Completed in 1983, the Cummins Corporate Office Building in downtown Columbus, Indiana, sits in an old railroad yard, and surrounds the company's first factory and administrative office building — the Cerealine Building — a late-nineteenth-century cereal mill since converted into an employee cafeteria and training center. The Cummins Engine Corporate Museum highlighted the past, present, and future of one of the world's leading engine-producing companies, enhancing the new headquarters' work environment and celebrating the company's history, from its beginnings in 1919 to the present. Employees, tour groups, architectural students, and clients were able to view a collection of restored early engines, including the first diesel-powered race car to run the Indianapolis 500 back in 1952; a video presentation showing the race car in action; cranks and camshafts; models of diesel engines currently in production; and a video and timeline of the company's history. The museum's centerpiece was — and remains — the company's largest diesel engine, disassembled into approximately 440 parts, and suspended in tension and in relation to each other by stainless-steel cables. The deconstructed engine appears to be floating in mid-air as if it is about to be reassembled within the two-story exhibition space — de Harak called it an 'exploded' diesel engine. The presence of this unique centerpiece, alongside a changing display of the company's current diesel engine line, gave the museum an additional function as a hands-on product marketing center for the company.

Throughout his career, de Harak always looked to reduce visual elements to their most fundamental. In many ways it was the ultimate goal in his approach to rational simplicity. Being simpler didn't necessarily mean the end result would be less profound.

The museum covered over 650 sq m (7,000 sq ft), and highlighted the relationship between the company's product — diesel engines — and its dedication to timeless design, as evidenced by both the engines themselves and the new headquarters building itself. To achieve this, industrial equipment was taken out of the manufacturing shop and treated as an art form.

In summarizing de Harak's masterful approach at the Cummins Engine Corporate Museum, and in his wider exhibition design work, Steven Heller wrote that 'presenting histories and stories became de Harak's prime talent and greatest pleasure. [It] is not only a masterpiece of corporate culture, but of retelling — what de Harak refers to as "real people's stories". He interviewed scores of Cummins workers to develop the museum's content. With the exploded engine as a dynamic focal point, de Harak created a living testament to the company's commitment to progress through artful displays that pull in history and contemporary practice without a hint of nostalgia. The combination of de Harak's Modernism and eclecticism are fully realized . . . He always referred to himself as a storyteller, so exhibition design was a logical direction and his most exceptional . . . and likewise his inspired exhibition designs for museums and expositions have transformed didactic displays into engaging environments. Dedicated to the efficient communication of information, de Harak uses detail the way a composer scores musical notes, creating melodies of sensation to underscore meaning. His exhibits are indeed symphonies that both enlighten and entertain.' [3]

A Growing Multidisciplinary Practice

Although these three major museum commissions tended to be all-encompassing and time-consuming, de Harak was also intent on making sure his now expanded design consultancy would still be able to take on a diverse body of work which included a multitude of print-related, branding and identity, publication, and environmental graphic design projects.

In 1980, de Harak began a long-term working relationship with John Hejduk, the dean of The Irwin S. Chanin School of Architecture, when he was asked to design several publications to coincide with its exhibition programs at the Arthur A. Houghton Jr Gallery, located in Cooper Union's Foundation Building in Greenwich Village. The first was a book on the life and work of Richard Stein, a New York City-based architect and faculty member of the School of Architecture from 1946 to 1990. Stein was well-known for his pioneering research in energy-conserving design and its applications in the building industry, but also notable for the furniture he designed in 1939 for hospitals, schools, housing, and other public facilities in New York State, when working for Walter Gropius and Marcel Breuer. *Richard Stein: Forty Years of Architectural Work*, a fifty-six-page monograph, was comprised of photographs, drawings, and narrative descriptions of both built and unbuilt projects. During this period, de Harak also designed an intimate, small-scale twenty-page exhibition catalog, *Michael Wurmfeld: European Travel Sketches 1963, 1964, 1965, 1970*, to coincide with an installation of sketchbooks by Michael Wurmfeld, a New York City-based architect and faculty member of the School of Architecture from 1972 to 1984.

The following year, the United States Postal Service approached de Harak with an unexpected request to design a commemorative stamp marking the centennial of the beginning of professional management education in the United States. The Professional Management Education Centenary Issue, an 18-cent stamp, was released on 18 June 1981 in Philadelphia, Pennsylvania, illustrated by Clarence Holbert, an engraver at the United States Bureau of Engraving and Printing, and designed by de Harak. On unveiling the stamp at the 1980 Postal Forum XIV, the Postmaster General, William F. Bolger, noted that the stamp's issuance date coincided with the centenary of the Wharton School of Business, 'where the principles of business education were founded for the entire nation.' [4] Joseph Wharton was an American manufacturer and industrialist, and anticipated the need for formal business

∨ Rudolph de Harak,
New York City, c. 1985.
Carol de Harak,
photographer.

education twenty years before the idea was implemented by any other institution. The stamp was printed in photogravure process and issued in panes of fifty stamps per sheet.

In 1984, IBM Corporation's lavish British-American made-for-television film adaptation of Charles Dickens's 1843 holiday classic, *A Christmas Carol*, starring Oscar-winning actor George C. Scott provided de Harak with another creative challenge, and one he drew on for both his unique point-of-view and his visual storytelling skills. *A Christmas Carol Christmas Book* was initially conceived as a commemorative publication for IBM clients and employees; however, de Harak proposed broadening its appeal by adding specific sections to the 160-page, full-color, hardbound book. He expanded it from a mere presentation of a movie script with accompanying stills, to include a biography of Dickens; a chapter on Victorian holiday crafts and traditions; a selection of holiday recipes and games from Dickens's time; a selection of traditional carols; a section on the custom of caroling, and the complete text of *A Christmas Carol*. These additional narratives were made richer by the use of monochromatic engravings and color drawings from the Victorian era; reproductions of pages from Dickens's handwritten manuscript, accompanied by the original illustrations by renowned British artist and caricaturist John Leech; and patterned end papers from the same time period. *A Christmas Carol Christmas Book* was so successful that a subsequent edition was released by publisher Little Brown & Company for distribution and purchase in bookstores nationwide during the holiday season.

In the 1960s, de Harak had been one of the first graphic designers to prompt the graphic design and architectural professions to collectively embrace the essential importance of graphic design in the built environment. By the 1980s, he was recognized as one of the leaders of the emerging design discipline of environmental graphic design (later to be known as experiential design). As a result, he was asked by leading architects to assist them in the development of comprehensive environmental graphics and wayfinding sign programs for a number of commercial office, public institutions, and cultural buildings including One Summit Square in Fort Wayne, Indiana; Owens-Illinois World Headquarters in Toledo, Ohio; Paradise Island Resort and Casino in Nassau, Bahamas; and the Grand Hyatt New York and The Main Research Libraries of the New York Public Library, both in New York City; and a multitude of New York office and mixed-use developments, including 31 West 52nd Street, 599 Lexington, 1585 Broadway, 712 Fifth Avenue, 750 Seventh Avenue, and World Financial Center.

World Financial Center (now known as Brookfield Place) is a large-scale, mixed-use, commercial real estate development project built on landfill from the construction of the adjoining World Trade Center, and covers a six-block area in Lower Manhattan. Developed by Olympia & York Properties, designed by American architects Cesar Pelli & Associates, and completed in 1988, World Financial Center revised the Manhattan skyline with its distinctive office towers, which form the west wall of Battery Park City. The 827,000 sq m (8,900,000 sq ft) complex consists of four commercial office towers, ranging in height from thirty-four to fifty-one stories; the Winter Garden, a glass-roofed public atrium; two nine-story octagonal gateway buildings; a retail mall; a landscaped public plaza and marina; and an esplanade along the Hudson River. Over the years, it has been the home to American Express, Deloitte, Merrill Lynch, Oppenheimer & Co., and the *Wall Street Journal*. This large-scale commission was awarded to de Harak and his design consultancy following an extensive interview process that involved twelve graphic design firms located throughout the United States. The four-year-long project culminated with a comprehensive environmental graphics and wayfinding sign program for all public areas of the complex, including identification for building tenants, sign requirements for exterior and interior public spaces, identification criteria for commercial and retail tenants, and an overall public orientation and directional system. De Harak's essential goal for this program was the integration of sign with architecture, as was the selection of typography, materials, profiles, and colors that all responded to the architectural vocabulary of the buildings. The project provided a unique opportunity to work closely with Cesar Pelli & Associates in developing a design solution that achieved a strong and integral relationship with a variety of architectural elements, forms, and conditions.

For over twenty years, Davis Brody and Associates served as the design architect for the restoration, adaptive reuse, and expansion of The Main Research Libraries of the New York Public Library, often cited as one of the five greatest libraries in the world. The landmark Beaux-Arts building was designed by American architects Carrère and Hastings and completed in 1911. A comprehensive master plan was initiated by Davis Brody and Associates in early 1980, and completed two decades later. De Harak and his design consultancy were invited to be part of their project team, responsible for developing an extensive environmental graphics, wayfinding, and donor recognition program for all newly renovated and restored, interior public spaces. This program included identification signs for all interior public spaces and library services, as well as informational and directional signs to facilitate their use by the general public. An extensive donor recognition program was also developed to facilitate and support the Library's fundraising efforts. De Harak's design solution involved the reapplication and reintroduction of the original typographic materials and methods that had been used throughout the landmark Beaux-Arts building when it first opened — these were found to be as effective and appropriate as they had been when the building first opened in 1911.

Another unusual and equally challenging commission came from Mount Sinai Medical Center's Patient Representative Department in New York City. Developed in cooperation with medical center staff and funded by research grants from a major philanthropic organization, the Robert Wood Johnson Foundation, Communi-Card was a visual communication tool that facilitated essential communication between speech-impaired patients, their family members, and clinical staff. Color-coded, easy-to-understand informational pictograms located on the front of a laminated card were developed to identify patients' symptoms and their medical, physical, and emotional needs, as well as to indicate specific health-care professionals with whom the patient wished to speak. A typographic alphabet was provided on the back of the card for the patient, caregiver, or family member to use in spelling out simple words or messages, along with a simplified human figure to help indicate locations of a physical problem. The card also contained

simple, one-word questions in English and in a second language, such as Spanish, Russian, or Japanese. Communi-Card was used in over 150 hospitals and health-care facilities throughout the United States and Canada. Based on the success of this innovative visual communication tool, a subsequent card, Communi-Card 2, was developed for cardiac patients communicating with hospital staff in emergency room and special care unit settings.

Due to the diversity and success of these projects, de Harak and his expanded practice became well-known as one of the most successful multidisciplinary design consultancies in the country.

Endings and New Beginnings

By the mid-1980s, the business and profession of graphic design were very different from when de Harak first started his small design studio in 1952. Now, thirty-five years later, his office, design staff, and clients came with increased demands and responsibilities, including project management, billing, collections, profit margins, marketing, human resources, and a reliance on new digital technologies. While he still experienced levels of personal fulfillment amidst this success, the constant challenges began to outweigh the positives. He started to re-evaluate everything about his role in the design consultancy, and about what was now important to him and to his personal and creative fulfillment. Whether he realized it or not, he was actually beginning to conceptualize and design the next chapter of his professional and personal life.

One of his first steps came in April 1986, when de Harak informed Cooper Union that, after thirty-four years, he would not be returning the following semester. Responding to de Harak's resignation, Bill N. Lacy, the President of Cooper Union, wrote that 'your presence here over the many years, both on the adjunct and full-time faculty, lent real stature to our design program and to the school as a whole. You will be sorely missed. Your international reputation as a designer has been an important part of Cooper Union's strong reputation. When the school received the endowment to establish the "Frank Stanton Professor of Graphic Design", it was a stroke of luck that you were here to be its first recipient and to give luster to the position. The publications and exhibitions you designed here

> De Harak with Massimo Vignelli (*right*) at Rochester Institute of Technology's 'Coming of Age: The First Symposium on the History of Graphic Design', Rochester, New York, April 1983.

∨ De Harak fishing on Saltaire, Fire Island, New York, c. 1984. Carol de Harak, photographer.

brought acclaim to the school and to the quality of the work done here. You always kept the school in touch with the most up-to-date developments in the design world, and you were in every respect a model of professionalism to your students and colleagues, someone everyone could be proud to emulate. I know that future generations of students are going to miss your conscientious attention, your good humor, your infectious dedication to good design, to good teaching, and to their personal growth and development.' [5]

Having taught at Cooper Union since 1952, de Harak had now made the difficult decision to start pursuing new creative challenges and modes of self-expression. While he stopped teaching in the traditional setting of the classroom environment, over the next few years he continued to share his experiences, knowledge, and insights enthusiastically with graphic design students and professionals throughout the country. In the later part of the 1980s, de Harak was invited to give numerous workshops and lectures at prominent educational institutions, including Alfred University in Alfred, New York; Maryland Institute of Art in Baltimore, Maryland; Rochester Institute of Technology (RIT) in Rochester, New York; and the University of Kansas in Lawrence, Kansas.

At the beginning of 1987, de Harak announced that his design consultancy, Rudolph de Harak & Associates Inc., was changing its name to de Harak & Poulin Associates Inc. This change was prompted by my own promotion to managing partner. In addition to my primary role as a Creative Director, I was now responsible for all creative and business aspects of the firm, including project direction, financial management, and business development. I had joined de Harak in 1981 as a designer and project director, was made an Associate in 1984, and a full partner in 1986.

In 1989, to honor his forty-year career, the Art Directors Club (ADC) inducted de Harak into its illustrious Hall of Fame, founded in 1971 to recognize those who have attained the highest standards of creative excellence in and made significant contributions to visual communications. In receiving this honor, de Harak was joining an elite group that includes, among others, Andy Warhol, Walt Disney, Charles and Ray Eames, Annie Leibovitz, Norman Rockwell, and Jim Henson, all honored for demonstrating outstanding artistry and craftsmanship throughout their careers.

As the 1980s came to a close, de Harak and his wife Carol finalized their decision to leave New York City, retire from full-time work, and relocate to the coast of Maine. They moved to a new home that they themselves had designed and built. Here, de Harak could devote himself to the creative pursuits that he had enjoyed forty years earlier when starting his career — abstract painting, black-and-white photography, and playing jazz saxophone. Later, when asked about his new way of life and surroundings, he considered his response for a moment and said, 'coming up here and being on the water and being amongst the trees . . . it gave me some calm'. [6]

1. Frank Bruni, 'New York City, 1981–1983: 36 Months that Changed the Culture', T: *The New York Times Style Magazine,* 17 April 2018, p. 1.
2. Steven Heller, 'ADC Hall of Fame: Rudolph de Harak', ADC, 1989, http://adcglobal.org/hall-of-fame/rudolph-de-harak/
3. Steven Heller, '1992 AIGA Medalist: Rudolph de Harak', AIGA, 02 September 1992, https://epi.aiga.org/medalist-rudolphdeharak
4. Postal Bulletin, *Professional Management Education Centenary Issue,* 14 February 1981.
5. Bill Lacy, letter acknowledging Rudolph de Harak's resignation from Cooper Union, April 1986.
6. Rudolph de Harak, 'Oral History Interview with Rudolph de Harak,' interview by Susan Larsen, 27 April 2000 (transcript), in Ellsworth, Maine. Archives of American Art, Smithsonian Institution, Washington, DC.
7. Rudolph de Harak, quote from *Connections* poster, Simpson Paper Company, 1987.

< Promotional poster,
*Rufus Porter
Rediscovered: Artist,
Inventor, Journalist
1792–1884,* The Hudson
River Museum, 1980.
The Museum of Modern
Art (MoMA) Design
Collection, New York.

Temporary exhibition and
interpretive graphics,
'Rufus Porter Rediscovered:
Artist, Inventor, Journalist
1792–1884', The Hudson
River Museum, Yonkers,
New York, 1980.

Temporary exhibition and
interpretive graphics, 'Irwin
S. Chanin: A Romance with
the City', Cooper Union,
The Irwin S. Chanin School
of Architecture, New York
City, 1982.

A Romance with the City
Irwin S. Chanin

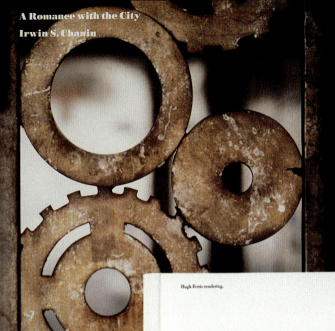

Hugh Ferris rendering.

From the Regional
Plan of New York and
its Environs, 1931.
Proposed Art Center
designed by Corbett,
Harrison and
MacMurray. A Hugh
Ferris rendering.

architecture as object – following the few existent precedents in the Upper West Side – and superimposes it to that of the towers as objects. These, however, do not stand as objects per se but are part of a larger sequence along the avenue. At the same time, in relation to the buildings themselves, the towers mark their frontality. Treated as front and back, they are both volume and frontal facade. The careful composition, detailing, fenestration and use of material emphasize this dual role of the towers.

There is a sense of theater in these facades with towers, in their frontality towards the park where there is an immediate relationship established between public and actor. But the influence of the theatrical world in their architecture is different in the theatricality of these buildings from the way that occurs in the Chanin Building.

These buildings are also some of the first modern apartment buildings in the city. We should not forget that most of the more audacious architecture was developed either for private residences or for corporate or institutional buildings. But even the Rockefeller Center was started later. Looking at other apartment buildings of the same period we notice that most of them are of a more "classic" style. In Chanin's two buildings there is no longer an attachment to old styles but a development of a new vocabulary, probably not as pure as its European models, but integrated into the specific conditions of New York City. What makes these buildings remarkable is that being the result of a commercial, financial venture, they manage to develop a modern and generous urban architecture. In fact I would say that they provide one of the few examples of truly urban contextual architecture for New York City.

It is quite clear that Chanin was aware of the architecture trends in the city; he had Hugh Ferris rendering his buildings, and he himself designed a visionary project, a 2000 foot high building, a multiple use building which was a precursor to the notion of a city within the city. It was visionary also in terms of materials. This building, which was supposed to be a reality in the city in 1981, was very much in the spirit of

projects that may be seen in the Regional Plan of New York of 1931. In this extraordinary document, New York is seen basically as a city of skyscrapers, but with the ideology of the City Beautiful; that is, with an emphasis on the aesthetic values and formal qualities of the city as the most important aspects for its development. Like in visionary projects or proposals of the New York Regional Plan, where the skyscrapers are in many instances discrete objects linked by bridges or freeways, in Chanin's vision the street tends to be a secondary element to the city. In this sense his built structures are more responsive urban statements than his visions and they are at the same time some of the very few examples that represent many of the principles of the Regional Plan.

It is probably the fact that Irwin Chanin came from Europe that allowed him not to take any given for granted and to transform entities into a positive driving force, which matched with the spirit of discovery, progress and adventure that prevailed in New York in the twenties made a formula that could only lead him to success. What made the work of Mr. Chanin and the Chanin office so special is the particular combination of an understanding of the dynamics of the city, the pride in the quality of the architecture that came out of their office, and most of all, the love for the life of the city.

1. "The Chanins
of Broadway",
American Magazine, August 1928
2. Diana Agrest,
"Architectural
Anagrams:
The Symbolic
Performance of
the Skyscraper"
OPPOSITIONS 11,
Winter 1977
3. Matlick Price, The
Chanin Building,
AF May 1929.

Exhibition research,
planning, programming,
and design; environmental
and interpretive graphics,
Philippine Pavilion, Expo
82, Knoxville, Tennessee,
The Government of the
Philippines, 1982.

Exhibition research, planning,
programming, and design;
interpretive graphics, General
Foods Collection, Rye Brook,
New York, General Foods
Corporation, 1983.

General Foods
Collection

Art is the imposing of a pattern
on experience, and our aesthetic
enjoyment in recognition of the
pattern.

Alfred North Whitehead, 1953

SERVI
stainle
Italian.

GRATE
Americ
1873

GRATE
Japane

It is in symbolic, visual terms that the designer ultimately realizes his perceptions and experiences; and it is in the world of symbols that man lives.

Paul Rand, 1970

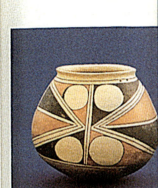

Y GRILL,
maker: Alessi,
porary

d iron,
nted June,

er, steel,
emporary

CHEESE BASKET, wood splint, probably Shaker, American, 19th C

CHOCOLATE MOLD, tinned lead, American, 20th C

WARMING PLATTER GRILL, brass, British, ca. 1810

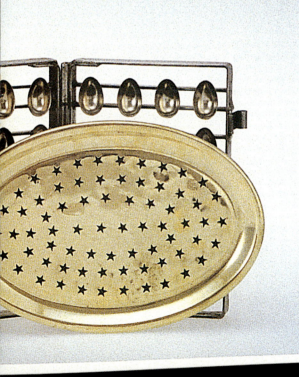

∨ Temporary exhibitions
and interpretive
graphics, General Foods
Collection, Rye Brook,
New York, General Foods
Corporation, 1983.

⌄ Temporary exhibition
catalogs, General Foods
Collection, General Foods
Corporation, 1983.

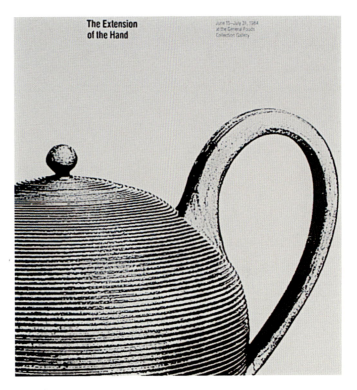

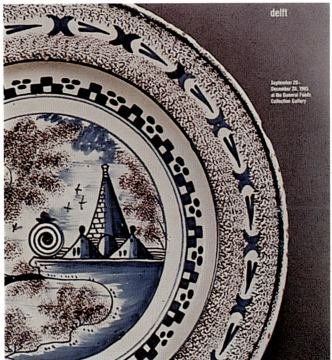

Exhibition research, planning,
programming, and design;
interpretive graphics,
Conoco Corporate Museum,
Houston, Texas, Conoco Inc.,
1984.

Exhibition research, planning, programming, and design; interpretive graphics, Cummins Engine Corporate Museum, Columbus, Indiana, Cummins Engine Company, 1983.

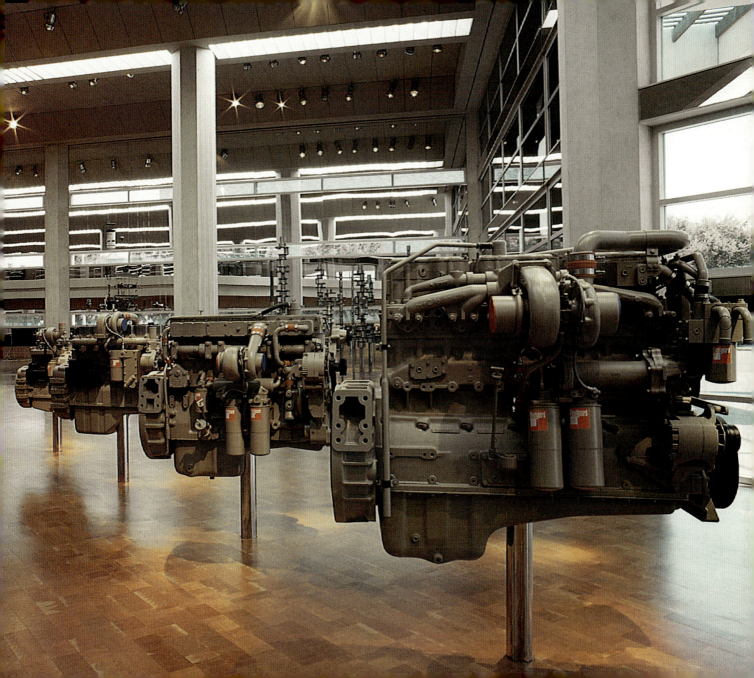

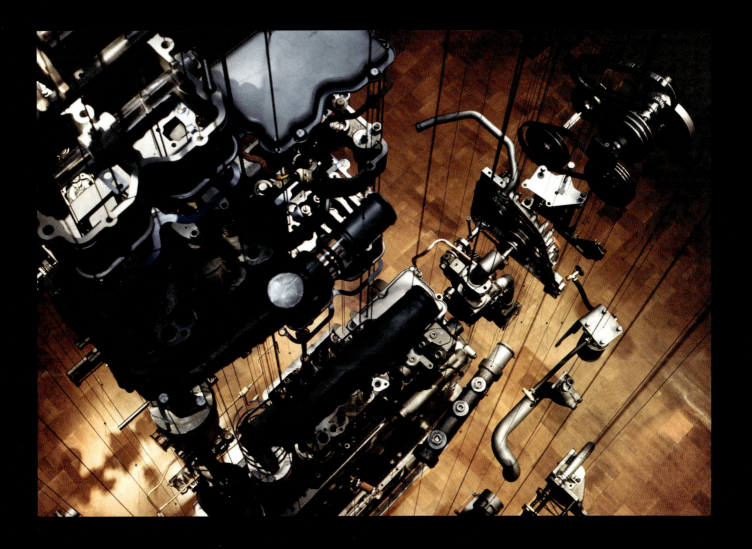

Environmental graphics,
wayfinding, and donor
recognition program,
The Main Research Libraries
of the New York Public
Library, New York City, New
York Public Library, 1984.

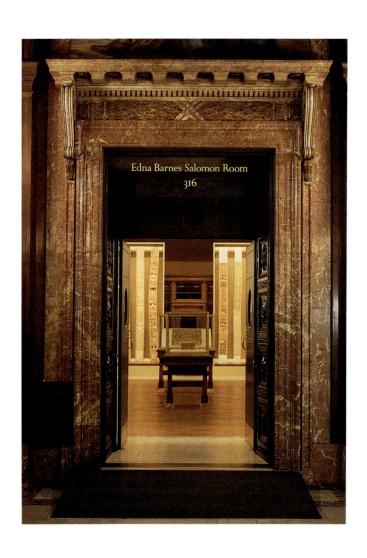

McGraw Rotunda

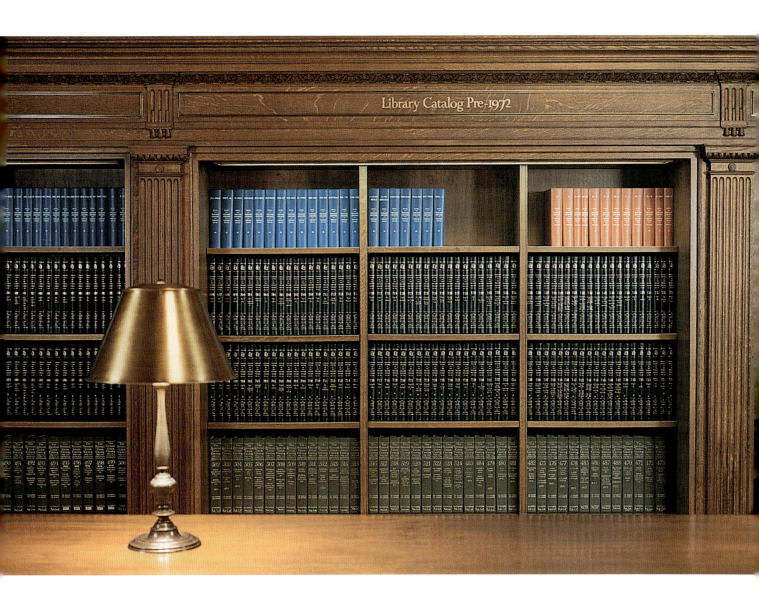

Dizzy
Mareado

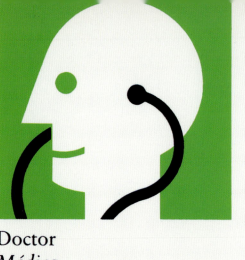

Doctor
Médico

Nurse
Enfermera

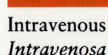

Intravenous
Intravenosa

Lower/Raise Bed
Subir/Bajar la Cama

Turn Me Ov
Dar Vuelta

nsado

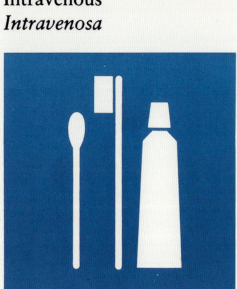

Mouth Care
Higiene Oral

Lotion
Crema

Pillow/Blank
Almohada/

are
dado de Pelo

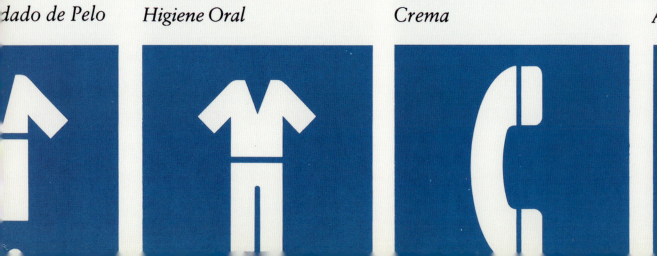

∨ Information design,
Communi-Card, Mount
Sinai Medical Center,
1987.

⌄ Stationery, 26 Beaver
   Street, 26 Beaver Street
   Homeowners Association,
   c. 1985.

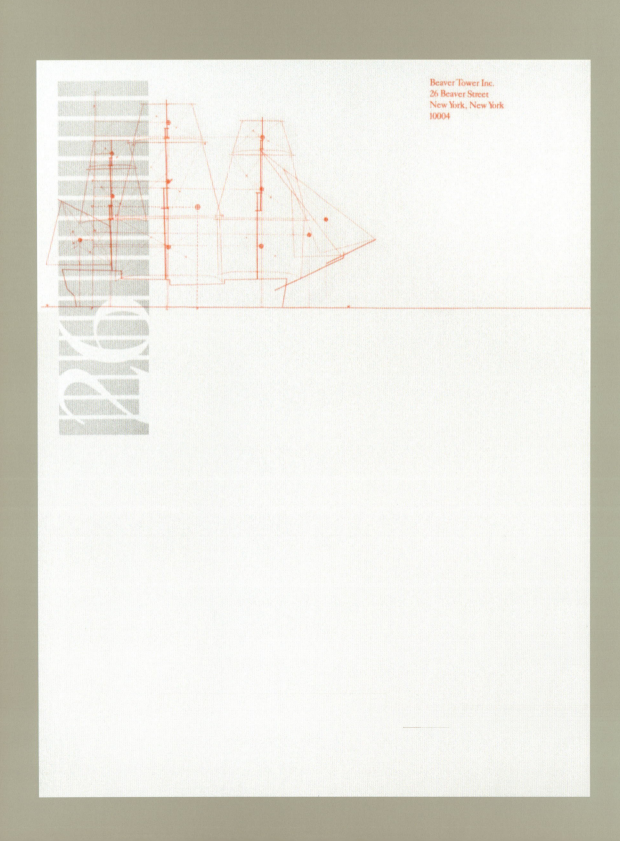

Beaver Tower Inc.
26 Beaver Street
New York, New York
10004

BONHEUR

Grand Central Oyster Bar, Inc.   Telephone: 212 245 5353   at sea
Grand Central Station   Telex: 239830 OBAR   Telephone: WRT 2553
New York, New York 10017   Telex: BONHEUR 11853

BONHEUR

Grand Central Oyster Bar, Inc.
Grand Central Station
New York, New York 10017

∨ Stationery, Beyer Blinder
   Belle, c. 1985.

Beyer
Blinder
Belle

Architects & Planners

41 East 11 Street
New York, New York 10003
212 777 7800

Robert T. Bayley, AIA

Beyer
Blinder
Belle

Architects & Planners

41 East 11 Street
New York, New York 10003

∨ Promotional poster, American Institute of Architects, New York Chapter Awards, American Institute of Architects, New York Chapter, 1983.

> Call-for-entry poster, *AIGA Functional Graphics,* American Institute of Graphic Arts (AIGA), 1984. As chairperson of AIGA's first 'Functional Graphics' competition and exhibition, de Harak designed its invitational call-for-entry poster as a history lesson in functional graphic form. The design jury included graphic designers Sam Antupit, Joel Katz, Tomoko Miho, Don Shanosky, and de Harak. Los Angeles County Museum of Art (LACMA) Design Collection, Los Angeles, California, USA.

New York Chapter
American Institute of Architects
Announces 3 Major Awards

Le Brun $ 5000
Stewardson $ 2000
Keefe $ 1500

Le Brun Traveling Fellowship
$5000

A biennial award to the competition winner for travel and study of architecture outside the U.S.A. Funds are provided in the will of Pierre Le Brun. Open to those with full time architectural office experience of at least 1½ years. Applicants must be residents of the U.S.A. and currently a beneficiary of no other traveling scholarship. Students are not eligible.

Subject of Competition:
"A Celebration of the Statue of Liberty"
Submissions limited to one sheet.

Make your request for the competition program and kit after April 1st.

Submissions are due by June 2.

Stewardson Traveling Fellowship
$2000

Open to architectural draftsmen (male/female), unlicensed and residents of the New York metropolitan area. A $2000 travel grant will be awarded.

Apply directly to the Committee by submitting a resume and a one page outline of your travel objectives and destination, reasons and justification for the travel grant.

Submission required by May 19.

Keefe Scholarship
$1500

$1500 is available to an American born architectural paraprofessional with no college education and at least 2 years experience as an employee in architectural offices to improve skills through technical school or community college training.

Apply directly to the committee by submitting a resume and a one page outline of your educational objectives.

Submission required by May 5.

Direct all correspondence to
Le Brun-Stewardson-Keefe
Committee
New York Chapter
American Institute of Architects
457 Madison Avenue
New York, New York
10022

212 799 5485

Winners will be announced within 3 weeks of submission.

Additional copies of this poster may be obtained by writing to the committee.

Designer Talks

The Work of Rudolph de Harak: 1947-1987

A Retrospective Presentation

Thursday, October 15, 1987
7:30 p.m.
The Alberta College of Art
Lecture Theatre
1407 14th Avenue N.W.
Calgary, Alberta T2N 4R3

Admission Free
For Information: 284-7600

Rudolph de Harak began his
career in 1946 working in
studios and agencies in Los
Angeles. Since 1950 he has
worked in New York City and
is a principal of de Harak
& Poulin Associates.

He is a designer with an
international reputation,
and has received many
awards for his work, which
has been featured in
publications, museums and
exhibitions throughout the
world.

Rudolph de Harak has also
been a teacher of design
since 1952 and is the
Frank Stanton Professor
of Design Emeritus at the
Cooper Union School of Art
and Architecture. He has
also taught and lectured
at many institutions
in the United States and
Europe.

Mr. de Harak is a member of
the Alliance Graphique
Internationale and American
Institute of Graphic Arts.
He has served as an advisor
to government agencies and
institutions.

Design: Rudolph de Harak, de Harak & Poulin Associates. Printed on Quintessence Dull 80 lb. Halftone courtesy of United Graphic Services Ltd.

< Promotional poster, *Designer Talks: The Work of Rudolph de Harak: 1947–1987 A Retrospective Exhibition,* Alberta College of Art, 1987. This promotional poster represented de Harak's lifelong interest in optical illusion and geometric form.

∨ Promotional poster, *Connections,* Simpson Paper Company, 1987. Los Angeles County Museum of Art (LACMA) Design Collection, Los Angeles, California, USA. Discussing this poster, de Harak stated: 'The joy of visual illusions exists in the perceptual attempt to make connections and logically order the specific information of optical experience. Mystically, magically, at precisely the moment the visual message is grasped, the connection eludes the viewer and presents another perspective.' [7]

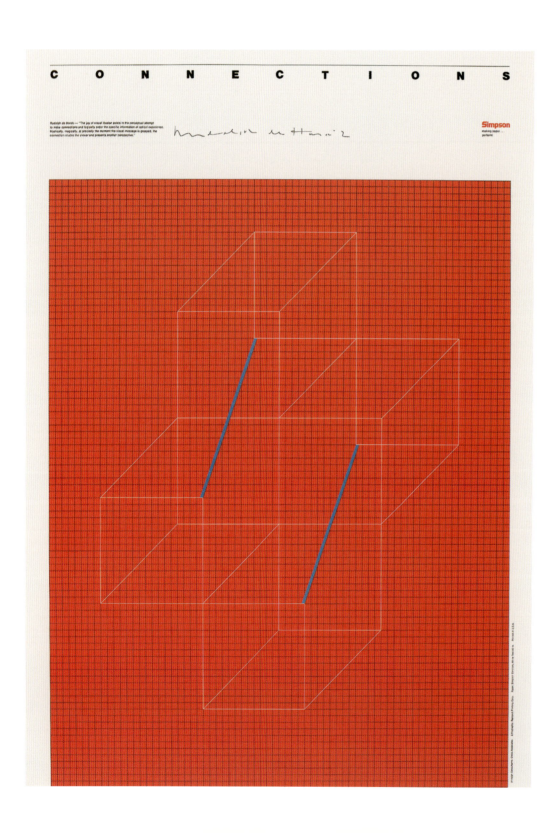

∨ Exhibition catalog,
Slutzky, Robert Slutzky,
1984. A fifty-six-page,
full-color exhibition
catalog designed in
conjunction with a 1984
exhibition of the artist's
work at the Modernism
Gallery, San Francisco,
California.

⌄ Promotional poster,
A Christmas Carol, IBM
Corporation, 1984.

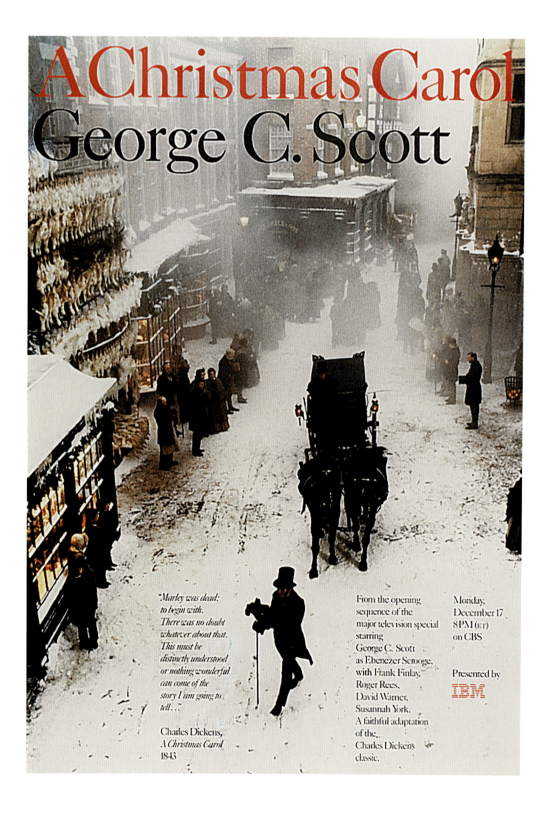

⌄ Publication, *A Christmas
Carol Christmas Book,*
IBM Corporation, 1984.

Posters
by Members
of the
Alliance
Graphique
Internationale
1960-1985

edited by Rudolph de Harak

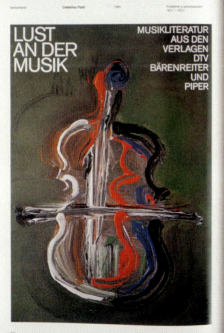

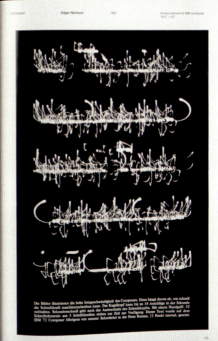

122 123 124 125

∨ Exhibition catalog, *Selections from the Reader's Digest Collection,* The Reader's Digest Association, Inc., 1985. An eighty-four-page, large-format exhibition catalog designed in conjunction with a traveling exhibition featuring thirty-seven works of art, including paintings, watercolors, and sculptures, collected by Lila Acheson Wallace.

> Book jacket, *AIGA Graphic Design USA: 9,* American Institute of Graphic Arts (AIGA), 1988. In the late 1980s, de Harak began producing more collages and paintings, like the one he used for this book jacket for *Graphic Design USA: 9,* the annual of the American Institute of Graphic Arts (AIGA) which celebrated the organization's competitive exhibitions and selected works that represented the highest standards in the field for the 1987–1988 season. Many of his friends and colleagues thought of this book jacket as de Harak's last 'official' design work while still head of his design consultancy.

graphic
design
USA:

9

The Annual of the American Institute of Graphic Arts

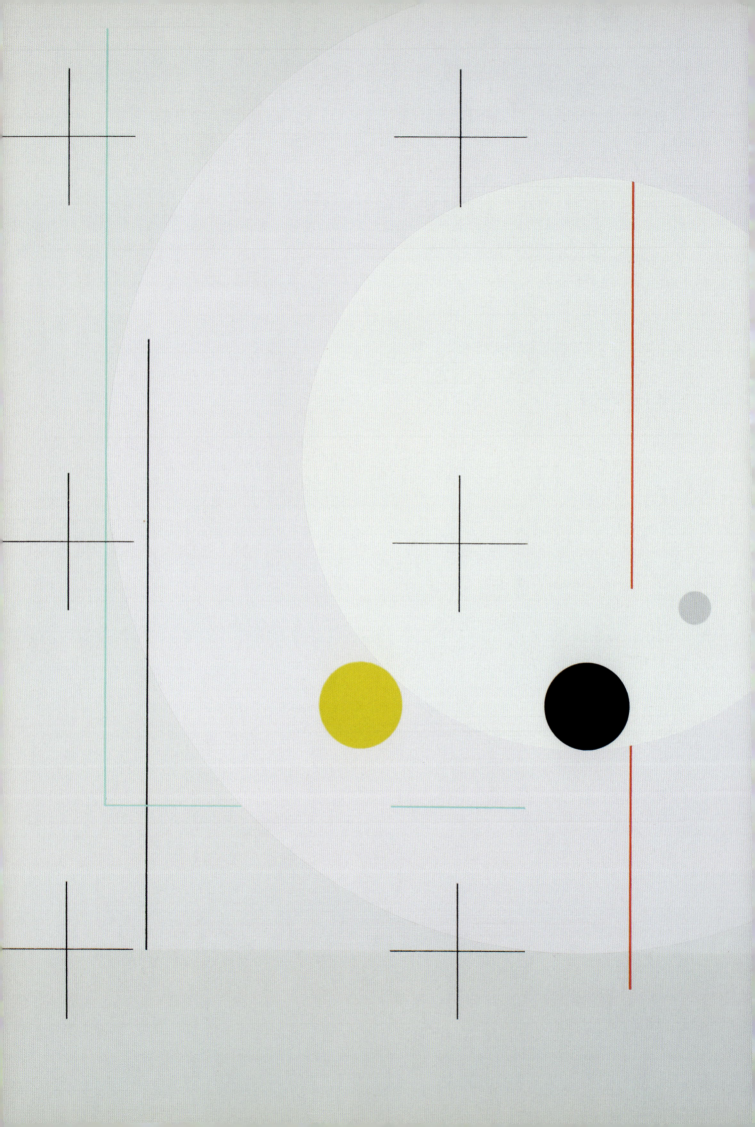

< *Three Moons* (detail),
  1999
  76.2 x 76.2 cm (30 x 30 in)
  Acrylic on canvas over
  wood panel.
  Collection of Susan C.
  Larsen and Laurie Martin

The digital revolution advanced at an extraordinary pace at the close of the twentieth century, transforming every aspect of human life. Globalization, fueled by the internet and social media, allowed people from all corners of the world to communicate on a level that they had never experienced before. Access to either a personal computer or smartphone provided anyone with a staggering and, to all intents and purposes, an endless amount of information and data, wherever they were in the world. New technologies were quickly embraced by graphic designers, allowing them to gain more control over the realization of their ideas. And, like other design disciplines, they now had an eclectic range of styles and idioms to choose from, as Postmodernism followed Modernism into the mainstream. Distinctions between different styles and idioms in graphic design started to blur, evolving into one single point of view. In addition, popular culture and visual forms such as film, video, and digital media began to have a tremendous influence on the graphic design profession.

At the beginning of the 1990s, New York City elected its first African-American mayor, David Dinkins, marking the beginning of a new era of multiculturalism. In 1993, a truck bomb planted by terrorists detonated at the World Trade Center's underground garage, killing six people and injuring over one thousand New Yorkers. In 1994, the city was deemed more 'livable' due to a crackdown on crime and real estate values skyrocketed. By the end of the decade, deaths in New York City from AIDS would exceed

75,000 people. In retrospect, the 1990s were one of the most sustained periods of economic growth and prosperity in the United States, as well as in New York City. However, it became painfully evident that the old rules governing the economy and the business world no longer applied — and it was equally obvious to most that no one knew what the new rules would be. This conundrum also applied to the practice and profession of graphic design. Running, maintaining, and expanding a design consultancy changed drastically during the 1990s, primarily due to digital technology, which both accelerated the receipt of information, and heightened clients' expectations with regard to response times.

At the start of the new decade, de Harak intentionally and methodically turned away from his demanding and all-encompassing graphic design practice, as well as from New York City, to pursue other creative passions that he had for so long placed on hold. While many of his friends and colleagues at the time thought this decision was unthinkable for someone of his stature and reputation, he eagerly looked forward to this new chapter in his life. Reflecting on his hometown, he said, 'I always felt that if someone didn't live in New York City, they were crazy, that it was the only place to experience life…every time I flew over LaGuardia and saw those lights…I was thrilled to be part of that.' [1] Now his perspective was different, but the results were just as satisfying and rewarding. As he and his wife Carol settled into their new home on the coast of Maine and made the transition from urban to rural life, several new opportunities were presented to him, many of which he enthusiastically accepted. The first overture was from Margo Halverson, a professor of graphic design at the nearby Portland School of Art, who invited de Harak to participate in a new and exciting educational design program.

Opportunities and Accolades

Founded in 1992, the Maine Summer Institute in Graphic Design was an annual series of three five-day residential workshops sponsored by the Portland School of Art and taught by prominent international faculty members. In its inaugural year, de Harak, along with graphic designers Bruno Monguzzi and James Cross, led the workshops that summer. Subsequent faculty members included Wolfgang Weingart, Dorothea Hofmann, Deborah Sussman, Ken Hiebert, and Nancy Skolos, among others. The program was developed for both novice and established graphic designers to provide methodical and structured exploration of theoretical and practical issues in visual communications in a studio environment, intended to foster strong faculty-student working relationships. Studio work was supplemented with related lectures and field trips to unique settings along the attractive Maine coast.

That same year, de Harak was awarded the AIGA Gold Medal for lifetime achievement from the American Institute of Graphic Artists (AIGA), the organization's highest honor, 'awarded since 1920 to individuals in recognition of their exceptional achievements to the advancement of the field of design as respected craft, strategic advantage, and vital cultural force. Medals have been awarded to individuals who have set standards of excellence over a lifetime of work or have made individual contributions to innovation within the practice of design.' [2] In October the following year, he was

presented the medal by his friend and collaborator Tom Geismar of Chermayeff & Geismar Associates, at AIGA's Fifth Biennial Graphic Design Conference, in Miami, Florida. In accepting this extraordinary recognition, he stated, 'This gold medal has been given to me for my few successes covering almost a fifty-year span of time…but what a wonderful time it has been. Having received this fine compliment, I feel obliged to continue to be worthy of this honor. I am grateful to the American Institute of Graphic Arts, its executive director Caroline Hightower, Kit Hinrichs and the medalist committee, to so many who have worked with me over these many years, and to the countless designers, artists, clients, and students past and present who have inspired me and had such a profound influence on my work.' [3]

At the time, American author Steven Heller movingly summarized the closing of one chapter in de Harak's life and the beginning of the next: 'For decades de Harak used his art to fulfill clients' needs. He stands poised to make art for himself. It is a meaningful conclusion to one career and the beginning of a new life of a man who has imbued graphic design with both a vocabulary and an ethic.' [4] In 1993, de Harak received another significant accolade when the Corcoran Museum School of Art in Washington, DC, presented him with an honorary doctorate in fine arts for his outstanding contributions to the fields of graphic design and graphic design education.

Lifelong Passions and Pursuits

Whatever de Harak's chosen creative endeavor at any particular stage of life, as his wife Carol explained, 'He went into it with an intense amount of effort, energy, and enthusiasm. If he didn't know specific aspects of any process, he would teach himself and learn along the way. That's the way he was with everything that he became involved with. Rudy possessed this inner strength that allowed him to keep on learning, absorbing, and observing and not giving up on anything nor on the dreams and aspirations that he had.' [5] During the last ten years of his life, de Harak not only painted practically every day, but also found the time to teach himself piano and clarinet (he had a lifelong love and passion for music and was a seasoned jazz saxophonist), make custom fishing rods and lures (he was also a highly skilled surf fisherman), and design and fabricate his own wood furniture.

Following his relocation to the coast of Maine, de Harak began to exhibit his paintings, constructions, and collages as part of several group and solo exhibitions at galleries and museums throughout the state, including the Leighton Gallery in Blue Hill (1991); Muse Gallery in Rockland (1996), Icon Contemporary Art Gallery in Brunswick (1998, 2000), the Clark House Gallery in Bangor (1999), and the John Edwards Art Gallery in Ellsworth (2001), as well as the Farnsworth Art Museum in Rockland and the Portland Museum of Art. One of his paintings, *Three Moons* (1999), was included in a major exhibition at the Katonah Museum of Art in July 2000, 'Maine and the Modern Spirit'. Exploring the myth perpetuated by artists, writers, reformers, and poets that Maine is a uniquely modern American Eden, it featured artists as diverse as Marsden Hartley, John Marin, Edward Hopper, Fairfield Porter, Louise Nevelson, Alex Katz, and Robert Indiana.

This was not the first time, however, that de Harak's fine art had been on view to the public. In 1964, following its relocation to new headquarters in New York City, the American Institute of Graphic Arts (AIGA) introduced an ongoing program of one-person exhibitions of member designers and illustrators, which included Herb Lubalin, Paul Rand, and James McMullan. In spring that year, an exhibition featuring de Harak's graphic design work and paintings revealed the remarkable duality of his practice. The exhibition raised the question: Which comes first — the painter or the designer? In an accompanying press release, de Harak himself answered the question: 'The position of the designer is unique … ambivalent. He is committed to industry, and he finds his vocational responsibilities in everyday realities. Yet there is part of him which parallels that of all other artists; that part — a spiritual need — which through discipline is shaped into the ability to look inward for answers, to questions even as yet not asked … that may be resented … that, perhaps, later cultures are measured by. Paradoxically, the designer's efforts are framed in the spirit of visual invention and the cold facts of commerce. He coordinates these ambivalent shapes and reshapes the aesthetic and communicative quality of forms in every conceivable category that make up our everyday lives and experiences. There are those who would say that working with the practical aspects of design is a commercial contest; is to compromise art, meaning that design is design, but art is art. However, art is not a thing — it can't be categorized as any specific medium, ever elusive, art hovers in a stratum of fantasy and spirit … available to those having the ability, discipline, energy, and force to transform mediocrity regardless of the purpose of which creative efforts are made.'[6]

The impact of the exhibition was also summarized in the press release: 'It is interesting to observe a linear-illusory drawing as a paperback book cover, to see across the gallery, a painting of transparent interpenetrating colors, and to observe that they are nearly identical. The drawing, strongly geometric — the painting, concrete and ablaze with color. There is color everywhere. As one enters the gallery there are three de Harak paintings brilliant with subtle and intense greens, lavenders, blues, shocking pinks, and turquoise. One painting, hung on a diagonal, is done in taupe, lavender and orange. The theme, with the exception of three examples, is always lucid, always saturated with colors identifiable with de Harak. Entering the main gallery, the eye experiences paintings as squares, some on point, manifested by close-knit color, and reminiscent of the Swiss concrete school. There is a small white-on-white construction whose pattern changes and is dependent on

the light source; a collage of American flags; a brown-on-brown varnish contrast and three paintings of an earlier period, entitled *Eight Visitors*, refusing any specific "school" identification. There are seventeen de Harak paintings on view.'[7]

Following the move to Maine almost thirty years later, one of de Harak's first solo exhibitions was at the Icon Contemporary Art Gallery in Brunswick, Maine. The exhibition of twenty paintings, constructions, and collages was reviewed in the *Maine Sunday Telegram* in August 1998 by art critic Ken Greenleaf, who described the show as a series of galleries filled with 'an air of studied elegance' characterizing de Harak as 'a master craftsman' and the exhibited work as reflecting 'the rules of visual interaction'.[8] At the time, Duane Paluska, founder and owner of the gallery, shared his reaction to the show: 'Rudolph de Harak's painting respects and alludes to an underlying system of grids, but it breaks away from the rigidity often found in hard-edge expression and strikes out on a more poetic path. While clearly influenced by the Dutch De Stijl school, de Harak replaces Mondrian's and van Doesburg's trademark palette of primary colors with a vocabulary of predominantly soft, close-value color relationships by high intensity, sharply articulated linear accents. De Harak does not think of himself as an abstract painter... his straight lines and hard, well-defined shapes and edges often suggest spatial and architectural references, craft, rationality, and precision that end up as a lyrical serenity that may have its closest analogy to music.'[9]

His paintings have been described as hard-edged, geometric, and abstract, yet he was always quick to counter such descriptions, saying in 1997 that he never saw his work as abstract, 'because geometry is as real as faces and landscapes'. He continued, 'Even though my work is considered non-figurative, I don't think of myself as an abstract painter. For me, the basic geometric forms (circle, square, triangle) are quite as real as a house, a tree, or the sun and are the building blocks upon which all of our visual world is constructed. I am, however, preoccupied with clean, straight lines and hard edges. This is because I am fascinated with conspicuous visual order... and for me, this is the most efficient and rewarding way to achieve it. What I compose is really a framework into which I can impose my feelings and expressions concerning color. What does it all mean? Like a cloud, a wave, the sound of music or the wind, it is all very personal for each viewer and elicits different responses.'[10] Throughout the decade, he worked intensely and continually on paintings and collages. His work was often identified with genres such as the De Stijl movement and Neoplasticism, or alternatively with the Minimalist art of the 1960s — such names as Piet Mondrian, Josef Albers, Ellsworth Kelly, and Sol LeWitt often cropped up in exhibition reviews. For de Harak, however, his art always remained rooted in nature.

De Harak's creative process involved a self-discipline that he always relied upon for reflection, refinement, and further experimentation. In a 1998 interview, he talked about his process and shared that, even after finishing a painting, he would always attempt to take his concept further. He said, 'I'll do very, very small pencil drawings of what kind of a configuration might be an interesting exploration. When you get older, you start to understand... how really naïve you were in your earlier years, of how to put something together, how to do something. When one first has an idea to do

⌄ De Harak with his friends
and fishing companions,
Ernie Rieger (*left*) and
Mark Baldwin (*middle*),
Fire Island, New York,
c. 1998.

something, they're generally drawing on some aspect of a previous learned experience — the sum total of technical abilities and your ability to translate and restate ideas that you've had before. Once I do that, then I try to take an additional step. That's very dangerous because you're trying to do something that you don't know.' [11] He would never allow himself to consider the easier solution or the familiar creative path; he always focused on the unknown and the path he hadn't taken yet.

Susan C. Larsen — an art historian, archivist, and curator specializing in American Modernism — first met de Harak while she was a collector for the Archives of American Art at the Smithsonian Institution, Washington, DC. In April 2000, she visited de Harak at his home in Maine and spent an afternoon interviewing him about his life and work for the Smithsonian's Archives of American Art Oral History Program, started in 1958 to document the history of the visual arts in the United States, primarily through interviews with artists, designers, historians, dealers, critics, and administrators. In reviewing de Harak's art following this interview, she described his paintings perfect for the dawn of a new millennium. She wrote, 'The paintings of Rudolph de Harak have always had a lean and confident beauty. With their taut edges, radiant color, and demanding visual syntax, they inspire one to look carefully and deeply. The ardent pursuit of painting has taken de Harak to a new realm of expression in the past few years. Suddenly, he has discovered a grandeur to touch the stars. His pictorial space has opened up, his color has gained warmth and tenderness. He has created a cosmic array of shapes and supported them with glowing planes of light. De Harak's new paintings stimulate the imagination with a sense of poetry that allows the viewer to dream and speculate along with the artist himself. They are friendly, surprising, invitingly playful and full of joy. Rudy de Harak is moving swiftly through a series of ideas and profound situations about painting and about nature in action, which is to say, the flow of life itself. He is full of new concepts but has the disciplined intellect and long experience to know that they find their way into his art through his own familiar language. How fortunate that years of experience and loving dedication to his vision have borne fruit in such a meaningful way. These paintings contain the best and the most generous aspects of the artist's knowledge and feelings about our world. He has only begun, like the century itself, and we look forward to sharing de Harak's long voyage of discovery and fulfillment.' [12]

In one of his last public appearances, de Harak closed his lecture by stating, 'It is important that the designer be an artist, for of all the artists, he is probably in the closest contact with the specific realities that stimulate, influence, and impose social and cultural change. Compensated only by his dreams, his dedication, energy, discipline and curiosity, he has walked a winding, windy path pitted with obstacles and directional uncertainties, trying to find his way. Trying to discover for himself, a new vision. How to see. How to look inward and simultaneously see outward. How to feel in those two directions, and how to understand in the same way. A lost and found chemistry that slowly, surely synthesizes emotional and intellectual capacities. The chemistry of understanding one's creative responses...and responding to one's creative understanding. Herein is his honor.' [13] Rudolph de Harak died at his home in Trenton, Maine on 24 April 2002. He was 78 years old and was survived by his wife,

Carol Sylbert, two sons, Bruno and Dimitri de Harak, and three stepsons, Doug, Jon, and Mark Sylbert. On that day, the world lost an honorable individual, dreamer, and visionary, who will continue to influence like-minded artists and designers for generations to come.

1. Donna Gold, 'De Harak's Geometry', *Maine Times*, vol. 34, no. 18, 23 September 2001, p. 16.
2. AIGA Awards, 'AIGA Medal', 6 May 2021, https://www.aiga.org/membership-community/aiga-awards/aiga-medal
3. Rudolph de Harak, acceptance speech at the presentation of the American Institute of Graphic Arts (AIGA) Gold Medal, AIGA Fifth Biennial Graphic Design Conference, Miami, Florida, October 1993.
4. Steven Heller, '1992 AIGA Medalist: Rudolph de Harak', AIGA, 2 September 1992, https://epi.aiga.org/medalist-rudolphdeharak
5. Richard Poulin, Interview with Carol de Harak, 12 August 2021.
6. 'The Design and Paintings of Rudolph de Harak', American Institute of Graphic Arts (AIGA), 28 February 1964. Press release.
7. Ibid.
8. Ken Greenleaf, 'De Harak Creates Studied Elegance', *Maine Sunday Telegram*, 23 August 1998.
9. Duane Paluska, exhibition brochure introduction on Rudolph de Harak and his new work, Icon Contemporary Art Gallery, Brunswick, Maine, August 1998.
10. Rudolph de Harak, 'Oral History Interview with Rudolph de Harak,' interview by Susan Larsen on 27 April 2000 (transcript), in Ellsworth, Maine. Archives of American Art, Smithsonian Institution, Washington, DC.
11. Ibid.
12. Trevor Merrill, 'A Designer's Discipline', *The Ellsworth American,* 13 August 1998.
13. Rudolph de Harak, Society for Experiential Graphic Design (SEGD) Lecture, New York City, 29 March 1997.

⌄ Rudolph and Carol de Harak's home, Trenton, Maine, 1990. De Harak and his wife, Carol, designed and built their post-and-beam home on two-and-a-half hectares (six acres) on the Atlantic Ocean waterfront of Union River Bay, near Acadia National Park. The open, loft-like interior included individual workspaces for each of them: an art studio and wood shop for de Harak and a photography studio, darkroom, and office for Carol. Carol de Harak, photographer.

> *Do Not Bend 1* (detail), 1987
30.5 x 30.5 cm (12 x 12 in)
Sewn canvas square, acrylic, oil, laundry tag, gum wrapper, and nails on wood panel
Collection of Farnsworth Art Museum

gum wrapper, and nails on
wood panel
Collection of Farnsworth
Art Museum

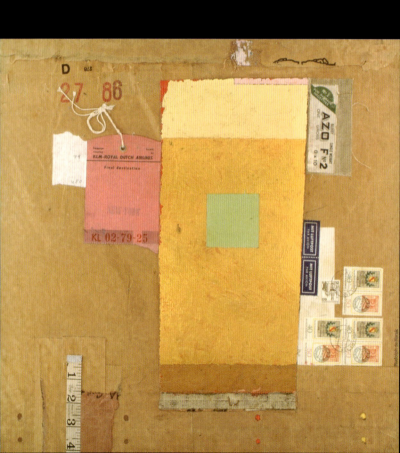

acrylic, oil, laundry tag,
gum wrapper, and nails
on wood panel
Collection of Farnsworth
Art Museum

acrylic, oil, laundry tag,
gum wrapper, and nails
on wood panel
Collection of Farnsworth
Art Museum

U.S. Off.

Coupon
de caisse
BALCON
DE CÔTÉ

Coupon
de contrôle
1re GALERIE
DE FACE

452448
LONDON W(e)

BAG STAMP ONLY

Bitte nicht biegen

8791

Chez
C...

...côté

VAPORS FROM HE...
AND RESPIRATORY IRRITANT

gum wrapper, and nails
on wood panel
Collection of author

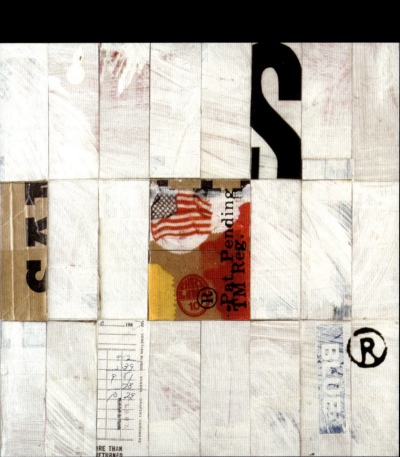

gum wrapper, and nails
on wood panel
Collection of Farnsworth
Art Museum

acrylic, oil, laundry tag,
gum wrapper, and nails
on wood panel
Collection of author

S

Pat Pending
TM Reg.

R

198

ASS — VENETIAN BLINDS — SHADES — DRAPERY HARDWARE

Rudolph de Harak

4/2
39
28
29 1987.

HAN

BLUE

R

30.5 x 30.5 cm (12 x 12 in)
Sewn canvas square,
acrylic, oil, laundry tag,
gum wrapper, and nails
on wood panel
Collection of Farnsworth
Art Museum

Sewn canvas square,
acrylic, oil, laundry tag,
gum wrapper, and nails
on wood panel
Collection of Farnsworth
Art Museum

acrylic, oil, laundry tag,
gum wrapper, and nails
on wood panel

Wrapping paper, fabric, tickets, photograph, staples, and aluminum with nails on wood panel

gum wrapper, and nails
on wood panel

acrylic, oil, laundry tag,
gum wrapper, and nails
on wood panel

acrylic, oil, laundry tag,
gum wrapper, and nails
on wood panel

Acrylic, labels, beer-can
fragments, nails, reprint,
and letters on wood panel
Collection of Farnsworth
Art Museum

gum wrapper, and nails
on wood panel
Collection of Farnsworth
Art Museum

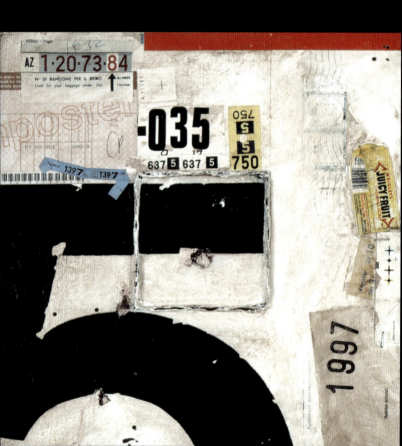

gum wrapper, and nails
on wood panel

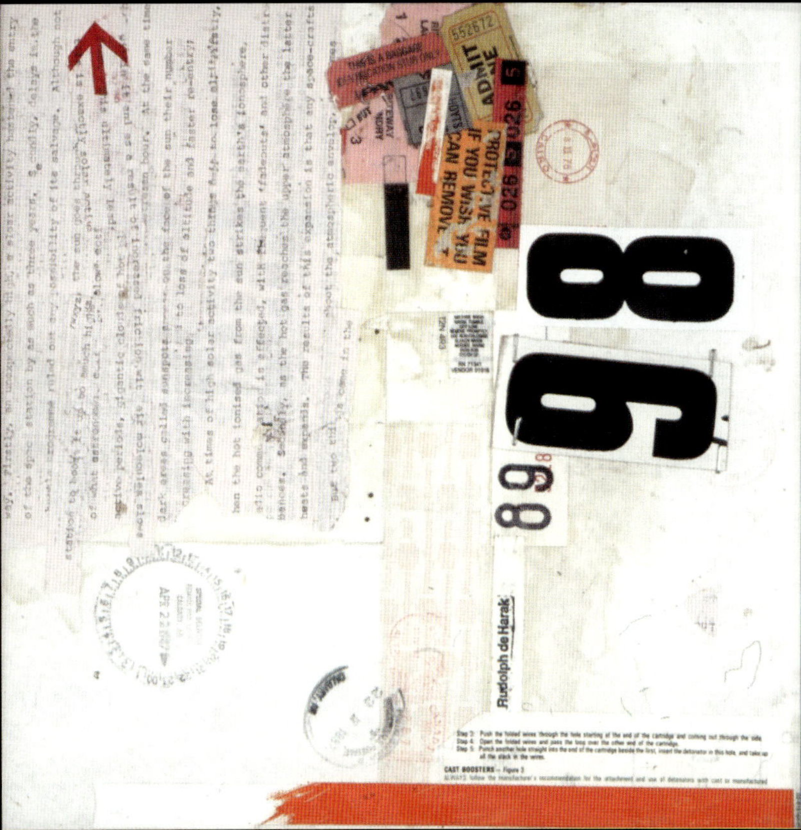

THIS IS A BAGGAGE
IDENTIFICATION STUB ONLY

552672

ADMIT 5

3

026 5 U26 5

PROTECT-A-FILM
YOU CAN REMOVE

98

96

89

Rudolph de Harak

Step 3: Push the folded wires through the hole starting at the end of the cartridge and coming out through the side.
Step 4: Open the folded wires and pass the loop over the other end of the cartridge.
Step 5: Punch another hole straight into the end of the cartridge beside the first, insert the detonator in this hole, and take up all the slack in the wires.

CAST BOOSTERS — Figure 3
ALWAYS follow the manufacturer's recommendation for the attachment and use of detonators with cast or manufactured

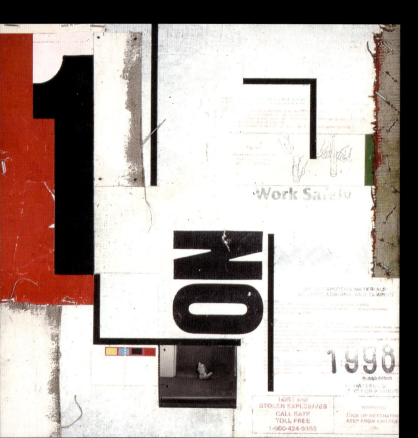

⌄ *Union River Bay, No. 1,*
1996
91.4 x 91.4 cm (36 x 36 in)
Acrylic on canvas

ˇ *Union River Bay, No. 2,*
1997
152.4 x 152.4 cm
(60 x 60 in)
Acrylic on canvas

∨ *Union River Bay, No. 3,*
1997
91.4 x 91.4 cm (36 x 36 in)
Acrylic on canvas
Collection of Farnsworth
Art Museum

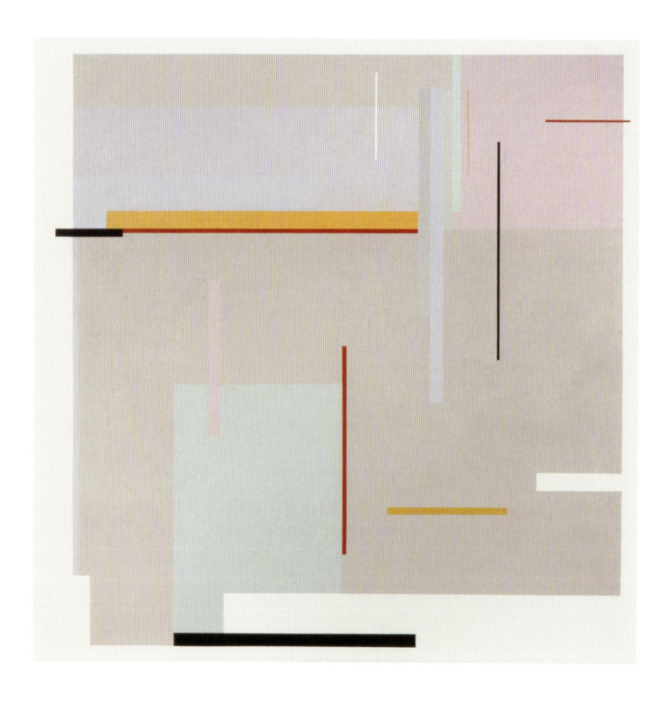

∨ *Union River Bay, No. 4,*
1997
91.4 x 91.4 cm (36 x 36 in)
Acrylic on canvas

∨ *Union River Bay, No. 7,*
1998
94 x 109.2 cm (37 x 43 in)
Acrylic on canvas

∨ *Tomahawk*, 1999
76.2 x 76.2 cm (30 x 30 in)
Acrylic on canvas

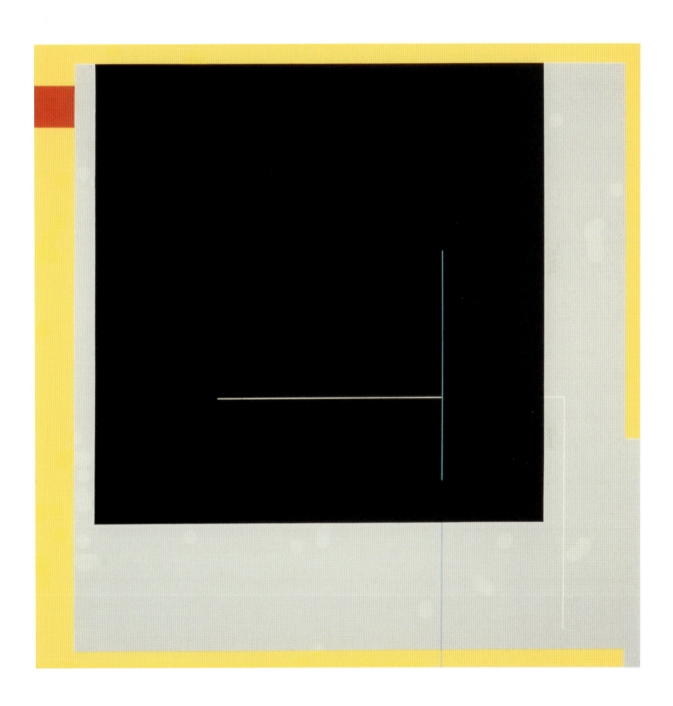

∨ *Black Patches,* 2000
121.9 x 121.9 cm
(48 x 48 in)
Acrylic on canvas

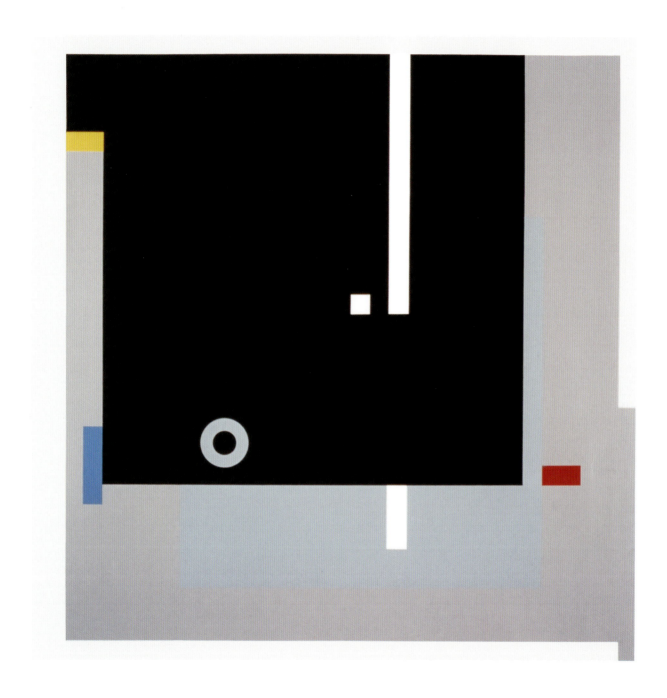

∨ *Three Moons*, 1999
76.2 x 76.2 cm (30 x 30 in)
Acrylic on canvas over
wood panel
Collection of Susan C.
Larsen and Laurie Martin

Remembrances and Recollections

In the past two years that I have been researching, writing, and designing this monograph on Rudolph de Harak, I have spoken with numerous individuals about his life, work, influence, and legacy — friends, colleagues, collaborators, former students and staff, designers, artists, and family members.

In writing this narrative so that the reader could visualize the life of a creative force that was energized with determination and imagination, I realized that there was an abundance of personal remembrances, recollections, and the like that I couldn't possibly leave out of this volume. To bring his story full circle, as well as share with the reader some of the personal insights that were shared with me during my research, I have included some remembrances and recollections in honor of my mentor, teacher, and creative inspiration — Rudolph de Harak.

Mark Baldwin
Founder, Borealis Press
Ellsworth, Maine
May 2021

'My life changed when Rudy walked in the door to get some typesetting and printing done, hijacking my graphic vision. He was one of the seminal graphic designers of the twentieth century; recipient of the AIGA Gold Medal for life achievement. Rudy was also big time in the smallest and the largest details. For example, when he wanted a better turntable for his LPs, or a set of speakers that suited his ear, he designed and built them. Fortunately, he took a liking to me and we became close friends. He was a constant mentor influencing everything I have done since I met him in 1991.'

Douglas Harp
Graphic Designer, Educator
Founder, Harp and Company Graphic Design
Hanover, New Hampshire
August 2020

'In 1980, Rudy was my professor in my second year at the Yale School of Art MFA Program in Graphic Design. He was at once warm and intense. It was corporate branding project, as I recall, and it was clear that this guy was the real deal — steeped in this kind of work daily. Rudy was the consummate educator: he was patient, clear in his explanations, encouraging, and demanding. And his body of work was nothing short of fantastically inspiring.

Upon graduation I had two job offers: one from Jack Hough Associates in Stamford, Connecticut, and the other from Rudy. I accepted the job with Rudy and found the experience invaluable as I sought to zero in on what area of the graphic design profession I wanted to concentrate on. That ended up being print and corporate identity, but had it not been for that job, I would have had little experience in environmental graphics and exhibition design, in both of which Rudy was a giant.

The model at Rudolph de Harak and Associates was based on the mentor and apprentice relationship. While Rudy delegated great responsibility and project management to his three associates, it was not unusual to have one-on-one meetings with him. One of my favorite memories was being called in to his impeccably neat office, comprised of an enormous, black wood table that he had designed, with the obligatory bent steel and leather chairs; a stainless-steel racing bike hanging from a polished stainless-steel wall rack that he had also designed; and then there was his Aurora clock . . .

We would sit together, and Rudy would make these masterful sketches on a roll of yellow tracing paper, outlining his thoughts on the project at hand. What was remarkable, though, is that he would ask my opinions, and unless I totally misread him, he often took them into account, and always made me feel as though I contributed something of value. Me, fresh out of

Remembrances and Recollections

graduate school; Rudy, the master with the international reputation. He was kind that way.

There is no doubt that Rudy was a powerful force in my formative years. If there is a cleanliness to my work, and a respect for the disciplined International Style, I can attribute this to having worked closely with him. I recall, after moving from New York to work in Corning's Corporate Design department, imagining Rudy looking over my shoulder, critiquing my work. That feeling of security, for lack of a better word, helped launch me into my own studio six years later.'

Jessica Helfand
Graphic Designer, Author, Educator
Founding Editor, Design Observer
Providence, Rhode Island
November 2020

'A modernist and a humanist, Rudy spent a lifetime considering the fusion of feeling and form, interrogating the many ways design takes flight in the imagination and in the world. His body of work reveals the mind of a true master, whose curiosity remains a boundless and beautiful gift.'

Jon Jicha
Professor Emeritus, School of Art and Design,
Western Carolina University
Cullowhee, North Carolina
February 2021

'My university teaching career in graphic design began in the mid-1970s. I realized then, as now, that the essential relationship between theory and studio practice is the foundation for effective instruction. My first invited visiting design speaker was the great Jacqueline Casey at MIT. She accepted the invitation to judge the *1982 Poster National: A Student Exhibition*, a project I had developed as a touring exhibition. My interest in curating exhibitions began with her advice and wonderfully pertinent observations about the international design field. I asked her for a name, another designer, who she thought I might contact. Without hesitation she responded, "You should talk to Rudy de Harak." She continued, "He's one of the best speakers, educators, and practitioners!"

Soon after, I accepted a faculty position at Western Carolina University as Coordinator of Graphic Design. Following Jacqueline's recommendation, I called Rudy to ask him if he would be interested in sharing with us (the University) his thoughts on design and (maybe) have an exhibition of some of his work. His generosity was overwhelming. We, along with Richard (Poulin) put together an exhibition in 1985, *Rudolph de Harak: A Thirty-Year Retrospective*, which travelled for several years. On campus, Rudy was a rock star. Captivating students and administrators in his lecture plus critiquing student projects in thoughtful reviews, he made me feel like I was I was doing the right thing as a teacher and, most importantly, inspired me as a designer and artist. To this day I can realistically say that he is one of my heroes and mentors. I learned much about why design matters through this association. Why it is relevant and necessary — like a river — always changing and yet being a constant reference of balance within our human condition.

On the way to the airport for his departure, we stopped at a roadside shop which had miscellaneous "stuff" scattered over the porch. His interest, I'm certain, was to find out more about this area of the Smoky Mountains through its artifacts. After entering, his attention was directed to a strangely complicated mechanical device, a hand-crank apple peeler. After purchasing it, we continued our drive as he talked about it through the lens of a philosopher, sociologist, artist, and designer. It occurred to me on my return trip home that he approached everything this way. He saw the complete picture — visible and invisible.'

∨ De Harak in his art
studio, Ellsworth, Maine,
c. 2001. Mark Baldwin,
photographer.

Jay Maisel
Photographer
New York, New York
June 2021

'I first met Rudy in 1954 right after I graduated from
Yale. I was just beginning my career and I had an
opportunity to show him my portfolio while he was
consulting art director for *Dance* Magazine. We became
good friends. He was even nice enough to lend me
his apartment while he was on his honeymoon with
his new wife, Berenice. Sometimes we would spend
time together walking around New York City and
experimenting with our cameras. I completed a few
assignments for him and *Dance* Magazine including
several rehearsals and classes for the New York Summer
Dance Festival. He was always inspiring and exciting to
be around.'

Sergio Correa de Jesus Medina
Graphic Designer, Educator
Barcelona, Spain
October 2020

'In the very first year (and the very first semester) of
my teaching graphic design at North Carolina State
University, Rudy gave a talk to my students. It was 1984.
At the end of our group discussion one of my students
asked him what made a good designer and his answer
was: "You have to be a jack-of-all-trades but a master of
one." His response has stayed with me to this very day.'

Armando Milani
Graphic Designer
Milan, Italy
August 2020

'Rudy was a fascinating and influential figure in the
design world, and a devout pioneer of modernist
graphic design. I met him at my first Alliance Graphique
Internationale (AGI) Congress in Montreal in 1984. I was
young and shy, surrounded by all these great designers
such as FHK Henrion, Saul Bass, Alan Fletcher, Shigeo
Fukuda, and Rudy. He understood my embarrassment
and invited me to dinner at their table introducing me
to all of them. I will never forget his kindness and for
opening the door at AGI to so many great creative minds.

I had just opened my studio in New York and he
invited me several times to his office for a personal tour
of his beautiful work. He liked my work as well, and
suggested I do some workshops at Cooper Union. He
told me that he was influenced when he was young by
the lectures of Will Burtin and György Kepes, and he
liked design that uncovered the unconscious, like me.
He merged Bauhaus Rationalism with the American
Eclecticism. We became real friends. Two years later I
invited Rudy to my studio in Milan and I introduced him
to Franco Grignani whom he highly admired.

He retired to Maine with his wife Carol where he
built his wood house on the shore dedicating himself
to painting, collages, and playing his jazz saxophone. I
visited both several times discussing our preferences
between Akzidenz-Grotesk and Helvetica typefaces,
American Expressionism, and Fellini and Truffaut movies.
Rudy was not only a great designer, but a generous and
caring friend, I love and miss him.'

Remembrances and Recollections

Jesse Reed
Graphic Designer
Co-Founder, Order and Standards Manual
November 2020

'I have a weakness, and Rudolph de Harak is at the heart of it. I simply cannot enter a bookstore, find a cover designed by Rudy, and place it back on the shelf.'

R. Roger Remington
Vignelli Distinguished Professor of Design Emeritus
Vignelli Center for Design Studies
College of Art and Design
Rochester Institute of Technology
February 2021

'Rudolph de Harak's work has always inspired me. It was a special delight when, in 2004, I was able to bring his career archive to the Cary Graphic Design Archive at Rochester Institute of Technology. This robust collection of quintessential de Harak graphic design is a treasured resource for students and researchers alike. There are important lessons to be learned from studying this body of work. It exists now in an archival setting of de Harak's contemporaries which provides the student with a rich context of design history. His design process exemplified key modernist values as indicated in the title of this book, namely an objective approach which leads consistently to simple, direct solutions. Looking back at his work inspires us because it exudes a quality of visual aesthetic formalism largely missing in today's world of graphic design. Whether in the many fine graphic expressions such as his classic paperback book covers for McGraw-Hill or in the Metropolitan Museum of Art's Egyptian Wing, de Harak was a master at creating forms that communicated, were memorable, and consistently solved the problem.'

Paul Rosenblatt
Architect, Educator, Artist
Founding Principal, Springboard Design
Pittsburgh, Pennsylvania
August 2020

'During my senior year in high school, I had a semester internship at Rudy's office. My dad, Arthur Rosenblatt, was working at The Metropolitan Museum of Art leading the museum's expansion and at the time was working on the Temple of Dendur and the Egyptian Wing with Rudy and his staff.

I took the subway downtown to Rudy's office to meet and talk to him about my upcoming internship. My time there that summer was an incredible experience. The office environment felt like a whirlwind of energy to me at the time. One room was being used to design and build full-size foam core mockups of new gas pumps for Hess Oil, never to my knowledge implemented. New shopping bags and other materials were being designed for The Metropolitan Museum of Art — this became the seed of the famous Met shopping bags that were used for decades. I remember remarking to myself that Rudy was comfortable flipping between the two-dimensional and three-dimensional worlds often within the same project, sometimes even within the same drawing or representation. Like the book and record covers that I so admired and do to this day. This oscillation is something that has defined my professional work as a designer, architect, and painter, ever since.

What did I learn from the time I spent working with and for Rudy? First, I think I began to internalize very high and rigorous standards of aspiration and craftsmanship. Aspiration was different from ambition. The work itself was of value inherently. The first idea was not necessarily the best and would always benefit from many revisions and refinements. Hard work. Discipline. Training your eye and demanding increasingly more of yourself. Not being satisfied with good or even great. Trusting your eye and standards and not others. I think I learned to abhor visual clichés from Rudy. I

∨ De Harak working in his
art studio, Ellsworth,
Maine, c. 2001. Mark
Baldwin, photographer.

began to avoid the flamboyant in favor of the refined. My
encounters with Rudy were very serious. He appeared
to treat me and my work with the same seriousness that
he treated his own staff and his collaborators. He was
demanding of me of work that I never had done before
and didn't accept something that didn't meet his exacting
standard, even though I had no experience or training at
the time. I eventually got there, I think, but it took a lot
more time and effort than it would someone with more
experience. More than anyone had asked of me before.
This instilled in me the belief that time and effort were as
equally important as raw talent, and that talent alone was
one thing, but how and how intensely you applied it was
much more important.

These lessons began as a high school senior with
Rudolph de Harak. I was fortunate to have so many
amazing teachers over the years, but Rudy was the first.
His expectations and standards set a high bar that
helped me aim high — and sometimes even succeed —
ever since.'

Adrian Shaughnessy
Graphic Designer, Author, Educator
Co-Founder, Unit Editions
November 2020

'Rudolph de Harak said that his work put him in the
"purist category". I can't think of a better description of
his work — pure. His record covers and book jackets
place him in the first rank of Mid-century Modernist
graphic designers.'

David Sutton
Design Consultant
Fort Collins, Colorado
April 2021

'I knew of Rudy only through colleagues who had worked
with him or had been his students. I had no knowledge
of his work. My eyes were opened wide when setting
up our office on 19th Street for Expo 67. I found a small
room lined with McGraw-Hill paperback books with
covers designed by Rudy. I think there must have been
about two hundred of them. Each was a stunning graphic
of creative genius.

In 1965, I was introduced to Rudy by Will Burtin, who
I was working for at the time, and with whom I began
my design career in New York. Rudy was looking for
someone with exhibit design experience to work with
him on the Canadian Pavilion at Expo 67 in Montreal,
Canada. I am an industrial designer who at Will's office
had worked on three exhibitions for the 1964 New York
World's Fair, including, with Will and Saul Bass, the
design for the Kodak Pavilion. I went to work for Rudy
as his Design Manager for the project. It began a most
exciting period of work for me and the development of a
relationship with Rudy as a lifelong friend and mentor.'

Bibliography

Books

Bass, Jennifer and Pat Kirkham, *Saul Bass: A Life in Film & Design* (London: Laurence King Publishing, 2011)

Bennett, Tony, *The Good Life: The Autobiography of Tony Bennett* (New York: Atria Books, 1998)

Bill, Max, *Typography, Advertising, Book Design* (Salenstein: Niggli Verlag, 2010)

Booth-Clibborn, Edward and Daniele Baroni, *The Language of Graphics* (New York: Harry N. Abrams, Inc., 1980)

Bradbury, Dominic, *Essential Modernism: Design Between the World Wars* (New Haven: Yale University Press, 2018)

Cerra, Julie Lugo, *Culver City: Images of America* (Charleston: Arcadia Publishing, 2004)

de Harak, Rudolph, ed., *Posters by Members of the Alliance Graphique Internationale 1960–1985* (New York: Rizzoli International Publications Inc., 1986)

de Harak, Rudolph, 'Some Thoughts on Modernism: Past, Present, and Future, Milton Glaser, Ivan Chermayeff and Rudolph de Harak', Steven Heller and Marie Finamore, eds., *Design Culture: An Anthology of Writing from the AIGA Journal for Graphic Design* (New York: Allworth Press, 2013)

Diamonstein-Spielvogel, Barbaralee, *The Landmarks of New York* (New York: The Monacelli Press, 2005)

Drew, Ned and Paul Sternberger, *By Its Cover: Modern American Book Cover Design* (New York: Princeton Architectural Press, 2005)

Eskilson, Stephen J., *Graphic Design: A New History* (New Haven: Yale University Press, 2007)

Evanier, David, *All the Things You Are: The Life of Tony Bennett* (Hoboken: John Wiley & Sons, Inc., 2011)

Friedl, Friedrich, Nicolaus Ott, and Bernard Stein, *Typography: An Encyclopedic Survey of Type Design and Techniques Through History* (New York: Black Dog & Leventhal, 1998)

Friedman, Mildred, *Graphic Design In America: A Visual Language History* (New York: Harry N. Abrams, Inc., 1989)

Heller, Steven, *Paul Rand* (London: Phaidon Press, 1990)

Heller, Steven and Georgette Ballance, eds., *Graphic Design History* (New York: Allworth Press, 2001)

Heller, Steven and Elaine Lustig Cohen, *Born Modern: The Life and Design of Alvin Lustig* (San Francisco: Chronicle Books, 2010)

Heller, Steven and Greg D'Onofrio, *The Moderns: Midcentury American Graphic Design* (New York: Abrams, 2017)

Heller, Steven and Marie Finamore, *Design Culture: An Anthology of Writing from the AIGA Journal of Graphic Design* (New York: Allworth Press, 1997)

Heller, Steven and Karen Pomeroy, *Design Literacy: Understanding Graphic Design* (New York: Allworth Press, 1997)

Henrion, FHK, *Top Graphic Design* (Zurich: ABC Verlag, 1983)

Herdeg, Walter, ed., *Archigraphia* (Zurich: Graphis, Inc., 1978)

Inglis, Theo, *Mid-Century Modern Graphic Design* (London: Batsford, 2019)

Jackson, Kenneth T., ed., *The Encyclopedia of New York City* (New Haven: Yale University Press, 1991)

Jacobs, Jane, *The Death and Life of Great American Cities* (New York: Random House, 1961)

James, Robert Rhodes, ed., *Winston S. Churchill: His Complete Speeches, 1897–1963, Vol. VII, 1943–1949* (New York: Chelsea House Publishers, 1974)

Kaplan, Wendy, ed., *Living in a Modern Way: California Design 1930–1965* (Cambridge: MIT Press, 2011)

Kepes, György, *Language of Vision* (Chicago: Paul Theobald and Company, 1944)

Kurlansky, Mervyn, *Masters of the 20th Century: The ICOGRADA Design Hall of Fame* (New York: Graphis, Inc., 2001)

Lupton, Ellen, *Mixing Messages: Graphic Design in Contemporary Culture* (New York: Princeton Architectural Press, 1996)

McKnight-Trontz, Jennifer and Alex Steinweiss, *For the Record: The Life and Work of Alex Steinweiss, Inventor of the Album Cover* (New York: Princeton Architectural Press, 2000)

Meggs, Philip B. and Alston W. Purvis, *Meggs' History of Graphic Design* (New York: John Wiley & Sons, Inc., 2006)

Nolan, Bernard Thomas, *Isaiah's Eagles Rising: A Generation of Airmen* (Bloomington: Xlibris Corporation, 2002)

Poulin, Richard, *Graphic Design and Architecture: A 20th-Century Design History* (Beverly: Rockport Publishers Inc., 2014)

Remington, R. Roger, *American Modernism: Graphic Design 1920–1960* (New Haven: Yale University Press, 2003)

Remington, R. Roger and Barbara J. Hodik, *Nine Pioneers in American Graphic Design* (Cambridge: MIT Press, 1989)

Remington, R. Roger and Robert S. P. Fripp, *Design and Science: The Life and Work of Will Burtin* (London: Lund Humphries Ltd., 2007)

Roberts, Caroline, *Graphic Design Visionaries* (London: Laurence King Publishing, 2015)

Saccani, Anna, *Letterscapes: A Global Survey of Typographic Installations* (London: Thames & Hudson, 2013)

Stern, Robert A. M., Gregory Gilmartin, and Thomas Mellins, *New York 1930: Architecture and Urbanism between the Two World Wars* (New York: Rizzoli International Publications Inc., 1987)

Stern, Robert A. M., Thomas Mellins, and David Fishman, *New York 1960: Architecture and Urbanism between the Second World War and the Bicentennial* (New York: The Monacelli Press, 1995)

Stern, Rudi, *Let There be Neon* (New York: Harry N. Abrams, Inc., 1979)

Tigerman, Bobbye, ed., *A Handbook of California Design: 1930–1965, Craftspeople, Designers, and Manufacturers* (Cambridge: MIT Press, 2013)

Venturi, Robert, *Complexity and Contradiction in Architecture* (New York: The Museum of Modern Art, 1966)

Periodicals
Blake, Peter, 'Biggest Big Top', *Architectural Forum*, Vol. 131, No. 5, December (1969), 68–69

Burtin, Will, 'Integration: The New Discipline in Design', *Graphis 5*, No. 27 (1949), 230–37

Cahn, Joel C, 'The Graphic Designer as Architect, as Landscape Architect, as Interior Designer', *Print*, November/December (1970), 52–55

Chaparos, Nicholas J, 'Rudolph de Harak', *Graphis*, No. 193, Vol. 33 (1977), 444–453

de Harak, Rudolph, 'Mimeo-Imagery', *Print XI: 2*, No. XI, Vol. 2 (1957), 68–72

Geismar, Thomas H, 'The U. S. Pavilion', *Graphis*, No. 150, Vol. 26 (1970), 328–335

Gottschall, Edward, ed., 'The Art of Typeface Design and Visual Communications', *U&lc*, Vol. 2, No. 1 (1975), 2–3, 24–26

Heller, Steven, 'Rudolph de Harak—A Playful Modernist', *Baseline 45* (2004), 25–32

Hölscher, Eberhard, 'Rudolph de Harak: An American Designer', *Gebrauchsgraphik*, No. 7 (1961), 2–9

Huxtable, Ada Louise, 'A New City is Emerging Downtown', *The New York Times* (29 March 1970), 239

Johnson, Pamela, 'Creating Emotional Involvement in Geography, Geology and Space Science: An Interview with Rudolph de Harak', *Dot Zero*, No. 4, Summer (1967), 24–29

Meggs, Philip B., '50 Years of Graphic Design: The Shape of the Decades; The 1940s: Rise of the Modernists,' *Print*, Vol. 43, No. 6, November/December (1989), 68

Müller, Rolf, ed., 'Rudolph de Harak,' *High Quality*, Issue No. 2 (1985), 10–17

Oeri, Georgine, 'Rudolph de Harak', *Graphis*, Vol. 13, No. 69, January/February (1957), 76–79, 89

Siegel, Rita Sue, 'Important U. S. Graphic Designers of the Last 25 Years: Rudolph de Harak', *IDEA*, Vol. 26, No. 151, November (1978), 112–113

Smith, C. Ray, ed., 'U.S. Pavilion: The Ultimate Understatement', *Progressive Architecture*, August (1970), 64–67

Wilson, Forrest, ed., '77 Water Street, New York, N.Y.', *Progressive Architecture*, March (1971), 66–75

Blogs
Heller, Steven, 'A Humanist's Modernist', *AIGA Medalists*, https://www.aiga.org

Heller, Steven, 'More de Harak Greatest Hits', *Print*, *The Daily Heller*, 13 November 2018, https://www.printmag.com/post/more-de-harak-greatest-hits

Heller, Steven, 'Now That's A Portfolio', *Print*, *The Daily Heller*, 24 October 2018, https://www.printmag.com/post/now-thats-a-portfolio

Heller, Steven, 'Rudolph de Harak's Abstract Purity', *Print, Design Culture*, 21 December 2017, https://www.printmag.com/post/rudolph-de-haraks-abstract-purity

Shaffer, Bill, 'Modern Survivor', *Design Observer*, 23 August 2017, https://designobserver.com/feature/modern-survivor/39644

Skidmore, Martin, 'Krazy Kat: Modernism and Influence', *FA The Comiczine*, 11 January 2011, http://comiczine-fa.com/features/krazy-kat-modernism-and-influence

Newspapers
Baldwin, Letitia, 'A Designer's Discipline' *The Ellsworth American* (13 August 1998)

Bruni, Frank, 'Culture New York City, 1981–1983: 36 Months That Changed The Culture', *The New York Times, T Magazine* (17 April 2018), 1

Gold, Donna, 'De Harak's Geometry' *Maine Times*, Vol. 34, No. 18 (23 September 2001), 16

Goldberger, Paul, 'Kevin Roche Finishes a Trio and Changes His Tune' *The New York Times*, Section II (29 November 1987), 42

Greenleaf, Ken, 'de Harak Creates Studied Elegance' *Maine Sunday Telegram* (23 August 1998)

Heller, Steven, 'Rudolph de Harak, 78, Artist And Environmental Designer' *The New York Times* (30 April 2002), 18

Huxtable, Ada Louise, 'Taking the Wraps Off Egypt' *The New York Times*, Section II (10 October 1976), 18

Kraner, Madeline R., 'Graphic Artists Lauded in New Universe Series' *Publishers Weekly*, Vol. 201 (7 February 1972)

Russell, John, 'The Romance of Egyptology' *The New York Times*, Section II, (10 October 1976) 1, 23

Wiederaenders, Tim, ed., 'Obituary: Harold (Hal) Tritel' *The Daily Courier* (17 June 2016)

Oral Histories
Larsen, Susan, 'Oral History with Rudolph de Harak,' Archives of American Art, Smithsonian Institution (27 April 2000)

Chronology

1924–1949

1924
Born 10 April, Culver City, California

1934
Moves to Chicago, Illinois
Moves to Astoria, Queens, New York

1938
Graduates from Public School 141, Queens,
    New York

1940
Graduates from School of Industrial Art,
    New York City

1943
Drafted into US Army 78th Infantry Division

1946
Discharged from US Army; returns to
    New York City
Moves to Los Angeles, California
Mechanical artist, California Advertising Art
    Service, Los Angeles, California
Promoted to Studio Manager

1947
Receives Merit Award, Los Angeles Art
    Directors Club
Attends Will Burton and György Kepes lectures,
    Art Center School, Los Angeles, California
Founding member, Los Angeles Society for
    Contemporary Designers

1948
Opens design studio with Hal Tritel

1950–1959

1950
Moves to New York City
Promotion art director, *Seventeen* magazine

1951
Freelance practice begins

1952
Begins teaching at Cooper Union

1953
Work selected for *Typographie et Publicité–
    Fifty Years of Art from the United States,
    Collection of the Museum of Modern Art
    (MoMA)* exhibition, Musée d'Art Moderne
    de la Ville de Paris
Work selected for Sixth Annual Exhibition
    of the Book Jacket Designers Guild,
    New York City

1953–1958
Esquire magazine spot illustrations

1954
Marries Berenice Migson Lipson

1954–1955
Studio photographer

1954–1964
Consulting art director, *Dance Magazine*

1955
Work selected for the Museum of Modern Art
    (MoMA) *American Art of the Twentieth
    Century,* Musée d'Art Moderne, Paris

1957
Son Dimitri born
Graphis magazine profile
Kurt Versen Lighting Company corporate
    identity

1958
Opens first design office, 795 Lexington Avenue,
    New York City

1960–1969

1960–1962
Westminster Records album covers

1961
Gebrauchsgraphik magazine profile

1960–1966
McGraw-Hill Paperbacks book covers

1962–1964
Visiting professor, School of Visual Arts

1963
Marries Orietta Giardino
Industrial Design magazine profile
Solo exhibition, Carnegie Institute of
    Technology, Pittsburgh, Pennsylvania

1964
Son Bruno born
Solo exhibition, American Institute of Graphic
    Arts (AIGA), New York City

1966
Marries Carol Sylbert
Moves design office to 112 East 19th Street,
    New York City
Work selected for the Museum of Modern Art
    (MoMA) Design Collection
Chairman, *AIGA Fifty Years of Graphic Arts
    in America*

1967
Canadian Pavilion at Expo 67, Montreal, Canada

1967–1970
Board member, American Institute of Graphic
    Arts (AIGA)

1968
127 John Street, New York City

1970–1979

1970
US Pavilion at Expo 70, Osaka, Japan
77 Water Street, New York City
Moves design office to 150 Fifth Avenue,
    New York City
Print magazine profile

1972–1983
The Metropolitan Museum of Art, Lila Acheson
    Wallace Galleries of Egyptian Art,
    New York City

1973–1978
Visiting professor, Parson School of Design
Visiting professor, Pratt Institute

1974
AIGA Symbol Signs
Speaker, 'The Art of Typeface Design and
    Visual Communications,' Washington, DC

1975
United Nations Plaza Hotel, New York City
Fleet graphics, *The New York Times*

1975–1977
US National President, Alliance Graphique
    Internationale (AGI)

1976
Visiting professor, Kent State University

1977
Graphis magazine profile
Awarded Residency, New Arts Program,
    Kutztown State University
Speaker, NEA's 'Studio Seminar for Federal
    Graphic Designers,' Washington, DC

1978
IDEA magazine profile
The Metropolitan Museum of Art Shopping Bags

1979
Named the Frank Stanton Professor of
    Graphic Design, Cooper Union

1979–1980
Visiting professor, Yale University

1980–1989

1980
Moves design office to 320 West 13th Street,
    New York City

1981
Speaker, Seventh Annual ICOGRADA Seminar,
    London, United Kingdom

1983
General Foods Corporate Museum, Rye Brook,
    New York
Cummins Engine Company Corporate Museum,
    Columbus, Indiana

1984
Chairperson, *AIGA Functional Graphics*
    competition and exhibition
Conoco Corporate Museum, Houston, Texas

1985
Awarded US Presidential Design Award
HQ, High Quality magazine profile
Retrospective exhibition, Western Carolina
    University, Cullowhee, North Carolina

1986
Retires from Cooper Union
Author, *Posters by Members of the Alliance
    Graphique Internationale 1960–1985*

1987
Office name changes to de Harak & Poulin
    Associates, Inc.
Visiting professor, Alfred University
Moves to Ellsworth, Maine

1988
AIGA Graphic Design USA: 9 book jacket

1989
Inducted into Art Directors Club (ADC) Hall
    of Fame

1990–2002

1991
Solo exhibition, Leighton Gallery,
    Blue Hill, Maine

1992
Awarded Gold Medal, American Institute of
    Graphic Arts (AIGA)
Inaugural faculty member, Maine Summer
    Institute in Graphic Design, Portland, Maine

1993
Receives Honorary Doctorate in Fine Arts,
    The Corcoran Museum School of Art,
    Washington, DC
Group exhibition, Fosdick-Nelson Gallery,
    Alfred, New York

1996
Group exhibition, Muse Gallery,
    Rockland, Maine

1998
Solo exhibition, Icon Contemporary Art Gallery,
    Brunswick, Maine
Group exhibition, Farnsworth Art Museum,
    Farnsworth, Maine
Group exhibition, Portland Museum of Art,
    Portland, Maine

1999
Group exhibition, Clark House Gallery,
    Bangor, Maine

2000
Group exhibition, Icon Contemporary Art
    Gallery, Brunswick, Maine
Group exhibition, Katonah Museum of Art,
    Katonah, New York

2001
Solo exhibition, John Edwards Art Gallery,
    Ellsworth, Maine

2002
Dies, 24 April, Ellsworth, Maine

Former Staff

Kenneth Alcorn
Eric Atherton
Frank Benedict
Janice Bergen
William Bevington
Laurie Binder
Todd Blank
Barbara Bowker
John Branigan
Barbara Caruana
Margie Chin
John Condon
Mary Condon
Ann Crews
Donald Crews
Margaret Desmond
James Dustin
Ann Ellis
Jennifer Fordjuor
Francine Gadson
Maude Gilman
Pauline Gobell
Donna Goldberg
Georgiana Goodwin
Pamela Grant
Douglas Harp
Lai Hom
Robin Horton
Linda Kondo

Deborah Kushma
Ellen Lupton
David Lustgarten
Terry Lynch
Heather McRae
Nilda Muñoz
Sheila Nichols
Mieko Oda
Ann Marie O'Kane
Richard Poulin
Carol Robinson
Paul Rosenblatt
Stewart Siskind
Brenda Sisson
Elizabeth Small
Tony Spagnola
Charles Spilman
Paul Steinglass
Kirsten Steinorth
David Sutton
Paulo Suzuki
Douglas Sylbert
James Tait
Ran VanKoten
Ruggero Vanni
Leslie Wengenroth
Jessica Wicken
Johanna Wirtz
Linda Wolf

Image Credits

6: Courtesy of Tom Geismar. 9: Collection of author. 16: Courtesy of Bruno de Harak. 18 top: Courtesy of R. Roger Remington. 18 bottom: Courtesy of Juliet Kepes Stone and the Department of Special Collections and University Archives, Stanford University Libraries, György Kepes Papers, Stanford, California. 19: National Portrait Gallery, Smithsonian Institution. 20: Courtesy of Bruno de Harak. 21 top: Security Pacific National Bank Photo Collection, Los Angeles Public Library. 21 bottom, 22: Courtesy of Joseph Schaffer. 23 left: Courtesy of Greater Astoria Historical Society. 23 right: Courtesy of Joseph Schaffer. 24: Collection of author. 25 top: Courtesy of Joseph Schaffer. 25 bottom: Collection of author. 26 top: Courtesy of Carol de Harak. 26 bottom: Courtesy of Bruno de Harak. 27, 28, 31: Courtesy of Carol de Harak. 33, 35, 36 bottom, 37: Collection of author. 42: Museum of the City of New York X2010.7.1.9800. 47: The Cooper Union Archives and Special Collections. 50: Courtesy of Jay Maisel, ©Jay Maisel, 51: ZHdK, Museum für Gestaltung Zürich, Poster Collection, ©2021 ARS NY/ProLitteris, Zürich, 52 top, 52 bottom, 53, 54, 56 bottom, 58, 59 top, 60 bottom, 61: Collection of author. 63 top: Reproduced with kind permission of Letterform Archive, Scott Lindberg Collection. 65, 67, 68 top, 68 bottom, 87, 101, 104: Collection of author. 107: Courtesy of David Sutton. 110, 112, 113, 116: Collection of author. 118 bottom left: Collection of Julian Montague. 119: Collection of author. 120: Collection of Julian Montague. 121 bottom, 122 top, 126, 128 top, 128 bottom, 129 top left, 130 top, 130 bottom: Collection of author. 132, 134: Collection of Julian Montague. 135: Collection of author. 137, 138, 139, 140, 142, 150: Collection of Julian Montague. 158 top left, 158 top right, 158 bottom, 160, 161 top, 161 bottom, 163: Collection of author. 172: Courtesy of Steven Heller. 173 top, 173 bottom, 174: Courtesy of David Sutton. 176: Courtesy

of Steven Heller. 177: Courtesy of David Sutton. 181, 182, 183: Courtesy of Steven Heller. 184: Courtesy of Nathaniel 'Thorney' Lieberman. 185: Stockfolio/Alamy Stock Photo. 186, 187, 191: Courtesy of Nathaniel 'Thorney' Lieberman. 192: ©The Museum of Modern Art/Licensed by SCALA/Art Resource, New York. 194: Courtesy of Don Shanosky. 199, 200: Courtesy of David Sutton. 203, 204, 205: Collection of author. 211: Courtesy of Nathaniel 'Thorney' Lieberman. 212: Courtesy of Steven Heller. 213: Courtesy of Nathaniel 'Thorney' Lieberman. 214 top: Courtesy of Steven Heller. 216, 217, 218, 219, 220, 221, 222, 223, 224, 225: Courtesy of Tom Geismar. 262: Courtesy of Don Shanosky. 266: Stockfolio/Alamy Stock Photo. 288, 297: Collection of author. 298 bottom: Courtesy of Carol de Harak. 307: Collection of author. 344: Los Angeles County Museum of Art., Marc Treib Collection, photography ©Museum Associates/ LACMA, by Paul Salveson. 354: Collection of Susan C. Larsen and Laurie Martin. 357, 359: Courtesy of Carol de Harak. 360: Courtesy of Mark Baldwin. 362: Courtesy of Carol de Harak. 391: Collection of Susan C. Larsen and Laurie Martin. 395, 397: Courtesy of Mark Baldwin.

Acknowledgements

I have worked for over two years on this project and in that time relied upon the help of many individuals. In particular, this monograph would not have become a reality without the enthusiastic support, encouragement, and generosity of Carol de Harak, Rudy's wife, who shared with me so many memories and rare insights into her husband and companion of over 35 years. I am forever grateful for her invaluable contributions and friendship. I am also indebted to friends and colleagues for their generous contributions and assistance, including R. Roger Remington, Vignelli Distinguished Professor of Design Emeritus, Vignelli Center for Design Studies, College of Art and Design, Rochester Institute of Technology for his continued enthusiasm and support, especially at the start of this project; Tom Geismar for his wonderful and heartfelt Foreword; Julian Montague, Montague Projects whose extensive collection of de Harak book and album covers were essential to the completion of this project; and Steven Heller and Susan C. Larsen, Ph. D, whose extensive oral history interviews with Rudy provided me with invaluable insights and perspectives. I have quoted extensively from both of these interviews and I am forever grateful for their earlier efforts in documenting his life and legacy.

To my publisher Thames & Hudson/ Volume, especially Lucas Dietrich, Editorial Director; Darren Wall, Co-founder, Volume; Evie Tarr, Assistant Editor and Project Manager; Augusta Pownall, Development Commissioning Editor, Architecture and Design; Beth Siveyer, Community Manager; Kate Thomas, Senior Production Controller; and my editor, John Jervis for their invaluable guidance and support throughout the evolution of this monograph. To Dr. Steven K. Galbraith, Curator; Amelia Hugill-Fontanel, Associate Curator; and Jiageng Lin, Photographer; Cary Graphic Arts Collection, RIT Libraries, Rochester Institute of Technology for their tireless support and assistance with my numerous requests, not only during my week-long research visit to RIT in the Spring of 2021, but the subsequent months following my visit.

I have also been very fortunate to have the support of many people who knew of Rudy's reputation, career, or work and offered their generous input and insights. Speaking with each of these individuals was one of the most rewarding experiences during my research. I want to particularly thank Mark Baldwin, Felix Beltram, Don Crews, Louis Danziger, Margo Halverson, Douglas Harp, Robin Plaskoff Horton, Jon Jicha, Burton Kramer, Jean Marcellino, Jay Maisel, Sergio Correa de Jesus Medina, Armando Milani, Paul Rosenblatt, Arnold Saks, Alan Siegel, and David Sutton.

The success of the monograph's initial funding campaign would not have become a reality without the generosity and support of Majid Abbasi, Studio Abbasi; Rafael Esquer, Creative Director, CEO, Alfalfa Studio; Robert Appleton; Sissa Morgado, Association of Registered Graphic Designers (RGD); Brian Collins, Chief Creative Office, Founder, COLLINS; Jessica Helfand, Founding Editor and Betsy Vardell, Executive Producer, *Design Observer*; Stephanie Mehta, Editor-in-Chief, Suzanne LaBarre, Editor, and Lilly Smith, Associate Editor, *Fast Company*; Gordon Kaye, Publisher, *Graphic Design USA (GDUSA)*; Marty Neumeier, Director, Liquid Agency; Nolan Giles, Senior Editor and Mae-Li Evans, Producer, *Monocle*; Jesse Reed, Co-Founder, Order and Standards Manual; Rudy Sanchez, *Print* Magazine; Cybelle Jones, CEO, Franck Mercurio, Writer, and Sarah Miorelli, Communications Manager, Society for Experiential Graphic Design (SEGD); Paul Carlos, Board Member, Type Directors Club (TDC); Peter Bilak, Typotheque; and Adrian Shaughnessy, Co-Founder, Unit Editions.

My design collaborators Derek Koch and Tyler Cheli were invaluable and indispensable throughout the process of assisting me with the development and design of this monograph and I will be forever indebted to them for their outstanding efforts.

My gratitude is also extended to those individuals who assisted me with and/or provided permission to reproduce images in this monograph, specifically Bruno de Harak, Greg D'Onofrio, Joseph Schaffer, Allen Shanosky, Don Shanosky, and Madeline Topp; Juliet Kepes Stone; Heather Strelecki, Director of Development, American Institute of Graphic Arts (AIGA); Mary Mann, Archives Librarian and Kim Newman, Media Relations Manager, The Cooper Union for the Advancement of Science and Art; Charlene Fox Clemens, Special Collections Cataloger, Ellsworth Public Library; Beth Kleiber, Archivist, Milton Glaser Design Study Center and Archives, School of Visual Arts; Robert Singleton, Greater Astoria Historical Society; Deborah Kushma, Photographer; Nathaniel 'Thorney' Lieberman, Photographer; Staci Steinberger, Associate Curator, Decorative Arts and Design, Los Angeles County Museum of Art (LACMA); Emily Arbuckle, Portland Museum of Art; and Leif Anderson, Department of Special Collections, Stanford University.

Lastly, and above all, this monograph is dedicated to the one person who has always given me the time, freedom, love, and support to pursue my dreams — my husband, Douglas Morris.

Index (A–I)

Index (I–Z)

A Note on the Design

About the Author

Rational Simplicity: Rudolph de Harak, Graphic Designer was designed and typeset by Richard Poulin, Derek Koch, and Tyler Cheli. Digital type composition, page layouts, and type design were originated on Apple iMac computers, utilizing Adobe InDesign CC 2021, Version 16.4 software. The text of this monograph is set in Akzidenz-Grotesk Next, a typeface designed and produced in 2006 by H. Berthold Typefoundry, Berlin, Germany.

Richard Poulin is a design consultant, educator, author, and artist living in Southern California. His forty-year career has focused on a generalist approach to all aspects of design, including graphic, environmental, interior, and exhibition design.

Since 1986, he has divided his time between professional practice and academia, as the co-founder and design director of Poulin + Morris Inc., an internationally recognized design consultancy in New York City, and as an adjunct professor at the School of Visual Arts and Cooper Union. He is also a frequent lecturer at colleges and universities; a contributor to design publications in the United States and abroad; and a recipient of a research grant in design history from the Graham Foundation for Advanced Studies in the Fine Arts. His design work has been published in periodicals and books worldwide; is included in private and public collections including the Library of Congress, Denver Art Museum, and Cooper Hewitt Smithsonian Design Museum; and has received awards and recognitions from national and international organizations and publications.

To date, he has written eight books on design, which have been translated into multiple languages and used by students and practitioners around the world. As an artist, his mixed-media collage constructions have been exhibited throughout the United States, and are in the collections of several private collectors.

You can follow his work at richardpoulin.net, on Instagram @richardpoulin, or contact him at richard@poulinmorris.com.